The Coming
Computer Industry Shakeout

The Coming
Computer Industry Shakeout

Winners, Losers, and Survivors

STEPHEN T. McCLELLAN

JOHN WILEY & SONS
New York · Chichester · Brisbane · Toronto · Singapore

Library of Congress Cataloging in Publication Data:

McClellan, Stephen T.
   The coming computer industry shakeout.

   Includes index.
   1. Computer industry.   I. Title.

HD9696.C62M4   1984   338.4'700164   84–7256
ISBN 0–471–88063–9

Printed in the United States of America

10 9 8 7 6 5 4 3 2 1

puter industry is struggling to come to grips with the changes in society and business that it is helping to bring about.

The personal styles of these industry leaders are also quite different. Some work in spacious offices at stand-up desks while others ensconce themselves in cubby hole sized offices, no different from those of low-level programmers. Some prefer to do business at the country club, while others surround themselves in libraries of books. Although there are no set rules for evaluating such things, the impressions you form can't help but become part of your opinion about a company's prospects.

My own interest and involvement in computers began after graduating from Syracuse University, during a stint in the U.S. Navy. I was an Operations Officer aboard the U.S.S. Suffolk County (LST–1173) during the Viet Nam era. All of the ship's radar, guns, navigation, and communications equipment were computer controlled. After leaving the service, and while attending graduate school at night at George Washington University for my MBA, I was an Office Equipment Industry Analyst at the U.S. Department of Commerce from 1968–71. I wrote the U.S. Industrial Outlook on the industry each year and was involved in such things as computer export promotion. In 1971 I came to Wall Street and joined the firm of Spencer Trask & Company as an investment research analyst. Since 1977 I have been a vice president at Salomon Brothers Inc. As part of my job I travel constantly, visiting computer companies, attending meetings, seeing clients, and preparing some 20 reports a year. I became a Chartered Financial Analyst in 1976 and was president of the Computer Industry Analysts Group on Wall Street in 1977, 1982, and again in 1984.

To do all of that and get this book done, I obviously had some help. Acknowledgment for invaluable assistance in helping prepare this book starts and ends with Joseph Kelly. Joe not only took raw McClellan text and helped make it comprehensible, he also came up with numerous suggestions and additions to enhance the content. My secretary, Jo Ann Turbiak, put the entire draft through a word processor not once, but twice (in draft and final form), spending innumerable hours at the keyboard, usually under deadline pressure. Her unending dedication and enthusiasm went far beyond the call of duty. Finally, I owe the greatest debt of all to my family, Jo Ann, Laurel, and Justin, for their patience and understanding during all of those weekday alarms at 4:40 am when I got up to write before leaving for work and those weekends spent in the basement at my desk. This book is more theirs than mine.

STEPHEN T. MCCLELLAN

New York, New York
May 1984

Contents

Continued on next page

PART 4: THE NEW INSURGENTS

CONCLUSION

GLOSSARY OF TERMS

INDEX

The Coming
Computer Industry Shakeout

Part 1

An Industry at a Crossroads

In the 1980s we are witnessing the start of a dramatic change in the business of computers. The structure of the industry—a structure that has prevailed largely without change since the 1950s and '60s—is coming undone.

A powerful convergence of forces—technological, economic, societal—is recasting the industry from top to bottom. The industry is no longer the private domain of the handful of companies that founded it. A new breed of company, better suited to the imperatives of the information age, is taking over.

A shakeout is in the offing. In the meantime, confusion reigns. The industry is struggling to come to grips with its own success. It is choking on the glut of new products that appear every day, and tripping over the enormous changes in the economy and society that it is helping to bring about.

When the transformation is complete—and it won't be for quite a while; it really is just beginning—things will never be the same again . . . not for the computer industry . . . not for anyone.

1

Never the Same Again

More than 30 years have passed since the first commercial computer, the Univac 1, appeared on the scene. The world's newest megaindustry, the computer business, has come a long way since then. A fledgling hybrid of the post-World War II electronics boom, computers blossomed in the 1960s and 1970s, emerging as *the* industry to watch. Today, the potential they showed then has become a reality. Computers are big business.

Revenues generated by the computer industry in 1983 totaled $110 billion, nearly double that of the steel industry and close enough to soon surpass the $120 billion made by the Big Three automobile makers that year. Only the oil companies are richer, with 1983 revenues of $500 billion. In time, however, they too will yield their preeminent position. The computer industry is on the eve of its ultimate triumph. By the end of this century (sometime in the 1990s), computers will become the world's leading business.

In almost every way possible, computers have exceeded the expectations anyone had for them 30 years ago. Who could have predicted that vacuum tube circuitry would become transistorized and put on microchips, enabling the entire contents of a computer processor to be placed on a component the size of a paper clip? Or that computers themselves would become consumer items, purchased in department stores, so commonplace that children (not to mention adults) would exchange them as gifts?

The unique achievement of the computer industry is to combine staggering technological achievement with enormous, sometimes mind-boggling market growth. But it is an achievement for which the companies that inhabit the industry are paying a mean price. The computer industry is not just growing, it is fragmenting. Success is pulling it apart, sending it off in dozens of different directions, into a myriad of specialized market niches. Twenty years ago, the industry had one basic product: the general purpose mainframe computer. The computer industry was built on sales of mainframes priced at $2 to $5 million. Today, the mainframe is just one of many offerings in the computer industry. As a market, mainframes no longer come even close to dominating the computer business.

The computer industry is no longer a one-product business. There is something for everyone, from the automated teller machines in banks to the point-of-sale terminals at local supermarkets; from the portable computers that people take along on business trips, to the home computers their children play games on in the living room; from the executive work stations that sit on the desks of some corporate vice presidents, to the word processors in front of their secretaries; from the computerized telephone systems that are replacing old, outdated switchboards, to the computerized manufacturing systems that are paving the way to the automated factory of the future.

Specialization is the name of the game in today's industry. No one makes general-purpose computers anymore. Computer products are designed today to appeal to specific market niches.

No one expected the industry to succumb quite so quickly to the lure of specialization. For most of the 1970s, the mainframe continued to reign supreme, although a number of challengers were beginning to appear on the horizon. A handful of upstart companies experienced extraordinary success selling smaller, less expensive computers known as minicomputers. Other companies did quite well providing data services, such as payroll processing, to customers who could not afford their own computers. And still others made a handsome living by manufacturing peripheral equipment, printers, disk drives, tape drives, and other auxiliary devices for the computer room. But none of these seemed to pose a serious threat to the reign of the mainframe.

As recently as 1975, seven mainframe companies (IBM, Burroughs, Univac/Sperry, NCR, Control Data, Honeywell, and Xerox*) were responsible for over 80% of all revenues generated in the industry. But when the end came, it came quickly. Since 1975, the fortunes of all but IBM have been in a steady decline. Mainframe sales, which used to grow by 15 to 20% a year, now increase at only a 6% rate. By 1988, mainframes will represent only 15% of all industry shipments. By the end of the decade, at least three of the mainframe companies will no longer be counted among the Top 10 computer companies.

The computer industry was exploding all around them, but the mainframe companies stood pat. In effect, they slept. When they finally awoke, it was too late. A wave of specialty companies had taken over the industry. The degree to which the real action in the industry had shifted away from the established mainframe companies (with the exception of IBM, of course) to the new insurgent specialty companies can be seen by looking at the list on the following page of some of the high-growth specialty markets and the companies that pioneered them. Conspicuously absent from this list is the name of any of the mainframe companies. Virtually no major specialty market that emerged in the past 10 years was pioneered by a mainframe company.

These markets may be specialized, but they are not necessarily small. Some of them are huge. The best known specialty market, personal computers (a market that did not even exist until the late 1970s) was $8 billion in 1983, and growing at 50% a year. The market for floppy disk drives, the memory devices that are used with most personal computers, was $400 million in 1983 and growing by leaps and bounds. The market for the actual floppy disks themselves was $200 million in 1983 and is expected to be $1 billion by 1988.

Even the smaller specialty markets are quite substantial. The market for automated teller machines is already approaching a half

---

* Xerox dropped out of the mainframe market in 1975.

Specialty Markets and Leaders

1. Automated teller machines	Diebold
2. CAD/CAM	Computervision
3. Data processing services	Automatic Data Processing
4. Disk and tape storage devices	Storage Technology
5. Small Winchester disk drives	Seagate Technology
6. Floppy disk drives	Tandon
7. Magnetic media supplies	Verbatim
8. Microprocessors	Intel
9. Minicomputers	Digital Equipment
10. Nonstop, fail-safe computers	Tandem Computers
11. PBXs	ROLM
12. Personal computers	Apple Computer
13. Plug compatible mainframes	Amdahl
14. Printers	Dataproducts
15. Software (data base management)	Cullinet
16. Software (application)	Management Sciences of America (MSA)
17. Supercomputers	Cray Research
18. Superminicomputers	Prime Computer
19. Turnkey minicomputer systems	Triad Systems
20. Word processing	Wang Laboratories

billion dollars (some 13,000 cash dispensing ATM machines were installed in 1983 alone) and is growing at a 30% rate.

And these specialty markets are not static. Once a market niche becomes established, it inevitably fragments into even smaller niches. You don't sell just word processors today, you sell either stand-

alone word processors (which are on the way out) or shared word processing systems (which are very definitely on the way in). If you sell printers, you don't sell just printers; you sell high-speed band printers, or daisy wheel letter-quality printers, or low-speed dot matrix printers, or perhaps electronic ink-jet or laser printers. How about disk drives? There are rigid disk drives, floppy disk drives, 14 inch and 5¼ inch disk drives, micro-floppy disk drives, and now thin film disk drives. Buying a minicomputer? Do you want a minicomputer, a superminicomputer, or perhaps a nonstop, fail-safe minicomputer? You don't want a minicomputer? Then try a microcomputer or a small business computer. What's the difference? Don't ask!

Where does it all end? It doesn't. The pervasive specialization and fragmentation are only part of a thoroughgoing transformation that is changing the way every computer company will do business now and in the future.

In today's industry, as we will explore in greater detail in Chapter 2, the competitive conditions are being radically altered. For starters, the industry is more price sensitive than ever before. Price cutting runs rampant on everything from home computers to the most sophisticated mainframes. The industry is no longer recession proof. The cyclical ups and downs of the economy affect computer companies the same way they do automobiles, steel, farm equipment, and other mature industries.

Technology cycles, which once paced the industry like clockwork, are now short and unpredictable. In some sectors of the industry, technology cycles are so brief a company is no longer guaranteed that it can recoup its R&D investment in a new product line.

Small companies now have distinct advantages over large firms. In the era of specialization, when a company has to be quick on its feet, large firms are too slow.

Markets do not develop according to established patterns. Although new specialty markets are popping up all the time, they seem to become overcrowded almost as soon as they appear.

The financing that supports the industry is in turmoil. Too many investors, looking for the next Apple Computer, put their money into companies that are not worth their weight in paper. The in-

dustry has become short-sighted, leaning heavily on the whims and expectations of Wall Street.

Customers are more demanding. As computers have become more commonplace, customers have gotten choosier.

Not every company can handle these new conditions. A shakeout is inevitable, and not just the widely predicted shakeout at the low end of the industry, where hundreds of microcomputer companies are vying for a piece of that explosive market. The shakeout we are talking about is one that will rattle the cages of the industry from top to bottom.

Even if a company survives the shakeout, there is no guarantee of a long-term presence in the industry. Even bigger changes are afoot. Hardware is becoming a profitless commodity. Software and data services will soon overtake hardware in importance. The companies that make computers will no longer rule the roost the way they do today. Many of the high flying specialty companies may find themselves coming down to earth in a hurry. But we are getting ahead of our story. What we are talking about now goes beyond just the computer industry. We are talking about the end of the industrial era and the rise of the *information age*, an era in which information is more valuable than machines, even when the machine is a computer.

THE INFORMATION AGE

Unfortunately, no simple demarcations accurately separate one age from another. Although it is commonly said that we are entering the information age, many of the key information technologies—radio, television, the telephone—already have been with us for quite a while. These technologies have helped prepare us for many of the changes we are about to experience as we leave the industrial era behind. It remains for the computer to occupy center stage.

In almost every way, the computer is truly the most appropriate symbol of this new age. Unlike its predecessors, it is a machine with virtually no moving parts. Although it is capable of enormous production, its product is an intangible one: information. Instead of being run by blue-collar workers, it was originally operated by

a select group of highly educated professionals. Sometimes they even wore white coats. Now the business has come full circle. Everyone has access to and operates computers in everyday life.

The computer is a machine ideally suited for managing the complexity and contradictions of a mass society. It can play games as easily as it can plan a war. It can simulate scientific experiments as easily as it can project profit-and-loss statements. It can teach a child the alphabet as easily as it can store the contents of an entire library.

As Daniel Bell, the Harvard sociologist, noted over a decade ago: "Technological revolutions . . . become symbolized, if not embodied, in some tangible 'thing,' and in the post-industrial society, that 'thing' is the computer." * Bell coined the term *post-industrial society* to describe the vast sea change occurring as society evolves from one driven by its commodity-producing industries (such as steel and automobiles) to one based on the sale and distribution of services. Although the service sector was once considered an unproductive segment of the economy, the enormous revenues created by such industries as health care have proved that not to be the case. Now economists are realizing that information plays a key role in a services economy. As early as 1967, according to the economist Marc Porat, nearly 50% of the gross national product and more than 50% of all wages and salaries were derived from work involving the creation, processing, and distribution of information.[†] Figure 1.1 shows the dramatic increase in the number of white-collar workers, whose primary job involves the handling of information.

In the post-industrial economy, Bell sees information and knowledge actually joining capital and labor as the economy's strategic

* Daniel Bell, "The Social Framework of the Information Society," in *The Microelectronics Revolution* (Cambridge, MA: MIT Press, 1981), Ed. Tom Forester, p. 509.
† Porat arrived at this figure by combining the contributions made by "primary" information industries (in which he includes computer manufacturing/services and telecommunications, as well as such industries as accounting, advertising, and education) together with the contribution of the vast public and private bureaucracies (planners, marketing personnel, clerks, analysts, etc.) that are directly engaged in information work, even though their contribution to the gross national product is not readily apparent.

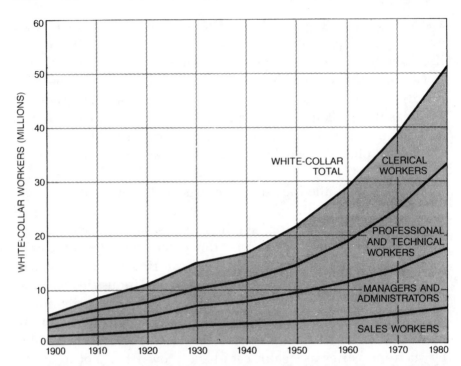

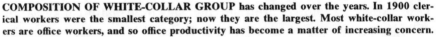

COMPOSITION OF WHITE-COLLAR GROUP has changed over the years. In 1900 clerical workers were the smallest category; now they are the largest. Most white-collar workers are office workers, and so office productivity has become a matter of increasing concern.

Figure 1.1. Increase in white-collar workers. From *Scientific American*, September 1982, *The Mechanization of Office Work*, Vincent E. Giuliano, p. 154. Reprinted with permission of Scientific American.

resources. Access to information is as important as ready supplies of cheap energy and raw materials were to the industrial era. Working networks of communication are as important as railways and highways. But if information is a commodity and a resource, it is one the likes of which we have never before seen. It doesn't spoil or go out of style, and there are no limits to its use or consumption. In fact, consumption enhances its value in the marketplace. The more one has, the more one wants. The object is not to compile a lot of information, though; it is to select only the right information. As John Naisbitt noted in his best-selling book, *Megatrends*, if people "can locate the information they need, they will pay for it. The emphasis of the whole information society shifts from supply to selection." *

A new term, *information poor*, has been coined to describe those organizations that are not adapting well to this new economy. In the past, a company that lacked a computer to generate quarterly financial results was considered information poor. Today a business is information poor if it does not have an on-line database of inventory, order entry, and pricing information so that at any moment it can find out what goods are selling, for how much, and what remains in stock. Tomorrow an organization may well be considered information poor if its computer cannot analyze its energy use, answer the telephones, and instantaneously produce management reports with multicolor bar charts.

Actually, most organizations today are information poor. They have not taken full advantage of what computers have to offer, either from lack of knowledge or, in some cases, out of fear of the power of these devices. But eventually they will. It is inevitable. The companies that make up the computer industry know that. There is a heady feeling in the industry today. It is the feeling that comes from the realization that enormous sums of money are yet to be made. It is the feeling that the information age is just beginning and will be with us for quite a while—and indeed it will be. But those who are enticed by visions of plunder may find their success shortlived. Beneath the surface of the computer industry, dangerous currents have been set in motion that could easily capsize those companies that are not careful.

REQUIEM FOR A HEAVYWEIGHT

The key factor that made the rise of the specialty markets possible is well known: the dramatic advances in integrated circuitry, culminating in the creation of the microprocessor at Intel in 1970. The microprocessor—the ubiquitous computer on a chip—made its presence felt like a primordial big bang explosion, causing the in-

---

* John Naisbitt, *Megatrends* (New York: Warner Books, 1982), p. 24.

dustry to scatter in dozens of different directions. The ripple effect of that blast is going to be felt for years and years to come.

The advent of the microprocessor brought about a complete change in the outlook of the industry. Almost overnight the business became market driven instead of technology driven. It is now possible for virtually anyone to form a company and enter the computer business. You don't even have to know how to build a computer anymore. Many of the products on the market today are built from the same components (such as the Motorola 68000 or Intel 8088 microprocessors) and for all practical purposes are exactly the same. The difference is in the extra value-added features that manufacturers put in to make their products appeal to a particular market segment.

In theory, the mainframe companies had the same opportunities as everyone else did to build computers around these new inexpensive, mass produced computer chips. As a practical matter, it never happened. First of all, it was hard for them to drop their mainframe orientation. The mainframe companies were accustomed to developing their products to be part of a large system. Any new product they did come up with was usually priced too high and not functional enough to be sold as a stand-alone specialty item.

Moreover, the mainframe companies were limited in the extent to which they could delve into the new microprocessor technology. By making a major commitment to the new microprocessor technology they would render obsolete the software at their existing customer locations, something they were loath to do.

Finally, the mainframe companies possessed little sensitivity to the needs of the new breed of unsophisticated customer who was now buying computers. The mainframe companies were accustomed to dealing with large firms that employed staffs of experts to make computer buying decisions. They had no idea how to talk to the customer who wanted to buy a computer just for word processing or the small business that wanted one to prepare the weekly payroll.

On top of everything else, the industry simply was moving too fast for the mainframe companies. A few of them tried to dabble in one or two of the specialty niches, while maintaining their main thrust in general-purpose computers. But they could never quite get it right. There is no way a generalist firm can stretch its resources so thinly and remain an effective competitor (only IBM has been effective in doing this). In today's market, the company that tries to cover more than a few hot niches is doomed to failure.

The young, insurgent specialty companies do not suffer from such problems. Small and voracious, they are able to concentrate their energy and resources—marketing, management, R&D, finances —on small product lines and attack the industry like piranhas. They enjoy the advantages of leading-edge products, specialized sales forces, higher profit margins, and accelerated growth.

The first of the insurgent specialty companies are now established leaders in their respective niches. Digital Equipment, Hewlett-Packard, Storage Technology, and Wang Laboratories rode the minicomputer, peripherals, and office automation booms. All four are among the top 12 companies in the industry, with sales of over $1 billion each. They have experienced combined revenue gains that are triple those of the non-IBM mainframe companies over the past decade.

Waiting in the wings is another echelon that has already passed the half billion mark in sales: Apple Computer, the Camelot company; Data General in minicomputers; Tandem Computers, the leader in fail-safe computers; and ROLM, one of AT&T's big competitors in the market for automated switchboards. And there are others— some on the rise, some on the decline.

Then there are countless baby insurgents, if one considers $50 to $500 million in sales to be the equivalent of infancy in the computer business. This is a diverse group that includes Convergent Technologies, Apollo Computer, Commodore International, Cray Research, Diebold, Tandon, and Verbatim, to name a few. It is from among the ranks of these type of insurgents that a new leading order in the industry is taking shape.

THE COMING IMPLOSION

Although they are riding high now, the future of these specialist companies is by no means a sure thing. Already some of them show signs of not keeping the pace. Digital Equipment is in a difficult transition period that could prove painful to a company so accustomed to uninterrupted growth. Data General began to suffer in 1980 after it had failed to come out with either a superminicomputer or a personal computer. Storage Technology is feeling the heat from IBM, and so is Apple.

Playing the niche market is a tricky business. Today's hot new niche is tomorrow's dated, price-competitive, overcrowded niche. Because there are so many of these specialty companies, the customer has trouble distinguishing among them. And those companies that are truly successful often have trouble handling their growth. They try to move into other niches, but then they aren't specialists anymore. They become just more high-flying, high-technology glamour companies, past their prime and experiencing growth problems.

In the long run, I am pessimistic about the future of many of these specialist hardware companies. The long-term trend of the industry is running against them. In the end, they may be undone by the very technology that made their existence possible in the first place: the microprocessor.

The microprocessor introduced the possibility of affordable computer hardware. It made possible the explosion of computer devices that we are seeing all around us and by doing so it is credited with opening up a whole new era in computing. Actually, the microprocessor did something far more profound. It ended an era. The invention of the microprocessor marked the end of the hardware era, a time when a company could expect to make money just by pumping iron.

The specialization occurring today involves custom solutions for a seemingly endless list of vertical industry markets, from hardware stores, to small insurance agents, to large Wall Street brokerage firms, to dentists' offices, to hospitals, to lawyers, to government agencies—you name it. But a custom solution ultimately means one thing: software. To appeal successfully to these markets, the instructions inside the computer are as important (if not more so) as the computer itself. Cheap hardware made it possible for all of these specialty markets to come into existence in the first place, but it is software that is going to reap the benefit over the long term. Software and data services firms are already making their presence felt in the industry. Electronic Data Systems, Computer Sciences, and Automatic Data Processing have all passed the half billion mark in sales, and several others, including Shared Medical Systems, National Data, Quotron Systems, Cullinet, and MSA, have established themselves as major players. By 1988, software and data services firms will account for nearly one out of every three dollars made in the industry.

To be sure, the hardware companies still have a few tricks up their sleeves. For one, the need for faster and more powerful computers will demand even more powerful computer chips. One start-up, Trilogy Systems (discussed in Chapter 11), is banking on its ability to create an extremely powerful new computer chip 4 inches square. Silicon, the material now used for most computer chips, may be replaced in many applications by chips made of gallium arsenide, which generates much less heat and therefore allows greater density. Today's storage devices—disks and tapes—which are based on principles of magnetism, may be replaced by devices whose elements are produced biologically in a test tube, rather than through a chemical process. Bulky cathode ray tubes will be replaced by flat panel displays less than a half inch thick. Keyboards will be supplemented by terminals capable of accepting input through direct speech and maybe even eye contact, eventually.

Nevertheless, the future clearly belongs to software. With the end of the hardware era, the computer industry finds itself in the throes of the same change it has forced on other industries: It is entering the information age. The programmer is replacing the design engineer in importance. The instructions that make the computer run are becoming more valuable than the computer itself.

As software gains ascendancy, a new word will arise to characterize the activities of the industry. The key words will no longer be *customization, specialization,* and *market niche.* The new word will be *integration.* All computer equipment will need to communicate. The mainframe must be able to share data with the personal computer. The minicomputer must be able to take information from the computerized telephone switchboard, or PBX (private branch exchange). The word processor must be able to speak to the typesetting machine. Communications networks will be needed to facilitate the attaching of equipment, regardless of make or location.

Satellites, phone lines, packet-switched networks, and local area networks will all play a role.

Systems integration, the job of attaching a far-flung proliferation of computer equipment into one large network, will be the most sophisticated and difficult task computer companies will have to undertake. It will be the most software-intensive, value-added aspect of the business. Ultimately, it will also be the most profitable. The commonly voiced prediction that electronic data networks will be our "highways and railroads" of the future is more than just talk. An enormous investment is going to be made in these new information networks that will result in billions of dollars in business for the firms that can provide systems integration services.

Already the federal government is awarding massive contracts, dubbed *megacontracts* in the industry, to upgrade existing information networks and also create new ones. At the Postal Service, for example, a contract is expected to be awarded that calls for the creation of a network of computers and other devices at 22,000 post offices around the country to automate the retail functions, such as stamp dispensing and package mailing. Total cost of this contract: $3 billion.

Such projects dwarf the traditional public works projects we read about in newspapers and hear debated in Congress. They are to our time what such projects as the Triborough Bridge, the Tennessee Valley Authority, and the Hoover Dam were to earlier generations. The creation of vast electronic information networks will be the new public works projects of the information age. And the government is not the only customer for such computer systems integration services. Many of the leading Fortune 500 firms with their worldwide operations will soon be awarding contracts just as big as those now being put out by Washington.

The trend toward the integration of vast numbers of computer devices into communicating networks may eventually play into the hands of the broad-based generalist mainframe companies—if they can survive until then. These companies are ideally suited for that kind of work, having both the knowledge and resources to build and tie together networks for customers. Other new industry leaders may well come from the ranks of the data services industry: companies, such as Electronic Data Systems, that are already experi-

enced at integrating hardware and software with information databases of all kinds. Electronic Data Systems, in fact, has already
scored some major victories in this area (see Chapter 9).

A classic match is now shaping up between the mainframe companies and the data services firms. If they can get their act together,
the mainframe companies can offer major economies of scale in the
creation of the hardware needed for these networks. Data services
firms will be competing based on their knowledge and expertise
in coordinating vast networks and satisfying the needs of diverse
users. In effect, the match-up will be brawn versus brains.

There will be no shortage of companies vying for a share of this
market. Already a host of companies have lined up to participate
in software, communications, and systems integration. They range
from AT&T (newly deregulated) and Satellite Business Systems (the
joint venture of IBM, Comsat General Corporation, and Aetna Life
& Casualty) to such network vendors as Tymnet and Telenet. Equipment within a building or complex will be able to communicate
over local area networks (LANs), such as Ethernet (supported by
Xerox, Digital Equipment, and Intel), WangNet (by Wang), Marlan
(by NCR), and the yet to be announced local area network by IBM.
Cullinet, MSA, and Informatics General have software that permits
personal computers to communicate with IBM mainframes.

IBM is virtually certain to be a major player both through Satellite
Business Systems and the local area network it plans to announce,
and because all communications protocols will have to be compatible with IBM's de facto communications standard, Systems Network Architecture (SNA).

Notably absent from among the ranks of these possible systems
integration competitors are many of the small, specialty hardware
companies that are rapidly populating today's market. They have
little talent for systems integration. Increasingly, they will find
themselves caught in a commodity business that is competitive and
price sensitive with little value added. They will no longer set the
pace in computers the way they do today.

The pendulum will have shifted. The industry will have come
full circle: from centralized data centers; to a plethora of incompatible, unattached computers; to the creation of integrated networks and systems. Computers will have evolved from a nucleus,

to an explosion, to an implosion. This is the McClellan Implosion
Theory. Those who choose to ignore it do so at their peril.

THE TOP 10

These changes that are dramatically altering the computer landscape will not occur overnight—but they will occur. For evidence
of that you need only look to the exclusive listing of Top 10 companies that lead the industry. The 1980s will see the greatest change
in this ranking of any previous decade.

Below are the Top 10 companies as they were listed by *Datamation* magazine in 1980 and my predictions as to the companies
that will hold those positions in 1990.

Top 10–1980[a]	Top 10–1990
1. IBM	1. IBM
2. NCR	2. Digital Equipment
3. Control Data	3. Wang Laboratories
4. Digital Equipment	4. Hewlett-Packard
5. Sperry	5. NCR
6. Burroughs	6. Electronic Data Systems
7. Honeywell	7. Control Data
8. Hewlett-Packard	8. Burroughs
9. Xerox	9. AT&T
10. Memorex	10. Japan, Inc.

[a]*Datamation*, June, 1981, p. 92.

The most noticeable difference is the departure of four major
companies that appeared in the 1980 listing. Sperry, Honeywell,

and Xerox will fall victim to the declining mainframe and, in the case of Xerox, copier markets. For Xerox, this situation is particularly tragic. Its foray into computers was eagerly awaited, but when it actually happened in the late 1960s, it was a complete disaster. Offered a second chance with the rise of the office automation market, Xerox has made a valiant effort but for the most part has missed the boat (see Chapter 6).

For Sperry and Honeywell, their story is all too familiar. They realized too late that the mainframe era was over and offered too little in their catch-up effort. Even in 1980, Memorex was already a troubled manufacturer of IBM plug-compatible peripherals. It would not have appeared on the 1990 listing even if it had not been acquired by Burroughs in 1981.

Three other mainframe companies will fall several notches. Even with the addition of Memorex, Burroughs falls in ranking, as do NCR and Control Data. Like Sperry and Honeywell, Burroughs realized too late that the mainframe market was maturing and that new strategies were called for. The turnaround being orchestrated by former Treasury Secretary Michael Blumenthal is a steep uphill battle. NCR and Control Data can be expected to make out the best of the non-IBM mainframe computer companies, although they will both experience a drop in the rankings. To its credit, NCR realized early that the mainframe market was going nowhere and that the company would also go nowhere in that market. So NCR established efforts in several specialty markets early on. Control Data began diversifying away from mainframes years ago and is now entrenched in data services, peripheral storage devices, printers, and other specialty markets, such as supercomputers. Perhaps if it had not diversified so much, Control Data could have done even better. (For a discussion of all the non-IBM mainframe companies, see Chapter 5.)

IBM, of course, remains No. 1. It has dominated the computer industry since 1956, when it surpassed Remington Rand (later to become part of the Sperry Corporation). It has never looked back since, and there is no reason to believe it will have to in the future. With 1983 revenues of $40 billion, IBM is equivalent in size to the next 13 computer companies combined and eight times bigger than its nearest competitor. Each year, IBM's growth is equivalent to more than the total size of Digital Equipment.

A fortunate early start and brute force (which led to charges that the company was guilty of antitrust violations) were keys to IBM's early success. Although IBM built its presence in the market through mainframes, it has more recently achieved leadership in several key specialty niches, including personal computers and peripheral equipment (disk drives), as well as some special-application machines (word processing) and software. Of all the generalist mainframe companies, IBM is the only one that successfully spread its tentacles into several different specialty markets. Today, it is management and marketing expertise, combined with an aggressive technological push, automated low-cost manufacturing, and a legal campaign against competitive infringement, that is enabling IBM to retain its premier position.

By dint of its enormous customer base, IBM will be the one to set industry compatibility and communications standards. In the coming era of systems integration, IBM will play the piper's tune that others will have to dance to. (See Chapter 4 for more on IBM.)

Immediately after IBM are the three major success stories of the computer industry. Digital Equipment, Wang Laboratories, and Hewlett-Packard were tiny companies a decade ago when they were staking out their claims in the emerging minicomputer and word processing markets. Their emphasis on products that were small and versatile enabled them to capitalize perfectly on the minicomputer boom. Though they face challenges from microcomputer upstarts and have all experienced growing pains that require a transition, these companies appear to be the new order in the industry for the next few years.

Electronic Data Systems should be the first of the new breed of systems integrator to break into the Top 10. Known best for its high-profile chairman and founder, H. Ross Perot, the company is already a leading data services firm within the industry. As such, it is positioned ideally to provide the software integration services that companies will increasingly need in the coming era.

At the bottom of the list are two new entrants that may not be surprising but are certainly controversial. First, with the consent of the Federal Communications Commission (provided in the 1981 decision known as Computer Inquiry No. II), AT&T is now permitted to enter the unregulated business of providing computer hardware and services. AT&T's debut has not been an auspicious one. The company seems to be concentrating first on making up for lost ground. Because it has given up a good chunk of its telecommunications equipment market to such competitors as ROLM and Northern Telecom, it has to first win some of that back before it can make a thrust in computers. But an even bigger question has to do with the fact that AT&T has never had to compete in the open market before. Can a formerly regulated company change its stripes?

Japan is the most controversial new competitor. Concern that Japanese companies will take over the computer industry the way they did automobiles and consumer electronics is a commonly voiced fear. Yet, there is really no reason to worry. Computer technology, products, and markets are changing so fast, accelerating to such a degree, that the Japanese will have trouble getting a foothold. The Japanese threat will remain just that: more a threat than an inroad, at least until the computer business matures.

Japanese influence will be felt the most in inexpensive, low-value-added products, such as personal computers, printers, terminals, and semiconductors. They are at a disadvantage providing more sophisticated kinds of computing, where software, systems integration, service, and marketing are more important. The computer industry may still be moving too fast for the Japanese to catch up. Yet, the Japanese influence on U.S. computer manufacturers may be telling. The mere threat of Japanese penetration will push U.S. computer companies to concentrate on quality, strive for low-cost production, pursue creative and varied marketing channels, and provide services equivalent to none other than IBM.

If any of these companies (or countries) can't cut the mustard, there are always others ready to take their place. ROLM, especially with its new alliance with IBM, could well be a competitor through its computerized telephone switchboards (or PBXs), which are capable of handling both voice and data. And then there is Tandem Computer, the inventor of one of the most novel but eagerly accepted computer systems: a fail-safe computer.

NEVER THE SAME AGAIN

As the decade unwinds, the computer industry will experience other changes, more subtle but perhaps more profound than the shake-up in the Top 10 lineup. Computers will become mundane, not arcane the way they are today. The awe and mystique that surround computers and the people who work with them will gradually dissipate. IBM is already as common to the populace as GE, General Motors, and Exxon. IBM made the cover of *Time* magazine in 1983. Its day of recognition is here.

The government will become more involved in the computer industry, to stimulate cooperation, safeguard against information abuses, thwart the theft of valuable trade secrets, and perhaps address protectionism. Consumers will become more active and aware of the business. Social issues will arise, such as concern over privacy invasion (already much talked about) and the fear that computers will only help widen the gap between the rich and poor. Legal issues of the information age, such as copyright protection and computer crime, will be debated through the courts.

Computers will become the single most valuable resource in the United States. They will replace automobiles in importance within the next year and oil by sometime in the 1990s; that is, sales will reach well over $500 billion by that time. Even with such giants as IBM and AT&T, control over the industry will be more diffuse than it is today. The business will belong to everyone, the computer users, the data suppliers, the computer engineers, the software programmers, the retail distributors . . . not just the stockholders and management of the computer companies. It will never be the same again.

2
Success Gone Wild

Y ou know an industry has arrived when even the most innocuous new products are announced with great fanfare at sumptuous luncheons in expensive restaurants where the attendees are sent away with slick, glossy handouts. The young computer company on the rise today would never dream of making its public debut without first signing up with one of the high-priced media firms that specialize in high-tech clients: Regis McKenna out West; Strayton Group, and for some recent high fliers, Miller Communications back East.

This attention to the finer points of image polishing is apparently one of the inevitable accompaniments of a growing successful industry. There are others, not all of them quite so benign. The changes that are occurring in the industry today—fragmentation, specialization, and (over the long term) integration—have unleashed a whole set of forces that are altering every nook and cranny of the industry, from product cycles and growth patterns, to marketing and management, to relations between the industry and its customers and investors. Things are not getting any easier. They are harder and more confusing than ever. The computer industry is struggling to accommodate the very success it has achieved in abundance.

It is almost enough to make one long for the old days, when there were fewer companies, fewer products, and you needed a degree in computer science to understand the press releases. But really, life wasn't any easier back then. It only seems that way now.

For a business that has the word *winner* written all across it, the computer industry, from the very beginning, has had a problematic relationship with its own winning ways. The heroic success stories that have occurred in the computer industry (lone inventor achieves breakthrough, founds company, makes millions, becomes famous, advises presidents, etc.), have not yet been elevated to the mythic level of Thomas Edison or Henry Ford, or been made into a film, a sign of sure acceptance.

In fact, if most people are a bit fuzzy about the origins of computers, there is good reason for their confusion. While the early days did see a number of significant breakthroughs by lone inventors, in many cases those early accomplishments have been overshadowed by subsequent patent disputes and personal quarrels as well as corporate mistakes and marketing errors that blurred their impact.

This confusion also extends to the companies that helped found the industry itself, such as Remington Rand (later Sperry), GE, RCA, Honeywell, NCR, and Burroughs. Far from plunging excitedly into a new realm, these companies could almost be accused of backing into the computer era reluctantly, prodded by the government. As noted in the book *The Computer Establishment*,* these corporations, which had all amassed considerable fortunes and reputations in the precomputer era, typically would be approached by a "small group of bright engineers" who had already begun work on designing computers but had lost their original financing and were fishing around for new benefactors. The corporation would buy the fledgling venture, relying on faith and a kind of imperial belief that these new fangled devices were nothing new under the sun and could be sold and supported like any other piece of capital equipment. How wrong they were. As *The Computer Establishment* explains it:

* Katherine Davis Fishman, *The Computer Establishment*, (New York: Harper & Row, 1981).

> The corporation was not quite sure what it had bought. It knew
> computers would be significant in business somehow; meanwhile,
> the bright young engineers who understood the machine would de-
> velop it, and the corporation would sell it in the traditional way.
> Later, however, the corporation discovered it was spending enor-
> mous sums on the computer division with little to show for it. Thus
> followed a reappraisal, a change in management, tight financial
> controls, slashes in the budget, and the departure of some of the
> young entrepreneurs, now middle-aged, but complaining that the
> game wasn't fun anymore.*

For a long time, the game wasn't very much fun. Companies that
entered the business in those early days had to contend with unexpected complexities as well as the fearsome competition of IBM,
which seemed to dominate any market having to do with office
equipment by means of its colossal marketing and maintenance
capability. Success stories, not to mention profitable years, came
few and far between. Sperry threw away an early lead and failed
to make a profit until 1966 (11 years after its merger with Remington
Rand), while NCR's computer operation did not make it into the
black until 1973, approximately two decades after it first acquired
a computer division. Some never made it. RCA, GE, and later Xerox
spent millions before throwing in the towel in the early 1970s.

As GE and RCA were making their exit, however, seeds of change
were being planted that would radically alter the industry. Developments in integrated circuitry began to make computers smaller
and easier to produce. Venture capital was becoming available. No
one backed into computers anymore. Bright young engineers increasingly exercised the option to form their own companies, make
computers of their own design, and keep a big share of the profits.
Even if no Thomas Edisons appeared, the 1970s did produce a
number of remarkable success stories.

Among the most successful was Digital Equipment, the company
that invented the minicomputer. Digital Equipment sold its first

* Fishman, The Computer Establishment, p. 157. In this description, Fishman is
referring specifically to Burroughs, Honeywell, NCR, and Sperry. The computer
divisions at GE and RCA were started internally but ultimately suffered from many
of the same difficulties. IBM, as we shall see, was not an early computer pioneer,
but it soon caught up with a vengence.

minicomputer for $120,000 in 1960, a time when the cheapest main-frames were still going for way over $1 million. By the mid-1960s, it had brought its prices down to under $20,000. Sales and profits soared (they have only recently begun to stall), putting Digital on the road to becoming the No. 2 computer company.

Digital was followed in the minicomputer market by Data General, a spin-off started by former Digital engineers in 1967. Data General exuded a certain brashness (many saw it as just plain arrogance) that even then was noted as being a manifestation of the quickening tempo of the business. In an industry where profits had been scarce, Data General declared in its first advertisement that it planned "to make a lot of money." And indeed it did. By the time Data General celebrated its tenth birthday, it had surpassed the half-billion mark in sales and earned a spot on the Fortune 500 listing.*

Other new companies were also moving up quickly, grabbing a piece of the exploding market that just a few years earlier had belonged entirely to a few mainframe companies. In data services, Automatic Data Processing and Electronic Data Systems were showing even then that hardware wasn't the only game in town. Both sustained a level of growth that put them over the half-billion mark in sales by the early 1980s.

In retrospect, however, these success stories of the 1970s now seem tame compared to what was to follow. As Data General was celebrating its tenth birthday in 1977, one of the industry's most unconventional start-ups was just getting off the ground. Whereas Data General typified the hyped-up East Coast aggressiveness, Steve Jobs and Steve Wozniak brought the computer industry its first, true-to-life, California counterculture success story. It took Apple Computer only 5 years to reach the half-billion-dollar sales mark. Jobs and Wozniak did it with a product—a *microcomputer*, a *home*

---

* Data General may also become the first computer company to take its place on the silver screen. Film rights were purchased by Columbia Pictures to *The Soul of a New Machine*, (Boston: Little, Brown, 1981), the best-selling book by Tracy Kidder detailing the creation of Data General's 32-bit Eclipse superminicomputer. The spirit of Edison may yet live on in the character of Tom West, Kidder's major protagonist.

computer, a *personal computer*; no one was quite sure at first what to dub it officially—far less sophisticated than any computer Data General ever produced. In fact, Apple earned the notable distinction of accomplishing the most spectacular rise in American business history, in the most complex industry in history, with a product that is probably less complicated than most toaster ovens.

A bit too simple? There obviously is something peculiar and as yet unfathomed about an industry that spurns the likes of GE and RCA and then a few years later rolls out the red carpet for grass roots start-ups like Data General and Apple.

There is a lesson to be learned here: First impressions are not to be trusted. All is not so simple. It never was and never will be. Although many of the original barriers to success (untried technology, lack of market acceptance, IBM's domination) have been eliminated or blunted, new ones have arisen to take their place. The main barrier is the reality of success itself. The computer market today is overcrowded, underpriced, and sensitive to every tiny shift in the economy.

At times, it seems to be operating on permanent overdrive. Eventually something will have to give. A shakeout is inevitable, not because the industry isn't big enough, but because it is too big—and too important—to be won simply by dumping millions of computers into homes and offices across the land. Success is spoiling the industry. Too many companies are believing what they hear at these expensive luncheons and what they read in their glossy press kits.

We will now take a look at the situation facing the industry by focusing on four key trends: the technology glut, turbulent growth patterns, economic sensitivity, and customer sophistication.

TECHNOLOGY GLUT

The technology revolution of the 1970s has become the technology glut of the 1980s. Too many companies are selling too many products. Computer trade shows, which were once respectable, professional affairs, now resemble carnivals. In 1982, at Comdex, a

semiannual trade show, there were some 3200 booths and literally hundreds of new products. By November 1983, the show, which was held in Las Vegas, boasted more than 5000 booths.

The original purpose for which these shows were created has long since been forgotten. Nobody can attend one of them and hope to get a perspective on where the industry is going. There is simply too much. A visitor to the four-day Comdex show in Las Vegas, going nonstop for 8 hours a day, would have had only 20 seconds to spend per booth. So many new products were announced that a new computer that seemed like a hit in the morning often found itself leapfrogged by a half-dozen competitors by midafternoon. And remember, at this particular convention, the entire computer industry was not represented—just microcomputers (which, despite their rapid rise, still account for a comparatively small segment of total industry revenues).

Although it seems as if there is room for everybody in the computer industry with its overall growth rates of more than 15% per year, this is really not the case. Even though the pie is getting bigger, in this era of specialization, no one can even attempt to munch the whole pie—just one or two slices at most. But the slices are getting thinner and thinner, and there are too many people looking for a bite.

In word processing, for example, six companies (IBM, Wang, Lanier, Xerox, CPT, and NBI) control 70% of the market. For the remaining 30%, there are more than 100 competitors. Obviously they can't all survive. Some of the early word processing casualties include Burroughs and Management Assistance. Even among the leaders, there is trouble. By concentrating on a market for the simpler, stand-alone word processor—a market that is now maturing—Lanier and CPT are losing ground.

In the explosive market for microcomputers, the situation is similar, with an added twist. Two million microcomputers were shipped in 1983, with IBM, Apple, Tandy, and Commodore commanding 75% of the market. What success will the 150 other competitors have chasing the remaining share, even with the incredible demand for these small computers? Add to that the problem these companies will have in just getting their products in front of customers. Limited shelf space in retail stores may be the undoing of many

vendors. There are only 2000 retail stores, and the battle for shelf space is heated. Too many vendors are clogging up too few distribution channels. Something has to give. While new companies spring up constantly, such as the latest whirlwind, Compaq Computers, microcomputer disasters are occurring with equal frequency, such as Xerox, Vector Graphic, Osborne, Texas Instruments, Atari, and Victor Technology.

Limited shelf space is not the only reason that many vendors' computers do not find their way into customers' hands. Although office automation equipment offers substantial productivity gains and cost savings, the reality is that during the next several years customer expenditures for such capital equipment will outpace any savings from improved efficiency. The success of many office automation vendors will depend on the patience of customers who are willing to purchase aggressively, despite the long-term nature of the payoff—a risky proposition at best.

The enormous implications of the technology glut are most evident in mainframes. Once the dominant source of revenues in the industry, mainframes are now just another market sector. Today there are 10 companies supplying many different models. But with demand growing at only 6% annually, there is room for only two or three. IBM sets the industry standard, and its already awesome dominance is becoming even more expansive. As IBM continues to gain share above 70%, the others must consolidate.

The technology glut is not only a matter of quantity. It is affecting quality as well. In any particular sector in today's computer industry, product leadership is almost impossible to maintain for very long. Product cycles, which once had a predictable ebb and flow, have shrunk into a series of stutter steps. Mainframes, which once could be counted on to have a viable life span of 5 years, now last no more than 3. The standard 4-year cycle of minicomputers has been cut in half. Microcomputers, terminals, and word processing products are made obsolete annually.

It is not unusual for a seemingly hot new product to be announced and then surpassed by several competitors before it even makes it into production. Manufacturers have adapted to this by making an attractive, follow-on model an important part of their product strategy. Yet this too encourages the trend toward shrinking product cycles, causing existing products to become obsolete sooner and more abruptly.

Compact technology cycles are causing havoc in all the other areas that a business needs to be successful in, such as personnel, production, marketing, and customer practices. In today's market, leading-edge technology companies almost inevitably end up as laggards, as illustrated by Storage Technology (peripheral storage devices), Prime Computer (superminicomputers), Osborne (personal computers), Memorex (peripheral storage devices), and National Advanced Systems (mainframes).

TURBULENT GROWTH PATTERNS

An ideal stage occurs in the development of a new market when the market is large enough to support several companies profitably, without too much head-on competition; is not yet overcrowded; and is still small enough to grow fast. Unfortunately, this ideal stage almost never occurs today, and the computer industry is suffering because of it.

Markets in the computer industry are currently at one extreme stage or another. Some are in their infancy: unprofitable, tiny, not yet a business. Executive-level office automation, artificial intelligence, and voice response terminals are in this stage now. Others are large, heavily exploited, and intensely price and product competitive. This category includes mainframes, traditional minicomputers, terminals, word processing, and many of the newer specialty markets. Microcomputers have also joined these ranks.

The ideal in-between stage almost never occurs because, in today's highly visible industry, too many competitors have designs on infant markets far in advance of their development. Investors now approach the industry with their wallets open. Capital is flowing from every conceivable direction. Every week during 1982 and 1983, various private computer firms went public, issuing their stock to outside investors and finding more than enough willing to help them raise capital for expansion and new product development. Rothchild, Unterberg, Tobin; Montgomery Securities; and Hambrecht & Quist are Wall Street brokerage firms that have been leaders in taking thousands of young high-technology companies public in recent years.

R&D limited partnership tax shelters are another form of capital being directed into the industry, in this case from individuals. Storage Technology, Anderson-Jacobson, Anacomp, and Matrix are among the firms using this vehicle for capital formation. Finally, many older established companies are altering courses to dip into one of the exploding niche markets. United Technologies, Schlumberger, McDonnell Douglas, Gould, and TRW have made major acquisitions and joint venture agreements, while GE and General Dynamics express interest in doing the same.

No matter how the investment is made, it all adds up to the same result: There is too much capital pursuing too few viable new companies. The result of this investment pressure is the emergence of a "cut off your nose to spite your face" attitude toward long-term growth. Managing computer companies beyond the start-up phase has become a no-win proposition. It is something akin to sprinting and running a marathon at the same time. The winner must be able to satisfy investors with a fast start and big profits, and yet conserve enough resources to survive over the long haul.

Most managers today have decided to become sprinters and forget about the marathon. They milk the business dry, take their high-flying companies public while they can, become millionaires, and cash in shortly thereafter, only to start another sprint elsewhere. Management invariably holds huge stock investments in their own companies through liberal use of stock options and stock incentives for employees. Management, therefore, gives undue attention to current profit performance and stock prices to keep this vested interest intact, to keep employee incentive worthwhile and valuable, and to keep morale up. They manage the stock price instead of the company.

Future growth is sacrificed in the face of investor demand for immediate stock performance. R&D, maintenance, and marketing are shortchanged. For a company to grow and prosper, it needs its original management. After the pioneers leave, so-called professional management is usually unable to foster the creative and entrepreneurial leadership and atmosphere that are necessary to compete in today's fast-paced, leading-edge computer markets.

ECONOMIC SENSITIVITY

Computers were once believed to be exempt from the ravaging effects of the economy. "Computers are always in demand because they help customers automate and save costs," ran one old adage. Another held that the computer business is a "growth industry immune to the economy." These old saws died hard in the 1970s and early 1980s.

External economic influences actually have been taking their toll for more than a decade, and with each recession the impact becomes more pronounced. Many people in the computer industry have been learning this fact the hard way. Digital Equipment was surprised in 1983 when demand fell and orders declined. Most of the industry experienced the same. But Digital did not take steps to deal with the situation, so costs remained high and profits plummeted.

There does not have to be a sales decline in order for problems to occur. A decline is actually a rarity. All that is necessary to create an adverse effect on profits is a slowdown in the *rate at which sales are growing.*

The main reason behind the industry's increased sensitivity to economic cycles is not hard to fathom. As the market has gone beyond general-purpose mainframes (used primarily by large organizations for accounting and financial tasks) and fragmented into dozens of specialty niches, the industry has become as sensitive to economic fluctuations as the broad and diverse group of end users it serves. Now when the economy goes into a slump, the computer industry lurches. When fewer houses are built, fewer cars are sold, or fewer banking transactions are made, these influences all add up to a temporarily weaker demand for computers.

Measures can be taken to lessen the impact of this decreased demand. A company can become more aggressive in selling and pricing; it can make use of more liberal payment terms and easier collection policies; inventory can be allowed to stack up in the pipeline; bad orders (that customers do not really want or are unable to pay for) can be shipped; products that are easier to sell, but lower in profit, can be emphasized. But these measures will not alleviate the overall impact of soft demand; they will only delay it for a few quarters at best. Eventually the slow bookings will catch up and the impact is often magnified as a result of the desperate measures taken earlier to offset the slowdown.

In a worst-case scenario, these measures could result in a loss of financial control, as happened at Datapoint in 1982 and Digital Equipment in 1983. More typically, overhead as a percentage of total costs will rise, sometimes dramatically. Computer companies historically are reluctant to reduce investments in plant, personnel, and R&D for fear of losing market share in the event of a rapid upturn. This will have to change. As is becoming evident to nearly everyone, the management of computer companies have a lot to learn from places like Detroit and Pittsburgh.

Even the high-flying specialty companies are not immune. Several notable earnings declines or slowdowns evident at specialized niche companies during the 1982–1983 recession go beyond mere coincidence (i.e., Tandem Computers, Automatic Data Processing, Prime Computer, Computervision, Triad Systems, NBI, Lanier, CPT, and Harris).*

As a rule, however, the newer specialty markets are less vulnerable to economic downturns than other more mature elements of the computer industry. The purchase of a mainframe, for example, represents a large capital expenditure, requiring the approval of upper-level management at most end-user organizations. The impact of the economy on mainframe orders is felt immediately, even though the actual effect on revenues may be delayed for a year.

In the case of minicomputers, the impact of the economy is immediate. Changes in the capital spending rate or the gross national product show up in minicomputer company revenues within a few months (see Figure 2.1). Part of the reason for the enormous sensitivity of the minicomputer companies to economic fluctuation is due to one-third of their sales are coming from original equipment manufacturers (OEMs). These firms are primarily small businesses that purchase minicomputers at a volume discount, jazz the com-

---

* Because few specialty companies have been in business 10 years, the effect of the recession is but one of several adverse influences that can disrupt progress. Small, growing explosively, and pushing the technology, these companies are highly vulnerable to wrenching product cycle transitions (Prime and NBI in 1983); changes in a market, while the firm stands pat (Tymshare in the data services market in 1982); mergers and acquisitions (Docutel in 1983); or new internal accounting procedures (Tandem in 1983). In some cases, the effect of the recession can actually camouflage such other influences.

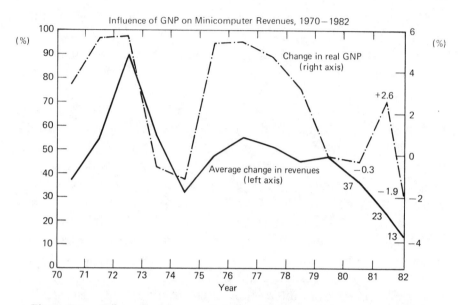

Figure 2.1. Influence of gross national product on minicomputer revenues, 1970–1982. Only in recent years has a strengthening economy failed to equally stimulate minicomputer demand due to inroads into that market by microcomputers. *Source:* Salomon Brothers Inc.

puters up with extra hardware and software, and resell the final system to various end-user markets. Hardware OEMs supply general-purpose systems to a broad market and are therefore very sensitive to reduced capital spending rates, high interest rates, or tight money. Software OEMs, on the other hand, add software to a standard minicomputer system to make it marketable to a specific market niche. The health of these OEMs is much more dependent on what is happening inside that particular market niche.

To offset economic sensitivity, minicomputer companies have increased their efforts to bypass the OEMs by building their own sales forces to market directly to end-user customers so as to penetrate new markets and control their own destiny more closely.

CUSTOMER SOPHISTICATION

Computers today are smaller, faster, lighter, cheaper, more powerful, more versatile, more popular, and, most importantly, more understood. Computers are losing their mystique. A new generation of professionals, managers, and white-collar personnel who have been exposed to the computer since high school is taking over. The next generation is being exposed to computers in grammar school.

In 1964, there were 24,000 computers installed, mostly IBM model 1401 mainframes that sold for about $1 million apiece in today's terms. By 1983, more than 7 million computer units were in use. More than half of them were microcomputers selling for under $10,000. Commercially available software programs now number over 32,000.

By the end of this decade, there will be almost 40 million computerized devices in offices. Almost 50% of all workers will use a computer terminal on a regular basis. Among white-collar workers, the ratio of personnel to computer devices will decline to nearly 1 to 1 from today's 5 to 1 ratio.

Computer-aided decision making is part of today's corporate youth culture—one of the essentials for a young man or woman on the rise. A computer is as important to this new generation as a desk or a telephone. Recent MBAs hired at major firms are demanding personal computers for their work.

This increase in user sophistication is the most expected and logical, yet the least controllable aspect of the fast-growing computer market. It is one that is almost unique to the computer industry. While consumers in other industries, such as the automobile industry, can express their preferences on such things as size, color, and extra add-ons, the needs of customers in the computer industry are integrated into the product to a degree not imaginable elsewhere. The permutations and combinations of features and products can be endless.

The immediate effect of this increase in customer sophistication is to further hasten the decline of the general-purpose mainframe companies. At one time, customers would seek to satisfy all their data processing needs from their mainframe vendor. Today, dependence on a single mainframe vendor has gone the way of the keypunch machine. It is no longer unusual to visit a large organization and find it using, for example, an IBM mainframe, Storage Technology disk or tape drives, Raytheon CRT terminals, Dataproducts printers, Hewlett-Packard color plotters, an in-house time-sharing network using Prime Computer or Tandem Computers equipment, Apple personal computers, and Wang word processors, all supplemented by an outside time-sharing network service.

With the end of the mainframe era, the domain of the management information services (MIS) director has greatly diminished. Spending on computers has become more democratic. Once responsible for nearly the entire data processing budget, the MIS department now directs only 75% of such expenditures, and the proportion is decreasing. Management and administrative personnel in the far-flung reaches of most organizations are now so familiar with word processing and personal computing that such buying decisions have become almost completely decentralized. Most large organizations today have no idea of exactly how many computers and office systems have sprung up in their offices.

The willingness of customers to go for it, to experiment, to be creative in automating the office and factory, has played a vital role in the emergence of the small specialized computer companies that are now proliferating throughout the industry. Once again, however, appearances are deceiving. This growing customer sophistication that has encouraged the rise of the specialty companies also contains the seeds of their demise. Customers may be more sophisticated today, but they still seem like kids in a candy store. They want more, more, more, but they want it for less, less, less. The mass, low-cost highly automated production techniques needed to compete in this market run counter to what small companies focusing on narrow market niches are capable of accomplishing. Something has to give.

But even before it does, customers will have a new demand: They will want all their shiny, new computers to be able to talk to each other. While this has not yet stopped the march toward more incompatible product offerings by new and different companies, it soon will. The way is being cleared for the rise of the systems integrators. Uniqueness will give way to compatibility. Explosion will be followed by implosion.

Technology is the straw that stirs the drink in the computer industry. By next decade, though, customers are going to have their say. And when they do, watch out!

3

The New Winning Formula for Computers

The computer industry is being turned on its head. Small companies are displacing big companies. Information contained inside the machines is valuable and proprietary, while the machines themselves are becoming a commodity. Specialized products are replacing general-purpose equipment. The companies emerging as winners have a lot in common—a new formula for success that enables a company to make the transition from the hardware era to the software era, to survive in an industry that is fragmenting and imploding at the same time, and to remain solvent in a business no longer immune from the vicissitudes of a troubled economy. This new formula has eight critical components. We'll call them the eight Ss. No one company has all eight, but to be successful, a company must be well positioned in most of these crucial areas.

The first three—selling, service, and software—are familiar to anyone following the industry. The virtues of this triumvirate have been stated and restated time and again. As the industry transforms, however, these three capabilities assume a position of heightened importance. In an industry where hardware has become an indistinguishable commodity, selling, service, and software will separate the winners from the losers.

A second group of four critical factors is evident from the analysis of the industry contained in Chapter 2. A company must be *small* and *specialized* to be able to act quickly in a fast-changing and fragmented industry. And a new *style of management* is necessary which departs from the professional management techniques honed by the broad-based computer companies of the hardware era. A successful company will also need access to financial resources that will not place heavy demands for repayment of interest expense during periods when the company might be experiencing a slow-down. *Stock financing* has this advantage over debt.

Finally, any company that hopes to survive and compete over the long haul will have to sell more than discrete computer products. It will have to offer *systems compatibility*. The features that now sell a computer product, such as the amount of memory or the speed of the processing unit, will become secondary to whether or not the product can share data and communicate with other equipment. As the computer industry fragments and new products blitz customers from all directions, systems compatibility, probably IBM compatibility, will be a prerequisite. A machine will not stand alone, out in the cold, unable to tie into other machines.

SELLING

Marketing is king in the computer industry—and it is going to stay that way. Since the 1950s, the army of dark-suited, white-shirted, IBM salespeople has been the major reason for the predominance of that company. Not only IBM but many of the big winners, including Digital Equipment, Hewlett-Packard, and Wang, as well as such newcomers as Tandem Computers and Tandy Radio Shack, owe a large measure of their success to the decision to create their own sales network.

A variety of marketing channels are being used extensively today, including dealers, distributors, and most recently retail stores where computers are sold like stereos. Yet the lessons learned by the big winners are more important than ever. In all but the mass consumer and OEM markets, a company-operated sales network is not a luxury, it is a necessity. Those who try to get around that fact are just fooling themselves. Sooner or later a sales force must be established.

The way a product is sold is more important than the product itself. This is true (albeit unpleasant to contemplate) whether the product is a car, a computer, or a new formula for shampoo. Marketing is even more important than product technology. A company that operates its own sales network ensures that it has control over this process. To entrust this function to a source outside the company places the integrity and reputation of the product in someone else's hands. A computer company must insure that the end customer is getting the message as to why the product is superior, why it is best suited to the needs of the user, how it can be used, and why its quality, reliability, price, software, and after service are the best. Such vital aspects of a product often are overlooked or misstated by third-party sellers running their own shows.

A dealer, distributor, or store may resort to overly aggressive sales techniques or heavy discount pricing that reflect poorly on both the manufacturer and the product. Financial control can be ruined through the creation of false order backlogs and excess inventory in the pipeline. A manufacturer that relies on a third-party vendor experiences an inevitable delay in obtaining critical market intelligence and customer feedback.

Because it is cheaper and easier to rely on outside marketing expertise than to employ your own, many start-up companies use third-party channels and experience an initial period of fast growth. Soon, however, they pay a price for such early success. It is almost impossible to sustain market position over the long haul when products are sold to the end user by a third party. When the time comes to make a transition to direct selling, a severe price must be paid that can cause a permanent setback. The problems experienced by such minicomputer companies as Datapoint, Data General, and Microdata are cases in point. Each spent vast sums bootstrapping a direct sales force, incurred stresses in competing with their OEM customers, and realized too late that a sales force should have been established much earlier.

Computer stores have caught the imagination of the public and many manufacturers, but retailing is a tricky business and ultimately a difficult way to sell computers. What kind of store should be used? Stores that carry the products of only one vendor have proved largely unsuccessful in selling to computer consumers because they are unable to draw enough traffic. Buyers want a choice; they want to compare. Yet in multiple-vendor stores, an intense battle for shelf space will be the undoing of many manufacturers. Personal computers from over 140 vendors just won't fit on the shelves of a typical store.

What market should the store address? Stores are a passive form of marketing. They have proved largely unsuccessful in appealing to the small-business market, where follow-up contact is essential. As a result, a split is now emerging between stores that sell to the consumer and those that target small or even large businesses. Increasingly, it will be important for stores to establish a definite image for themselves, if only because there are so many stores. Already there were almost 4,000 U.S. computer specialty stores at the end of 1983, not including more than 600 manufacturer-owned stores, such as Radio Shack Computer Centers. Coupled with the shelf-space squeeze and the problems of single-vendor stores in drawing traffic, the outlook for computer retailing is unsettled.

Even in the consumer market, a vertically integrated manufacturer, such as Tandy Radio Shack, which can directly control its own end marketing, enjoys a lasting advantage. For that reason, IBM, Digital Equipment, Xerox, and Hewlett-Packard are all using their own stores to supplement other outside retail distribution channels.

SOFTWARE AND SERVICES

Software and services have always lurked in the background of the computer industry. If only because it can't be seen by the naked eye, software for a long time has played second fiddle to hardware, although it is of undeniably more importance. Software is finally now rising to prominence. As hardware drops in price, both software and services of all types—systems engineering, systems integration, training, maintenance—are taking on tremendous added value and becoming important profit centers for computer companies.

The growth of software and services should come as no surprise. Over the past 30 years, computer hardware performance per unit of cost has advanced by a factor of nearly one million. Total user expenditures for computers (including hardware, software, and services) have increased 320-fold. Yet, despite tremendous advances in hardware performance, software programmer productivity lags far behind. Systems design, integration, and installation are major bottlenecks. As computers and their applications proliferate into sophisticated networks, the need for such services increases dramatically. Customers are being snowed under, unable to program fast enough to meet the computerization demands of their organizations and unable to hook all their machines into a common network. Software and data services companies are flourishing, filling this void.

Software and services are the kind of proprietary, easily differentiated business with high value-added potential that computer companies need in order to survive the hardware war. Software is expensive, and therefore highly profitable, costing in the neighborhood of $10 to produce a single line of programming code, which is higher than the cost of an entire microprocessor chip. Both software and services require highly skilled, experienced technical talent, of which there is a severe shortage. Programmers cannot be rushed or force fed without dire consequences. Computer equipment companies that do not have a major stake in software and services are losing position in the industry, as the profit squeeze in hardware intensifies.

The data services and software industry is expanding at a 21% rate—far faster than computer hardware. Software alone is growing 28% annually.

Company	Service Growth (%) 1978–1983	Equipment Sales Growth (%) 1978–1983
IBM	22	14
Digital Equipment	35	20
NCR	10	7
Hewlett-Packard	40	25
Wang Laboratories	60	49

The scales are tipping toward data services and software, as applications proliferate and huge sophisticated networks emerge. Several data services firms, already at the half-billion revenue size, have led the trend: Automatic Data Processing, Electronic Data Systems, and Computer Sciences. Such software companies as Management Sciences of America, Cullinet, and Computer Associates are thriving.

Systems integration specialists are replacing the general-purpose hardware manufacturers as prime contractors on big government and defense computer contracts. The U.S. Army VIABLE contract, to computerize all U.S. Army base administrative functions, and the U.S. Navy inventory control program contract were both won by Electronic Data Systems as the prime contractor, with IBM and Amdahl as subcontractors. Data services firms, like systems integrators, are also likely to win the Postal Service and Social Security Administration business. Systems integration and software are the critical elements of these projects.

Maintenance of computer equipment is emerging as a distinctive, lucrative profit center for computer hardware manufacturers. And as several companies have learned the hard way, a poor reputation for service can seriously alter fortunes in this business. Wang Laboratories suffered a slump in growth in 1981 when its sales outran its ability to supply proper after service. Burroughs also suffered from an inadequate service reputation during the latter half of the 1970s. One of the key reasons behind IBM's dominance of the industry, and what permits it to charge premium prices for its equipment, is its reliable, responsive maintenance and service.

In a highly fragmented, specialized industry, software and services are common denominators, required for all products, the glue that holds the industry together.

SIZE AND SPECIALIZATION

What is the proper size a company should attain in order to flourish, to have enough resources, yet to be responsive and on the leading edge? This matter of critical mass is often debated among economists and management theorists, and ultimately exposes the inadequacies of such theories. In the early days of capitalism, the development of an industry was likened to the growth of a forest. Companies began as tiny acorns and grew to become mighty, towering oaks. Not every acorn enjoyed such good fortune, of course. But the theory held that there was always room for another acorn to put down roots and reach for the sun.

In the modern era of capitalism, the forest scenario has been subject to some major pruning and alteration. Principles of scientific management have spawned such axioms as the "economies of scale" and the "experience curve," which argue in favor of the benefits of being big. These ideas have been joined by the analyses of such economists as John Kenneth Galbraith, who argue that, because capitalism now operates on world-scale dimensions, only large firms can successfully compete.

Lately, there has been a backlash against this scenario. In the best-selling book *Wealth and Poverty*, George Gilder sees the future of the economy in smallness and looks to the computer industry, to the "vale of cubistic new factories across the bay from San Francisco—Santa Clara's Silicon Valley where worlds indeed unfold in grains of sand."* It is Gilder's theory, apparently, that it is time we all abandon the forest and head for the beach.

Who is right? As far as an analysis of the computer industry is concerned, small size is more often than not a virtue. But it is that way partly because of the awesome domination of the industry by IBM. In the early days, big firms dominated the market. Big was considered beautiful until one by one these firms discovered the difficulty of both competing against IBM and at the same time staying abreast of a market continually being transformed by young specialty companies.

Virtually every important computer innovation has been pioneered by a small technical company, from microprocessors to minicomputers. Small firms are ideally suited for the computer market. Having little to defend, they are inherent risk takers. They can enter new markets quickly, with short R&D cycles, and not worry about

* George Gilder, *Wealth and Poverty* (New York: Bantam Books, 1981), p. 96. Actually, the proliferation of high-technology companies is down the peninsula from San Francisco, not across the bay in Oakland or up in Marin County.

damaging an existing rental or product base. And in such areas as software development, where economies of scale are of virtually no benefit, small size is ideal.

Small companies experience high growth rates, fueling spectacular increases in stock prices. Selling shares can be used to finance additional development and expansion and attract the best people—no small consideration in the computer industry, where skilled talent is hard to come by. Financial incentives are not the only aspect of small firms that employees find appealing. A small firm with an entrepreneurial atmosphere and direct access to management is an exciting place to work. Hotshot computer engineers and programmers just out of school prefer the sweatshop environment, long hours, and low pay at a small firm to the structured organization of a larger company. Actions translate directly into results. Great responsibility is obtained quickly: "I got an offer at IBM to work on a memory chip," one of Data General's young engineers told Tracy Kidder. "Here I got an offer to work on a major new machine, which was gonna be the backbone of the company sales. I'd get to do *computer* design. It wasn't hard to make that choice."*

The ideal size for a computer company is about $1 billion. Any bigger and specialization and incentive begin to suffer. The advantages of large size—more funds for R&D, more marketing clout, more products, and greater credibility—do not hold up well in an industry that is fragmenting into specialty niches. In today's computer industry, a company must do one or two things well. By concentrating in a narrow market sector on one type of product or service, efforts are not spread too thinly. Reaction times to competitive developments and market changes are short. The elapsed time between market intelligence, new strategies, management decisions, product development, and sales force product rollout is minimal. For example, Convergent Technologies conceived of its workslate portable microprocessor and delivered the product in only 9 months.

Once a company gets too big, it finds itself in competition with IBM, which is always a perilous position to be in. IBM can make life difficult for a firm too successful on IBM's turf, as Control Data, the plug-compatible mainframe and peripheral manufacturers, and the leasing companies discovered in the 1960s and 1970s, and as

---

* Tracy Kidder, *The Soul of a New Machine* (Boston: Little, Brown, 1981), p. 62.

the personal computer and compatible data terminal companies are discovering in the 1980s. Of course, once a specialty market is a proven success, IBM can swoop in for a landing, apply its enormous resources, and capture a significant share of the market. Even for IBM, however, large size is a problem, but one that it appears to be managing quite well. To obtain the benefits of smallness within bigness, IBM has established several independent business units (IBUs), free of corporate and bureaucratic overhead, to tackle such specialty niches as personal computers, software, robotics, and CAD/CAM (computer-aided design/computer-aided manufacturing.) Even for a giant such as IBM, small is beautiful.

STYLE OF MANAGEMENT

The management style of the small, specialist computer company of today's industry is altogether different from that of the larger, broader based computer companies of years past. The key to this new style is the preservation of an entrepreneurial atmosphere that animates the organization from top to bottom. Small size makes it possible for such an atmosphere to flourish. A small firm permits formal and informal lines of communication to operate side by side and does not encourage the formal regimented procedures that are the inevitable accompaniment to growth. Individual accomplishment is more easily recognized. Office politics, while inevitable anywhere, can be kept to a minimum.

But small size is not in itself enough to create an entrepreneurial atmosphere. It is up to management first to plant the seed. Leadership by the founders seems essential. When management has an individual style, whether it is fun and colorful or the underdog on the hustle, it rubs off on the employees. Team spirit, enthusiasm, common goals, and a feeling of identity are all encouraged. Management really has to care about its people and show an interest—to have beer busts, sabbaticals, company nautilus equipment, and a pool. A creative nonconformist at the top means there is room for the same throughout the ranks. In theory, this air of creativity can be instilled by professional management, but this rarely happens. In almost every successful specialist computer company, its pioneer and founder is active in its affairs: Kenneth H. Olsen at

Digital Equipment (minicomputers), An Wang at Wang Laboratories (office automation), H. Ross Perot at Electronic Data Systems (data services), James H. Treybig at Tandem Computers (fault-tolerant computers), Jugi Tandon at Tandon (floppy disk drives), and John J. Cullinane at Cullinet (database software).

Preservation of an entrepreneurial atmosphere requires a delicate balancing act. A manager must be able to rein in the egocentric energies that founded the company in the first place and apply them to the more mundane tasks of managing the company's growth. Assuming the company has reached the point where it can go public, management must be able to withstand investor pressure for short-term results and make the sacrifices necessary to ensure survival over the long haul. Finally, management must be able to instill the discipline needed to withstand the upturns and downturns that are part of a cyclical economy, while still allowing an atmosphere conducive to creativity.

Ultimately, however, the most profound demand on management will occur as the computer industry continues to shift away from hardware toward software. Traditional management techniques that were developed during the industrial era are proving inadequate. The most successful companies will be those where management is able to make the adjustment to the fast-paced changes wrought by developments in microprocessors as well as the new era of software development. Management in the information society requires a new set of rules. The successful managers of the information companies themselves will be the first to write them, as the president of Intel, Andrew S. Grove, has done in his book *High Output Management*.*

STOCK FINANCING

It takes a lot of money to start a computer company and keep it going. Those who try to do it on a shoestring usually end up tripping over themselves. The way in which capital is raised—equity versus debt financing—is as important as the amount. Going public has

---

* Andrew S. Grove, *High Output Management* (New York: Random House, 1983).

all sorts of problems attached to it. The timing must be right, and anyone who thinks it is rough to manage a privately held company should try it with a bunch of anxious investors, focusing on quarter-to-quarter results. Prior to going public, cocky entrepreneurs could gamble on their own success while being accountable to virtually no one but themselves. In comparison debt financing retains a certain element of the machismo that is at the heart of capitalist lore: the gutsy entrepreneur holding off his creditors while he struggles to perfect his invention. Above all, it is a statement of faith in the future.

Since the road to a future of abundance is an awfully rocky one, and it is almost always uphill, debt financing, borrowing by issuing bonds, can be disastrous. Stock financing, issuing stock to raise money that is interest free and never has to be paid back, even though ownership is then shared, is the way to go. This is true even after a company is publicly held. The rush to the equity window by small high-technology companies making an initial public offering became almost a panic in 1983.

The computer industry today—an industry of shrinking product cycles, dramatic increases in both pre- and postproduction costs (from R&D to customer service), and major uncertainties connected with software development—simply does not lend itself to carrying a heavy debt load. Business risks are high enough without being compounded by financial risks. Debt leverage leads to higher earnings volatility, which may be pleasant on the upside when business is good but can be a heavy cost burden during slowdowns. Earnings expectations become overinflated in good times and overly disappointed in bad times. Return ratios are good enough in this industry without being magnified by debt.

By reducing or eliminating this one fixed cost, equity financing also gives a company the flexibility to finance through debt as a last resort. This feature alone is one that is healthy for an industry already suffering from a glut of products and companies. A company that relies on equity financing and does well will enjoy the benefits of high-priced stock and the easier access which that brings to financial markets. Whatever success debt financing might have in other industries, in the computer industry equity financing is the one method with a proven track record. The most successful companies in the industry have little or no debt. Those that do well and are in debt, keep it to under 30% of capitalization. And as can be seen from the following examples based on 1983 data, there is a marked difference in quality between those companies with over 30% capitalization in the form of debt and the purely equity-financed firms.

Little or No Debt	Under 30% Debt	Over 30% Debt
IBM	Wang Laboratories	Sperry
Digital Equipment	Harris	Honeywell
Hewlett-Packard	Burroughs	AT&T
Tandem Computers	Computervision	Xerox
Electronic Data Systems	NCR	Prime Computer
Data General	Control Data	Storage Technology
Automatic Data Processing	Computer Sciences	AM International
Diebold	Dataproducts	Mohawk Data Sciences

SYSTEMS COMPATIBILITY

Computer companies of the 1980s would do well to borrow from the experience of another industry that suddenly was turned on its head in a shakeout 60 years ago. Hollywood of the 1920s was home to a glamorous but nonetheless reliably profitable industry that boasted highly paid stars and built scores of gaudy movie houses. It was the silent film era, and Hollywood was convinced that things could only get better.

And things did get better. The talking picture soon arrived, and the movie business was never the same again. Another boom set in, but not all the studios took part. Many of the high fliers of the silent era found themselves with stars blessed with good looks but not so well endowed when it came to vocal cords. Other studios simply did not see the potential in sound. At first, only Fox and

Warner Brothers were willing to take the plunge. The rest held back and watched the future slip away. Most of the reigning titans of Hollywood, as one film historian put it several years later, "were blinded by their own vast empire, by the bricks and mortar of their temple-theaters . . . . they had grown cautious, fearful of endangering the solid position they so comfortably enjoyed. And thus, they missed their opportunity."*

Woe to the executives of today's computer industry who are blinded by dazzling growth rates, by the dizzying array of new products, by the seemingly limitless market potential of the industry. Woe indeed to the computer executives who grow cautious or overconfident, fearful of endangering a "solid" position. They too will be left as high and dry as those shortsighted studio heads of the 1920s. The computer industry is in for a change that will be just as dramatic as the changeover to talking pictures. We are witnessing the end of the silent era of computing. In the not-too-distant future, this era will seem as crude and archaic as silent pictures are in an age of Dolby Stereo sound.

Computers will soon be talking. In a few years, virtually no office automation or data processing equipment will stand alone. Equipment that stands alone today, such as personal computers, stand-alone word processors, and even telephones and copiers, will be tied into larger data communications and computer networks. Data will be shared and will be the most valuable aspect of the system. Voice, video, and data will intermingle. Equipment may still be sold individually, but the customer will buy it in order to make it part of an overall network. Systems compatibility will be the key feature that will sell information processing equipment. Even waste baskets will not stand alone. They will be electronic, compatible, and even equipped with "uncrumple" features.

All this is still to come. Right now, we are still in the silent era. Corporate data networks are in the early formative stages, still on the drawing board. Computers have already been distributed far and wide throughout the lower echelons of businesses, but because

---

* Benjamin Hampton, *A History of the Movies* as cited in Richard J. Whalen, *The Founding Father: The Story of Joseph P. Kennedy* (New York: New American Library, 1964), p. 83.

of systems incompatibility, exchange of data is virtually impossible. When it does occur, it is often labor intensive, requiring an operator to take data manually from one system and reenter it in another.

Solutions to the incompatibility of today's systems will not come easily. Data communications is a veritable Tower of Babel of competing technologies, standards, and protocols. But a coming together into a data and communications network is inevitable. In an information economy, there is too much at stake to prevent the talking era of computers from becoming a reality. Even today in its rudimentary stages, systems compatibility is having an explosive effect on the market. Office, data, and MIS managers are hesitant to purchase new equipment that might be unable to communicate.

Wang, which initiated the office automation market almost single-handedly, saw sales of its word processor surge after it introduced the Alliance software programs enabling its word processors to share data with its other data processing computers. In the world of personal computers, the blockbuster success of IBM's PC, which far exceeded the wildest dreams of even the most optimistic observers, is largely due to the concern among corporate customers that, if they buy an Apple, they will be stuck with a device that cannot communicate with their installed IBM mainframe or other computer systems.

Many computer manufacturers are attempting to deal with this problem by introducing local area networks—communications systems that enable any number of differing computers within a building to share data with each other as well as with disk drives, printers, and other devices. Xerox, which knows well what can happen when a technology becomes a commodity and price sensitive, was actually one of the first companies to introduce a local area network. Called EtherNet, Xerox's offering is its way of making its copier business viable in the talking era of computers. It won't be easy. Because of its overwhelming domination of the computer market, systems compatibility standards will be set largely by IBM. Plenty of small companies can get under the IBM umbrella—provided they remain small—but it may be tough for major players like Xerox. Much of the industry will have to be compatible with IBM equipment. The talking era—make no mistake about it—will be once again an IBM era.

Part 2

The New Information Titans—Old and New Guard

An upheaval is occurring in computers. The old guard—the multibillion dollar companies that dominated the industry through the 1960s and 1970s—is breaking up and losing its grip. A new guard of information titans is taking its place. This new guard includes the recently unleashed AT&T and the much feared Japan, Inc. It also includes IBM, but a vastly different IBM than the one that dragged itself sluggishly through the 1970s. And it includes Digital Equipment, along with some of the other young insurgents that have made their mark in recent years.*

The members of the old guard that are losing ground—Xerox and the BUNCH (Burroughs, Univac/Sperry, NCR, Control Data, and Honeywell)—suffer from the fact that they are indeed multibillion dollar titans. Although size was originally the advantage that brought these companies into computers, now it may be their undoing. The

---

* Digital Equipment will be discussed in Part 3 and the insurgent companies in Part 4.

small, specialized, insurgent companies have changed the way the industry operates. Large size is a liability in the era of specialization. These titans are too heavy to run the fast race, much less to be leaders.

IBM has pointed the way toward overcoming the problems of size. Overweight through much of the 1970s, IBM slimmed down and altered its diet. Now it is scoring knockout punches in many of the key specialty markets. IBM has, in effect, regained peak form so it can once again use its overwhelming size to its advantage.

The other behemoths of the old guard have not been so fortunate. They allowed themselves to stay flabby too long and lost their ability to react quickly. They can barely stay abreast in this fast race. Although they still have a looming presence in the industry, they are now more like the dinosaurs of the prehistoric era that grew so huge they could no longer eat. For the dinosaurs, it was only a matter of time before they became extinct.

Yet nothing is a sure thing in computers, even for the new guard. IBM could well find itself spread too thin. AT&T has to make up lost ground in its communications business and survive a massive reorganization before it can be a force in computers. Japan is stymied because its ability to adapt and refine is of limited advantage in such a tumultuous market. And Xerox and the BUNCH companies are not necessarily headed for extinction. They have certain strengths: experience in computers, extensive customer lists, mature maintenance and service organizations, branch name recognition, and money. All of them have either implemented turnaround strategies or are in the midst of formulating them. As they struggle for life, their thrashing about may cause some big waves and even some renewed vigor. Some may be able to flourish, or at least muddle through. For others, their days of glory in computers may well be behind them.

4

The Elephant Romps Again: IBM

Year in and year out, few things in the computer industry are as predictable as IBM's No. 1 status. IBM has been Numero Uno for so long it seems to own the position by a sort of divine endowment—a notion that, given its record of antitrust problems, the company does nothing to discourage.

IBM has enjoyed a remarkable history that began in 1911 when 13 firms making cheese slicers, grocery store scales, tabulating machines, and other helpful devices were assembled into a holding company by Charles R. Flint, a noted financier of the time. The Computing-Tabulating-Recording Co., as IBM was originally known, had plenty of competition, notably Burroughs and National Cash Register (NCR), but it soon surpassed these companies. Much of its success was due to the talents of the man Flint chose to lead his company: Thomas J. Watson, Sr., an ex-NCR executive whose uncanny instincts and homiletic style are now something of a legend in the business world. Declaring the whole world a market, Watson in 1923 renamed his firm the International Business Machines Corporation. Before long, the company began to live up to its new name.

Among the 13 companies originally brought together to form IBM was the Tabulating Machine Co., the firm founded by Herman Hollerith to market the punch card machine he invented. On the strength of this machine, which revolutionized office record keeping, the IBM empire was built. In the 1930s with the help of a contract from the Social Security Administration, IBM became the punch card king of the world. Revenues, already growing nicely, more than doubled to $46.3 million. Watson himself became the nation's highest paid business executive, a published fact about which Watson was quite defensive but that did not deter him from either collecting his pay or pushing his firm onward to greater success. In the 1940s, IBM's last precomputer decade, revenues multiplied more than fourfold to $214.9 million.

It was in the 1950s, however, that IBM truly proved its mettle. Under the elder Watson's son, Thomas J. Watson, Jr., IBM was transformed from the patriarchal, family-run doyen of the punch card industry and emerged as the gleaming thoroughbred of the electronic era. Although IBM did not invent the computer, it may just as well have. It stomped through the early days of the industry like an elephant in a tulip bed. By 1955, IBM's Model 705 computer, aggressively priced and intensely marketed by T. Vincent Learson (a future chairman of the company), catapulted IBM into the lead in computers, surpassing the early front-runner, Remington Rand, with its famous Univac. In the 1960s, on the strength of the 360 line of computers, IBM enjoyed its most fabulous decade, its revenues increasing more than fivefold to $7.5 billion. IBM's long-term growth record is shown in the following table:

Year	Revenues[a]	Percentage Change	Net Income[a]	Percentage Change
1928	19.7	n.a.	5.3	n.a.
1929	19.4	(2)	6.6	25
1930	20.3	5	7.3	11
1931	20.3	—	7.4	1
1932	18.4	(9)	6.7	(9)
1933	17.6	(4)	5.7	(15)
1934	20.9	19	6.6	16
1935	21.9	5	7.1	8

Year	Revenues[a]	Percentage Change	Net Income[a]	Percentage Change
1936	26.3	20	7.6	7
1937	31.9	21	8.1	7
1938	34.7	9	8.7	7
1939	39.5	14	9.1	5
1940	46.3	17	9.4	3
1941	62.9	36	9.8	4
1942	90.7	44	8.7	(11)
1943	134.9	49	9.2	6
1944	143.3	6	9.7	5
1945	141.7	(1)	10.9	12
1946	119.4	(16)	18.8	72
1947	144.5	21	23.6	26
1948	162.0	12	28.1	19
1949	183.5	13	33.3	19
1950	214.9	17	33.3	—
1951	266.8	24	27.9	(16)
1952	333.7	25	29.9	7
1953	410.0	23	34.1	14
1954	461.4	13	46.5	36
1955	696.8[b]	n.m.	55.9	20
1956	891.7	28	68.8	23
1957	1203	35	89.3	30
1958	1418	18	126.3	41
1959	1607	13	185.8[b]	n.m.
1960	1808	13	217.0	12
1961	2192	21	272.2	25
1962	2591	18	304.7	12
1963	2863	10	364.3	20
1964	3239	13	431.2	18

Year	Revenues[a]	Percentage Change	Net Income[a]	Percentage Change
1965	3573	10	476.9	11
1966	4248	19	526.1	10
1967	5345	26	651.5	24
1968	6889	29	871.5	34
1969	7197	4	933.9	7
1970	7504	4	1018	9
1971	8274	10	1079	6
1972	9533	15	1279	19
1973	10,993	15	1575	23
1974	12,675	16	1838	17
1975	14,440	14	1990	8
1976	16,304	13	2398	21
1977	18,133	11	2719	13
1978	21,076	16	3111	14
1979	22,863	8	3011	(3)
1980	26,213	15	3397	13
1981	19,070	11	3610	6
1982	34,364	18	4409	22
1983	40,180	17	5485	24
1984E	46,000	15	6500	19

Note the slowdown in revenue and profit growth during the latter half of the 1970s and the subsequent acceleration in 1982, 1983, and 1984.

Sources: IBM annual reports and Robert Sobel, IBM (New York: Times Book Company, 1981).
[a]Dollars in millions.
[b]Including World Trade international business for first time.

While companies with the stature of GE and RCA tried unsuccessfully to crack the market, IBM was giving the industry its official imprimatur, taking it from a fledgling supplier of highly specialized equipment for the government, defense, and scientific communities, to the role it has today as a purveyor of indispensable business machines.

IBM TODAY

The IBM of the 1980s is reminiscent of those early days. Once again IBM is a company on the march, transforming both itself and the industry it leads. Alone among the early founders of the industry, IBM is adapting successfully to yet another new era in computers, the age of computer chips and software, of low-cost hardware and systems integration. The IBM of today is earning substantial revenues from product lines that barely existed for the company before 1980. Its stunning coup in personal computers—IBM will sell over 2 million of them in 1984—is a telling sign of the company's ability to adapt to the new computer marketplace. No other company—including Xerox, which rushed to beat IBM with its own personal computer—has come even close to matching IBM's success in this mushrooming sector. The PC will account for over $2.5 billion or 5% of the company's sales in 1984, from nothing in 1981.

Although its reputation is that of a classic hardware company, IBM is now the world's leading supplier of data services and software, almost three times the size of the largest independent software companies, such as Computer Sciences. Separate software sales (that is, software sales not connected to a specific hardware purchase) were worth $2 billion to IBM in 1983 (6% of overall revenues) and are growing at a rate of 40% a year.

IBM's record in office automation is perhaps the most significant element in its transformation. Although office automation began as a specialty market, pioneered by such companies as Wang Laboratories, Datapoint, and Lanier Business Products, it rapidly has become the main battlefield of the computer industry. The records of other computer companies, from Burroughs to Digital Equipment, and even Xerox, have been dismal or spotty at best in this market. IBM might have suffered a similar fate. It dipped into the office automation market in the early 1970s and had nearly all the word processing market to itself, largely on the strength of its memory typewriters. It then neglected word processing, introducing virtually no new products, until around 1981. The company is now back with a vengeance. Office systems (including word processors) accounted for 20% of IBM's revenues in 1983. By the end of this decade, once a local area network is introduced (enabling various equipment scattered around an office building to communicate) that percentage will increase to nearly a third of IBM's revenues. When that occurs, a major element in IBM's metamorphosis will have been completed. IBM will leave behind its status as predominantly a computer mainframe company, becoming instead a broad-range office automation firm encompassing all sizes and types of computer-related devices.

IBM is the undisputed industry leader; at times, in fact, it seems to be an industry all to itself. In virtually every respect, the size of the company is awesome. IBM's buildings and facilities worldwide total some 78 million square feet, the equivalent of 16 World Trade Center towers. It represents a constituency of over a million people—375,000 employees and 725,000 stockholders. Millions more are represented indirectly by pension or mutual fund investments. Countless suppliers and customers—corporations, small businesses, governments, hospitals, and now even consumers—have a vested interest in the company's success. Its products and services cover the entire gamut of computers and data processing. Its customers are numerous, loyal, and worldwide, including virtually the entire Fortune 1000. Internationally, its presence in each country is indigenous in terms of personnel, manufacturing, research, and even finances. It is the largest exporter of computers in most countries, including Japan.

In 1983, IBM had revenues of over $40 billion, eight times that of its closest competitor, Digital Equipment. IBM's revenues actually are equal to the combined revenues of the next 13 largest companies in the computer business. Put another way, its revenues are the equivalent of 45 Apple Computer Corporations. IBM's profits are more than the sales of any other company in the field, except Xerox. The money IBM spends on R&D alone (over $2 billion) is greater than the revenues of most computer companies and four times the amount spent on R&D by Xerox, Hewlett-Packard, and Digital Equipment, which rank two, three, and four in that area.

IBM is one of the wealthiest companies in the world, with $5.5 billion in cash and securities. Spending on new plant and facilities tops $2.5 billion annually, 10 times what Xerox and Burroughs spend. IBM's inventory does not sit around long, it turns over (it is sold) every 37 days; bills (receivables) are collected in 58 days on average, which is very fast. Return on equity (the annual percentage profit return on the net worth of the company) is the best among the top 30 U.S. industrial companies.

THE 1970S: WAS THE PARTY OVER?

Despite these strengths, IBM did not flourish in the 1970s. In fact, it languished. The decade was a period of extreme discomfort for IBM. The company's worldwide market share slipped from 60% in 1967 to 40% by 1980. Profit margins that ranged from 24 to 28% in the 1960s hit 21.5% by 1981, still excellent but far below the lofty heights of previous years. While the industry as a whole was bringing down manufacturing costs at more than 20% a year, IBM's were falling by only 15%. The stock price went nowhere but down, from the equivalent of $91 all the way to $68 during the 1970s, not exactly a growth stock. Rock bottom was hit in 1979, when earnings declined for the first time in 28 years and only the fourth time in the company's history (two were in wartime, 1941 and 1952, and the other was in the Depression, 1933). Serious questions were raised about IBM's prospects for long-term growth. Even as recently as 1982, IBM was described as a "fortress under siege."

IBM's decade of discomfort coincided with the antitrust suit filed against it in 1969 by the U.S. Justice Department. The government charged IBM with monopolizing the industry, citing as evidence IBM's overwhelming market share and the inability of such companies as GE and RCA to gain a foothold in it. The government also charged that IBM made use of certain anticompetitive practices, such as introducing "fighting machines"—computers created, not for the purpose of generating a profit, but solely to damage the competition—and giving favorable treatment to universities in order to gain an advantage later, once students trained on IBM computers entered the business world. The allegations had a familiar ring because some of the charges were identical to those made by William C. Norris, president of Control Data Corporation, in a separate antitrust suit filed against IBM.

Norris's suit grew out of the intense battle he had with IBM over its high-end, 360/90 computer. A very powerful computer for its time, the 360/90 was to compete directly with a computer that Control Data was about to unleash, the 6600 designed by Seymour Cray. After IBM announced the 360/90, many Control Data customers hesitated, most choosing to lease their computer instead of purchasing it outright, depriving the company of needed income. IBM's competitive announcement also drove Norris to lop $2 million from the price of his 6600.

One can imagine Norris's anger when in 1967 IBM announced that it was abandoning the 360/90, although none had yet been delivered. Only the handful of machines currently on order would be manufactured. Norris felt he had been fighting a phantom computer—as had happened, he charged, twice before with IBM—and therefore filed suit against IBM in December 1968, one month before the government filed its suit. Lengthy discovery procedures ensued, and IBM counterattacked with a suit of its own against Control Data. But Norris hung on. In January 1972, Control Data received overtures that IBM might be willing to settle out of court. A year later it was done. Control Data benefited handsomely from the settlement. It purchased IBM's Service Bureau Corporation for $16 million, only a third of its value on the open market, and received a package of subsidies totaling $101 million. IBM also picked up the tab for the legal fees.

IBM benefited too. As part of the settlement, a computerized index created by Control Data to the more than 75,000 pages of internal IBM memoranda obtained during discovery proceedings was destroyed. Many of these memoranda were also available to the government. The Justice Department lawyers, needing help in sorting them all out, were looking forward to using the index. In fact, they were depending on it. But they never got it. The government's legal offensive was dealt a crippling blow before it ever got off the ground.

The government suit dragged on, tied up over definitions of market share and the always thorny question of whether IBM "intended" to monopolize the industry. The fact that computers are a highly complicated matter did not help any. Nor did the changing political climate and the rapidly shifting, intensifying competitive conditions in the industry. The case was initiated on the last day of the administration of Lyndon Johnson by Attorney General Ramsey Clark, one of the most liberal attorneys general in recent times. It then languished during the more conservative Nixon and Ford administrations. Democrats returned to power in 1977 with Jimmy Carter, who promptly placed three IBM board members in his cabinet and was thus just as happy to stay away from the whole case. The trial was brought to a close in 1982 during the Reagan administration, when the Justice Department announced it was completely dismissing the suit. The government announced its decision on the same day that it revealed an out-of-court agreement had been reached ending another antitrust suit: the United States versus AT&T. In return for dropping the suit, AT&T agreed to divest itself of its operating companies—a momentous day all around for the information business.

Although it is unlikely that the IBM case would have ended in divestiture, after such a lengthy trial it was at least probable that the trial judge, David Edelstein, would have imposed some restrictions on the company, despite the fact that the computer business was by then dotted by thousands of successful specialty start-up companies, casting further doubt on the IBM monopoly theory. Instead, IBM got off without even a slap on the wrist.

As for IBM's lackluster performance during the 1970s, that was its own fault. To attribute it to the antitrust case lets IBM off the hook too easily and also minimizes the significance of its recent turnaround.

SETTING THE STAGE

IBM needed to change its ways. The computer industry of the 1970s was a world apart from the industry of the 1950s and 1960s. IBM was due for another massive shift in character—not quite as dramatic as the changeover from punch cards to computers, but a transformation that was potentially explosive not only to IBM but to the entire industry. IBM needed to move away from mainframes into the new high-growth specialty markets that were popping up all around it. Much more basic, however, was its need to push its product development and technology much faster than before.

No More Rentals

In the old days, life in the computer industry was much more predictable. IBM would introduce a new generation of computers in orderly succession every 5 or 6 years. The new generation would offer a lot more performance for only a little more money. Customers who were renting computers in the previous generation would simply change to the new one. IBM had always rented its equipment, long before it got into computers. Renting had distinct advantages for both the company and its customers. For the customers, it is far easier to spend several hundred thousand dollars a year renting new equipment than to spend the several million required for an outright purchase. And if the equipment or the manufacturer's support were unsatisfactory, or if the product became obsolete, the computer could be returned. For the company, profits were higher in renting than in outright sales, and they were assured over a continuous period of time. Renting also allowed for better control over the customer and, because of the capital requirement to finance rental equipment, was a barrier to competitive new entrants.

In a fast-moving business, however, renting becomes a serious disadvantage, as IBM came to realize. Renting causes an overly cautious attitude and a defensive posture. A company that operates with a rental policy introduces new products only when existing products are fully depreciated and are old enough so as to minimize the impact of their displacement. A sort of Napa Valley winery approach to new product development is practiced: We shall do no research and marketing before its time. While IBM was slowly fermenting its next generation of mainframes, the computer industry was exploding with specialty markets like so many champagne corks at a wedding—minicomputers, word processors, data services, microcomputers, applications software, and so on. IBM needed to start doing things differently, quickly—and it did.

The first realization that IBM was beginning to change its ways came in January 1979 with the announcement of a new line of medium-sized mainframes, the 4300 series. With these computers, IBM established a dramatic new price/performance curve in the industry (see Figure 4.1). The price per MIPS (million instructions executed per second—the common measure of computer performance) plummeted more than twice that of any previous new IBM

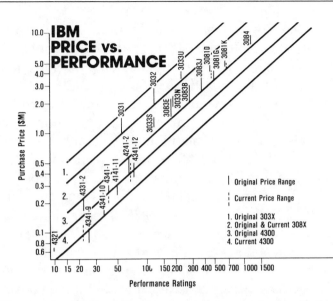

Figure 4.1. IBM mainframe price/performance curves. Notice the dramatic improvement in the price/performance ratio with the 4321, 4331, and 4341 product lines, which fell into a whole new realm when introduced in 1979. *Source:* International Data Corporation.

computer since 1964. The 4300 series offered a price/performance ratio that was eight times greater than that of the generation of IBM computers it replaced. While each generation is expected to improve on the one before it, the gap between these two generations was staggering. A computer in the 4300 series that sold for $70,000 (the 4341) took the place of a computer in the previous generation that sold for $500,000, even though that did include considerable peripherals and software. The reaction was immediate. Customers went crazy, ordering more than 40,000 units in 3 weeks, double the number anticipated by IBM over the entire 3- to 5-year life span of the whole product cycle.

Observers speculated that IBM had priced its new computers too low. After all, why would a company with the vast knowledge and experience of IBM improve the ratio of price to performance in a way that completely devastated the value of its existing computers? If there was any confusion over this question, it has since been dispelled. With the kind of prices IBM charged for the 4300 computers, its customers had no choice but to be purchase oriented. Customers once paid 40 to 45 months of rental payments before they equaled the purchase price of a computer; now it was down to 30 months. It was not very economical to rent anymore if in a little over 2 years the customer had paid the equivalent of the purchase price but might end up using the computer for a much longer period. Better to buy it at the beginning.

And while the price/performance curve took a big jump with the 4300 series, that was only the beginning. The succeeding generation, the larger scale 308X line of mainframes, sells at half the price of the 4341 in terms of cost per MIPS and is years ahead of the equivalent product offered by any other mainframe company. In disk storage, the thin film model 3380 disk drive using all new technology leapfrogged the existing model 3350 generation in 1982, dropping the cost per megabyte of storage by over half, 2 years ahead of competitive products that would not hit the market until 1984.

IBM has made its attitude of discouraging rentals clear in other ways as well. Long-term leases are still available through the IBM Credit Corporation, the new wholly owned financial subsidiary, in conjunction with other outside partners. The pricing terms are similar to those of any bank or third-party lessor—not particularly aggressive. Any customer who would need to lease equipment for over 2 years is better off buying. By terminating the pass-through investment tax credits to rental customers, IBM effectively used yet another stick to encourage outright purchasing or full payout sales-type leases. The result is clear: Rental business, which comprised 46% of all revenues in 1978, made up only 24% of the total in 1983.

Pricing

IBM has gone far beyond merely eliminating rentals. It is on the offensive, seeking to enlarge its market share, using pricing as a weapon. This is a polite way of saying that IBM is doing again what it has always done best: attacking the competition.

Ten years ago, IBM had a 10-point gross profit margin advantage over its competitors. Today, manufacturing plant automation still gives it a major edge, but IBM is willing to sacrifice some of the margin in pursuit of market share. As a result, IBM's pretax profit margins will not rise beyond the mid-20s percentage area.

Pricing and terms are aggressive on all fronts, from the PC to the popular Displaywriter word processor, which has been cut 30% in price several times. Today, IBM offers volume discounts on every product. If the purchase is a large system containing varying equipment and services, IBM will mix and match for a special low price. IBM will give as much as a 40% discount on the model 3178 terminal if it's bought in volumes of over 3000 units. If the deal is with a critical customer—a Fortune 500 company, a university, or a federal government agency—IBM will bid a special price that the customers often cannot disclose under the terms of the contract.

IBM also offers volume purchase agreements (VPAs) wherein, if customers will commit to taking delivery on a large volume of equipment over a period of 2 or 3 years, IBM will give the discounted price on the entire amount. Who needs rentals? Volume purchase agreements are a handy way to lock in future business before the competition can catch up—and it's working. IBM's model 3380 thin film disk drive is attracting substantial volume purchase agreements and multiyear commitments before Storage Technology, Control Data, and Memorex can even ship their equivalent products.

Hidden price competition takes less obvious forms. When IBM causes its competition additional costs, it in effect reduces its own prices. The restriction (or more controlled distribution) of such things as licensed source code materials that were once free to all competitors inevitably makes life more expensive and time consuming for IBM's challengers. The impact is the greatest on the plug-compatible manufacturers, such as Amdahl, as well as their Japanese suppliers (Hitachi and Fujitsu).

Indeed, it is the plug-compatible companies, the firms that benefited most from IBM's discomfort in the 1970s, that are now feeling the full effect of its new competitive thrust. Itel, which was both a plug-compatible manufacturer and a lessor, was the first to feel the heat generated by the 4300. Itel melted—evaporated really—losing $438 million in 1979, becoming one of the largest business disasters in history.

Amdahl and National Advanced Systems, which represent about 10% of the mainframe market, have undergone severe setbacks. Amdahl's earnings growth has stalled ever since the 4300 appeared. Its newest computers, the 580 series, were late, had technology problems, and will be only a temporary respite. National Advanced

Systems is in the red and no longer builds mainframes. (It will buy its computers from Hitachi.) In 1982, another plug-compatible maker, Magnuson, bit the dust, following Itel into bankruptcy.

The damage has also been heavy to the plug-compatible peripheral competitors. Storage Technology was caught over 2 years behind IBM in thin film disk drive technology and paid the price in 1983 and early 1984 with several quarters of red ink. Memorex (Burroughs) is only minimally profitable and, like Storage Technology, has fallen behind IBM in product technology. It has not grown in the last few years. Control Data is now reducing its exposure and investment in IBM plug-compatible mainframes and disk drives. It has seen the light. The plug-compatible game will never be the same now that IBM is going gang busters on both technological and pricing fronts.

Who is next? In personal computers, IBM has the leading share. The squeeze is on. There isn't room for almost 150 participants if IBM is to have a 25 to 50% market share. In office automation, the heat will be on once IBM gets serious with a local area network, a ROLM-based PBX digital switch, more competitive word processing products, and low-cost terminals stamped out by the hundreds of thousands in its highly automated Raleigh facility. There may be room for Wang Laboratories or even Xerox (if it gets its act together) and for some niche entrants, but the pressures will mount. IBM can be expected to make it more difficult for competitors in such other areas as distributed processing, PBXs, terminals, small business computers, software, and CAD/CAM.

THE NEW IBM

A typhoon has rocked the industry. Competitors are reeling. Almost none will escape unscathed. In an interview with the author, IBM Chairman John Opel surveyed the carnage from the lofty heights of IBM headquarters in Armonk, New York, and described the battle with typical understatement:

> *The shift of gears was really nothing more than a response to the need to be competitive, accentuated by the rest of the industry that*

formerly assumed IBM would not be competitive. [The industry as-
sumed IBM] would not dare introduce new machines, be our own
largest competitor, to stay ahead. Their assumption was wrong.

Wasting no more rhetorical flourish than Opel, Honeywell Chairman Edson W. Spencer, says simply but frankly, "It's a much tougher
business today to make money than [it was] in the '60s and '70s
with a protective, conservative IBM."

A revamped price structure was a key element in IBM's more
aggressive posture, but it was not the only change. There were
several others: a major commitment to automating its factories; a
new, streamlined marketing thrust; a reorganization to focus on
emerging specialty markets; a commitment to technology leadership; unprecedented joint ventures in marketing, manufacturing,
and product development; and a major legal offensive against competitors and potential competitors.

Factory Automation

Amid the confusion following the introduction of the 4300, IBM
issued a $1 billion debt offering. Its stock split four shares for one.
IBM was obviously up to something, but what? Actually, what IBM
was up to was already well under way. It started in 1978 when
IBM doubled its spending on plant and equipment to $1 billion.
By 1980, IBM had doubled that annual investment to $2 billion,
and by 1983, it was spending $2.5 billion. In the 5 years beginning
in 1978, IBM shoved $12 billion into its plants and facilities—the
equivalent of building six Navy aircraft carriers. This automation
and expansion required considerable outside financing, which was
done with Saudi Arabian debt, European debt, and U.S. issues. A
convertible debenture was even announced but withdrawn at the
last minute.

Other changes began even earlier. In 1975, the company realized
it was too fat in staff, production, and managerial levels. Thousands
of personnel were transferred back into field marketing operations
that year. Thousands more departed from IBM altogether when
confronted with this alternative. Branch offices were closed and
merged, from 240 down to 160. Staff jobs were releveled, having
become oversalaried and redundant with too many heavyweights.

With the advances in product technology and reliability, field engineering offices needed only 50 such engineers to maintain customer equipment, not 80 as in the past. Early retirement incentive programs were instituted in manufacturing. It was the first such streamlining in memory, and although there were no layoffs (IBM preserved its historic no-layoff policy), the reorganization served its purpose. Overall employment declined by 4000, or 1%, to 289,000 in 1975 and was held fairly flat again in 1976. IBM had shed some weight and was ready to step into the ring. It dedicated itself to be the low cost producer. By 1982 the payoff was evident. The cost of goods sold began to fall, volume surged ahead, and backlog and delivery lead times shrank. Between 1977 and 1982, revenue per employee moved from $60,000 to $95,000, a 58% improvement, better than the gains at Burroughs (50%), Digital Equipment (41%), Xerox (38%), or NCR (33%).

Marketing

A new marketing tack commenced in 1981. IBM signed up Sears and Computerland to sell its newly announced personal computer. Seven other distributors, including Arrow Electronics and Schweber Electronics, were selected to carry its low-priced CRT display terminals and desk-top printers. These items were sold at volume discounts to the distributors and stores. IBM never before utilized outside marketing channels. Its own sales force always sold direct. Alternative marketing channels are now proliferating, Matsushita in Japan for personal computers and Nippon Office Systems there for typewriters, word processors, and small computers.

In early 1982, another marketing shift occurred. The entire sales force was split into the national accounts division, to cater exclusively to the 1200 largest customers national in scope, and the national marketing division, to address all smaller organizations. In this manner, only one IBM sales group is responsible for each customer, selling all IBM products and services. Salespeople no longer trip over each other at the door, proposing different IBM products to solve a particular customer's data processing requirement. Customer confusion abates. IBM no longer competes with itself. And customers are handled with a singleness of purpose.

Specialty Markets

After missing the minicomputer boom in the 1970s, IBM began to notice the emergence of a personal computer explosion. Minicomputers and data services together represented $23 billion in business by 1983, almost a quarter of the industry. Talk about a missed opportunity. Would personal computers be similar? Could IBM dance fast enough to participate against such entrepreneurial, specialized companies as Apple, Tandy, and Commodore, which were doing only one thing and doing it well? There were also other explosive niches springing up right and left. The entire computer business was fragmenting into dozens of specialized sectors dominated by smaller computer companies. The industry had shifted. Mainframe computer systems were growing only in single-digit terms. IBM knew it could not make the mistake of passing up new niches again.

To address specialty niche markets, IBM created the independent business unit (IBU). Like an independent specialty computer company, the IBU is simple and small. Protected from the rest of the corporation and having no staff reviews, an IBU enjoys freedom of action. Originally, there were six such units at IBM: personal computers (PCs), software, computer-aided design and manufacturing (CAD/CAM), robotics, network computing services, and medical test equipment. Now there are many more in such areas as academic information systems, graphics, large displays, retail marketing, and workstations. In fact, personal computers have come so far so fast that their independent status has ceased and the unit has been folded back into the corporate structure. IBM vaulted from a new entrant in personal computers in summer 1981 to first place in sales by 1983, ahead of Apple Computer, Tandy Radio Shack, Commodore, and all the others. The company shipped over 700,000 PCs in 1983 and will ship almost 3 million, worth over $3 billion, in 1984. After stumbling in half-hearted pursuit of the minicomputer market in the late 1970s, even IBM itself was caught off guard by its surprising coup in personal computers. The company never dreamed it would catapult to the top so fast. In the words of IBM's Chairman, John Opel, IBM's personal computer effort is "one of the most successful entrepreneurial feats in modern times." It was the IBU structure, the freedom to compete as a specialty company, that made the difference since the minicomputer experience.

There has also been notable progress in other specialized markets where IBM has established IBUs, such as in applications software, currently a $2 billion business and expanding 35 to 40% annually. IBM is by far the leader in this sector, dwarfing such companies as Computer Sciences, Management Sciences of America, and Cullinet. In CAD/CAM, IBM started in fifth place in 1980 but by 1982 had leaped ahead to No. 2, behind only Computervision, surpassing Intergraph, Applicon (Schlumberger), Calma (GE), and Auto-Trol Technology. IBM's CAD/CAM revenues were over $300 million in 1983. Other specialty markets are coming along slower, mainly due to the lesser opportunity rather than to IBM's resources or emphasis.

Technological Leadership

In products, IBM no longer follows the pack. It is now the technological and price leader. One indication of IBM's new technological offensive is its thermal conduction module (TCM) that packages the semiconductor logic circuitry in the 308X mainframe central processing unit. This provides liquid cooling that will be increasingly necessary in the future with higher density semiconductor chips. IBM can change circuit design easily now to even higher density and stay ahead of other mainframe competitors over the next decade without regard to cooling requirements. In another example of its technological attack, IBM was first with thin film head disk drive technology. It shipped its 3380 product in volume by late 1982, almost 2 years ahead of such competitors as Storage Technology and Control Data. IBM is also likely to be first with emitter-coupled logic (ECL) semiconductor chips in mainframes with the Sierra—the follow-on generation to the 308X line, expected to be shipped in early 1985. And it will likely be first in vertical recording, the next generation of disk storage, around mid-decade. The fact that IBM experienced technology-related problems in recent years in the early phases of the System 38 small business computer, the 8100 computer, the 3081 large-scale mainframe, and the 3380 disk drive reveals the new, more aggressive pace the company is pursuing. The shift from routine technological development to the leading edge has not been smooth.

Outside Help

IBM realized early that an immediate cost effective way it could remain a broad-based, full product line computer system supplier was to go for outside help in manufacturing, development, and distribution. Going for outside assistance in so many important areas was unprecedented at IBM. The boldest such move was the $250 million 12% stake purchased in Intel, subsequently increased to 18%. This assures IBM of the leading-edge semiconductor components that it is dependent on—microprocessors (the 8088 is used in the PC), memory chips, and metal-oxide-semiconductor (MOS) technology. A $228 million purchase of 22% stock ownership in ROLM gives IBM similar product development and production access in PBXs, a telecommunications device essential in tying together computer networks and automated office equipment. IBM's prior relationship with Mitel for PBX technology was terminated once that company fell behind in software for its new-generation PBX product.

Expect to see more equity ownership by IBM in such areas as software, data services, CAD/CAM, automated teller machines, and floppy storage media, for example. IBM has licenses or other types of working agreements with Texas Instruments for MOS, VLSI, and local area network circuits; Matsushita, SCI Systems, and Teledyne for personal computer manufacturing; Minolta for copiers; Sanyo Seiki Manufacturing for robots; and Comsat General in partnership for Satellite Business Systems. A joint venture with Matsushita is aimed at manufacturing IBM PCs and other office automation equipment, such as terminals and small business computers, initially for the Japanese market but eventually for other international markets as well. The combination of Matsushita's low-cost and high-quality production, and IBM's brand name recognition and marketing capability will be formidable. SCI Systems produces all the circuit boards for IBM's domestic PCs and the newer PC XT model. Teledyne is producing IBM's home microcomputer, the PCjr, shipping the assembled product directly from its Tennessee plant.

IBM is no longer going it alone. Its new outside joint ventures and investments for development and production are with first-class companies, leaders in their respective markets. This new tack of going outside for the best help available will give IBM a major position in vital market niches and products.

Legal Action

The dismissal of the government antitrust suit in January 1982 was the final chapter of IBM defending itself on the legal front. Only the European Economic Community (EEC) antitrust charge remains, a vestige of the 1970s antitrust era. Now the roles are reversed. IBM is on the legal offensive, initiating suits against others rather than being sued. Most notable was the trade-secret theft civil suit against Hitachi in 1982, settled favorably to IBM in 1983. Hitachi agreed to pay IBM some $300 million and make available its new product designs for IBM inspection. Federal grand jury indictments against Hitachi, Mitsubishi, and various individuals were also handed down on the same matter. IBM is taking legal action against former employees for stealing technology, designs, and know-how when starting up competitive spin-off companies. It is serious about using legal means to protect itself and pressure potential competitors. In view of IBM's outstanding legal record and awesome legal resources, it is a sobering challenge to be sued by IBM.

WHAT HATH GOD WROUGHT?

IBM is on the attack. The benign umbrella under which the rest of the industry became used to operating—high prices, rentals, slow product cycles, and mundane product development—now appears more like a bayonet.

IBM is now expanding at a 15 to 20% rate in revenue and earnings each year, compared to the 12 to 15% rate it saw in the 1970s. Profit margins are back at 25% before tax, after dipping to 20% in 1981. Market share is rising. IBM is the only mainframe computer company gaining net competitive crossover business from other mainframers, including the plug-compatible manufacturers. The company is a leader in certain specialty niches, such as personal computers, software, and CAD/CAM. Additional IBUs are being formed to place even more concentration on the high-growth niche sectors.

John F. Akers became president of IBM in 1983 at the youthful age of 48. That alone tells the world IBM is taking on a new look, a faster pace. Nine additional senior vice-presidents are now on the top corporate management board, along with the prior seven, dispensing decision making wider, allowing faster response time, and keeping upper management more closely abreast of the market and customer requirements.

IBM is flexing its muscles—capital formation, R&D, automated manufacturing, revamped marketing, specialty market thrust, new products and technology, low prices, outside relationships, a legal offensive, and more youthful management—and it is pressing its advantage. The shock waves are being felt by competitors.

IBM is now an orchestra playing several instruments (i.e., markets and products), rather than a soloist as in the past, when only mainframes counted. In the future, IBM will have several multibillion dollar revenue segments—such as storage peripherals, software, maintenance, personal computers, small business computers, terminals, CAD/CAM and factory automation, lease financing, and, most importantly, office automation—offering rapid expansion opportunities. Many products will tie into large mainframe computer systems, but overall demand will be largely unrelated to mainframe shipments. In fact, the boom in microcomputers and office automation equipment will be the driving force and may stimulate the need for more computer mainframes, possibly hyping their growth back above 10% again. An additional mainframe may be required for every several hundred microcomputers once they are connected into a network and have access to common data. The tail will be wagging the dog. Once office automation displaces mainframes as the company's leading revenue contributor, IBM's growth will be more balanced. Mainframe product cycles will no longer be as important an influence on year-to-year sales and earnings progress. The broader product and market balance will offset the volatility caused by the shift away from rentals toward more outright purchases and by shorter product cycles.

Still, at least a few caveats must be noted. Even though IBM's prospects for the 1980s appear bright, the company faces risks.

Participating in so many different areas, manageability and control will be more difficult. Revenues will top $100 billion by 1990, perhaps over $175 billion by 1993 or 1994, accounting for 2% of the GNP, strung out in a myriad of different sectors. Profits will be over $25 billion by the early 1990s. Choosing the right opportunities will be tricky. Should the company sell communications products or more telecommunications services; supercomputers or specialty fault-tolerant computers; semiconductors, applications data services, or data bases? The new aggressive style is causing competitive disruption and upheaval. Reactions by competitors may backfire. Price wars and fierce product one-upmanship battles may become commonplace. Success may spoil the business. Industry conditions will be more turbulent. More competition, products, marketing channels, available money and technology, personnel jumping, and eventually slowdown and consolidation could lead to a profitless boom. Such factors pose a serious challenge to what appears to be a favorable outlook for IBM into the 1990s. Chairman Opel, who is at his best when walking around his office, leaning on his stand-up draftsman desk, thinking, will be doing a lot of thinking the company through the challenges that lie ahead. In the world of computers, as in horse racing, there is no such thing as a sure thing. But IBM is about as close as we are going to get.

5

Survivability at Stake:
The BUNCH

In the computer industry of the late 1950s and early 1960s, the job of competing against IBM was considered something akin to a rite of passage. A company was not accepted as serious unless its computers challenged those of IBM across the board. There was even a furtively held belief that a company could be as successful as IBM and surpass it in some areas. After all, some of the early computer companies, such as GE and RCA, were bigger and much more solidly entrenched in electronics. *Datamation* told its readers in 1965 that "the smart money for the short run is on GE and RCA." * Even IBM worried. The unexpected success of the Honeywell 200 computer in 1963 was one of the factors that caused IBM to rush ahead with its historic 360 line.

By the late 1960s, however, it was obvious no one was going to surpass IBM. The other companies were destined to operate in IBM's shadow, if not at its sufferance. Because they numbered seven—besides GE and RCA, there were Burroughs, Univac (now Sperry Computer Systems), NCR, Control Data, and Honeywell—these companies came to be known as the Seven Dwarfs. (Although the

* Quoted in *Datamation*, 25th Anniversary Issue, Sept. 1982, p. 81.

IBM public relations department labors mightily to cloak the corporation in a veil of pristine white, hardly anybody calls IBM Snow White.) When GE and RCA abandoned the computer business in the early 1970s (a very, very short-run investment), the group of five remaining companies came to be known collectively by their first initials as the BUNCH.

The BUNCH did not exactly flourish in the 1970s, but they did reasonably well, basking in a balmy period of industry stability. A conservative, protective, uncharacteristically benign IBM made it easy for the BUNCH companies to introduce new mainframe generations regularly, each one progressively better in price and performance than the last. Customers, while not numerous by IBM standards, were loyal—or, more precisely, locked in. Profit margins, however, were not so hot. Growth was well below 20%. New specialty markets, such as minicomputers, were emerging, but the BUNCH stuck with mainframes. After all, the ever powerful mainframe represented the mainstay of the industry, right?

Assuming that they had finally arrived and their position was secure—NCR, in 1973, became the last of the group to achieve profitability in its computer division—the BUNCH promptly lulled themselves to sleep. While they napped, things began to happen. The microprocessor hit with full force. Specialty markets proliferated. The industry shifted. IBM transfigured. Customers wondered. Yet, the BUNCH slept on. When they awoke they couldn't believe their eyes—but it was too late. They were not the BUNCH anymore. Now it was IBM and the five Whimps.

The BUNCH companies are suffering today, but it is hard to muster much sympathy for them. They were complacent too long. Through their own inertia, they failed to capitalize on the new specialty markets, including the most important one in which they should now reign supreme: the Fortune 500 office automation market. When BUNCH mainframe salespeople make their calls, it is usually on the MIS manager down in the computer room. But the MIS manager rarely controls the expenditures for today's office systems. As a result, less than 15% of BUNCH company customers are sticking with them for office systems, compared to nearly 50% for IBM.

Meanwhile, the revitalized IBM of the 1980s has radically changed the rules of the mainframe game. It is no longer possible for the BUNCH to keep up with IBM, let alone have the price/performance advantage that they once had. The BUNCH's over 30% share of the mainframe market in 1977 declined to under 20% by 1983.

Despite several attempts at turnarounds in the mid-1970s, the BUNCH companies never seemed to come up with the right formula. NCR's growth exceeded 10% only once over the past 10 years. Honeywell and Sperry Computer profits fell apart in 1982 and again in 1983. The industry is simply moving too quickly for the BUNCH companies. Defense of their customer base is still their main market strategy. And they suffer the disadvantage of being big in an era that favors small. Decisions are slow. Innovation is not natural. Boldness and risk-taking are limited. Product cycles, once an important and favorable influence on earnings, have lost their impact. Cycles are now both shorter and less profitable. Economic sensitivity has heightened. All the BUNCH companies experienced sharp order and earnings declines in the 1980–1982 recession.

To flourish again, the BUNCH companies must specialize, decentralize, and diversify away from mainframes. Control Data has gone the furthest toward this goal (mainframes account for only 21% of computer revenues) and is therefore the one member of the group that is almost assured of survival. But Control Data has diversified itself perhaps too much. In return for survival, it has traded away profit margins and any chance of exerting leadership in most of its niches. NCR has also diversified. In a major break with its strategy of the 1970s, NCR is deemphasizing systems and pushing technologically advanced superminicomputers, word processors, personal computers, and other specialty products. But NCR lacks a strong customer base among Fortune 500 companies (because it was never really a factor in mainframes), and this could seriously hamper the high growth it is seeking to achieve. NCR's long-term strategy does not come to grips with the coming era of systems integration and of compatibility.

At the remaining three BUNCH companies—Burroughs, Honeywell, and Sperry—mainframes still account for over half of the computer business. As a result, these three may be stuck in the mainframe market, trapped by past corporate strategy commitments. It does not help that all three have been late in trying to change their ways. Burroughs is the most tragic story. It was a stunning success in the 1970s, with widely praised products. When the mainframe market began to deteriorate, Burroughs tried to hide the fact. Financial problems and a loss of technological leadership quickly followed. In 1980 the company brought in W. Michael Blumenthal, the former treasury secretary, to execute a turnaround. It's been far tougher than he thought, and many of his strategy moves are late. Both Honeywell and Sperry have called in outside consultants to help them find their way out of the darkness. Because the other parts of the company—farm machinery and hydraulic equipment—are not doing so well, Sperry is banking on computers to bring the company around. That may be the incentive it needs to survive. Honeywell has a profitable defense and controls business to look to. It does not really need computers. It might do well to consider a graceful withdrawal from the computer industry.

This is not to say that there is no room in the computer industry for all the BUNCH companies. There is room, provided they know how to position themselves. To flourish again, the BUNCH companies need to adopt radical new strategies. They have to leave the 1960s and 1970s behind and realign themselves in an era that calls for small size, specialization, and an entrepreneurial style of management.

One possible solution would be for individual BUNCH companies to establish partially held, independent, publicly owned subsidiaries in selected specialty markets. The parent holding company could orchestrate finances and certain corporate overhead matters. These public subsidiaries could use stock financing to create the kind of entrepreneurial atmosphere that attracts creative employees. Being smaller and free of corporation overhead, the subsidiaries could react faster and take risks. Another route to survival for the BUNCH companies would be to concentrate on systems integration: buying the best products of all manufacturers and putting them together into comprehensive, coordinated networks for customers. Insatiable demand for such integration services is beginning to mushroom.

It may be wishful thinking to hope for such bold moves, but without them or something like them, we foresee an era of consolidation among the BUNCH. The world does not need five incompatible computer mainframe vendors. Business will diminish. By 1990, two of the five will be out of the mainframe business, have merged with other noncomputer companies, or have greatly transformed into specialty companies. In any case, their market share is declining, as indicated by the following table:

Company	Mainframe Market Share-Revenues (%)	
	1984	1975
IBM	76	59
Honeywell	6	7
Sperry	6	9
Plug-compatible manufacturers	5	3
Burroughs	3	8
Control Data	2	7
NCR	2	7

Sources: International Data Corporation; Salomon Brothers Inc.

Backing out of the large systems market in a graceful manner is next to impossible. Too much capital is invested, and too much past management commitment is influencing decisions.

Some members of the BUNCH now recognize the error of their ways, but new strategic actions are late. Although they are not without their strengths—customers, sales forces, maintenance and service capabilities, systems integration ability—none of these aspects is being properly leveraged to enable the BUNCH to realize their maximum value. The BUNCH companies are still headed down the hardware road. In fact, they are still riding along on the strength of incompatible mainframes, and it is a dead-end road. IBM and the specialists control the road map.

NCR: YET ANOTHER TURNAROUND?

It can never be said that NCR has not tried to better itself over the years. Since the early 1970s, it has made several efforts at what could be considered a turnaround. One of these years, it is going to get it right. This may be the time.

NCR has some distinct advantages that finally may work for it in the 1980s. Of all the BUNCH companies, it has the least exposure in mainframes—it did not really get into computers at all until the 1960s. Perhaps because of that, it was one of the first BUNCH companies to come up with a coherent strategy for dealing with the 1980s and 1990s. By 1979, when IBM was beginning to make its major moves, NCR had already altered its course and implemented some new strategies, which are now paying off. If any of the BUNCH companies can adapt and prosper in the new computer marketplace, it is NCR. But can a general-purpose computer company dance fast enough to stay up in the specialty markets of today? And can NCR achieve the high growth rates—20% a year in revenues—that its management has identified as the linchpin to its strategy? Only time will tell. Unfortunately, time is of the essence.

Throughout the 1970s, NCR followed a typical BUNCH company strategy of attempting to best IBM at its own game. This course required NCR to be proprietary on all fronts, invent everything in house, and sell unique NCR products that could tie into only NCR systems. As with all the BUNCH companies, NCR ran out of steam in the 1970s, and was forced to pursue a turnaround through the entire decade. By 1977, it had shored up its financial condition, after a write-off and management change in 1972 and a false-start second write-off in the mid-1970s. Around that time NCR correctly realized that its proprietary strategy would not pay off in terms of the huge growth that it sought then and still wants today.

The turning point seems to have come with the arrival of Charles E. Exley, Jr., as president in 1977. Exley came over from a position as vice-president of finance at Burroughs. His pullout caused notable bad blood there. This, however, did not stop Exley from recruiting away another Burroughs star, Manuel Garcia, now No. 3 in command at NCR as senior vice-president. Exley, Garcia, and

NCR's chairman, William S. Anderson, together represented the most savvy managerial leaders among the five BUNCH companies.* Their objective for NCR is clear. In Exley's words, they want NCR "to grow as a large company at a very high rate, 20 percent revenue growth in a normal economy, over a sustained period of time, and to be able to finance the growth, so balance sheet ratios stay at Double A rated levels." To accomplish this goal, NCR management embarked on a strategy that represents the earliest and most well thought out effort to break out of the BUNCH mentality of the 1970s. There are five main elements in NCR's strategy.

Products Will Communicate with IBM. After trying for years, NCR recognized that few customers were ever willing to get locked into an entire computer system offered by a BUNCH company. NCR will still try to sell end-to-end systems, but customers will also be given the option of buying only those products in which NCR is superior. NCR products are being designed to communicate with equipment of IBM and other vendors. Large computers will be designed with the same Systems Network Architecture (SNA) communications protocol as IBM. To its credit, NCR put this element of its strategy into place in 1979 with the acquisition of COMTEN, a manufacturer of IBM-compatible communications controllers, and COMTEN's chief executive officer remains a key member of NCR management. For small computers and peripherals, NCR has adopted industry standards, such as the UNIX operating system for minicomputers and the CP/M system for personal computers.

Advanced Competitive Products for Specialty Markets. The company is backing up its IBM-compatible communications strategy with competitive products aimed at key specialty markets. Recent examples include the low-end computer mainframe (the 9300) using NCR's own 32-bit 1LSI microprocessor; a 16-bit minicomputer (the Tower 1632); a personal computer (Decisionmate); a word processor (Worksaver), based on Convergent Technologies Computer; the Bank Branch Automation System; and the POS Scanning Terminal. To develop new products, NCR is not hesitant to go

---

* Exley was promoted to chairman in April 1984 taking over for Anderson, who retired.

outside, buying products from other specialty companies or the Japanese.

Standard Industry Components.   Although NCR has made a big bet on developing its own semiconductor technology—the 32-bit NCR/32 microprocessor chip set "must be successful or the company will not be brilliantly successful," according to Exley—at the same time, however, NCR is making full use of standard industry components, such as the Motorola 68000 microprocessor. This minimizes custom, high-cost components and thus makes NCR's products less expensive. The "not invented here" myopia has been discarded.

Specialized Marketing Techniques and New Distribution Channels.   The company's sales force was previously organized along market or industry guidelines. Now NCR has adopted the approach of successful specialty companies by having its sales representatives sell individual products, not the entire line. Such specialization (including hiring from the outside) was completed in both the financial and retail product areas in 1983. The 150-person special computer sales force will be fully in place later in 1984. Hiring of 500 new trainees to supplement the sales force commenced in late 1983. In addition to direct sales, NCR also sells its products through OEMs, systems integrators, and software houses.

Decentralized Strategic Business Units.   Development and manufacturing have been integrated in each of its sectors. Separate profit-and-loss units compete for the attention of the marketing divisions. Strategic business units that have been established include such areas as medium-to-large computers, financial terminals, electronic cash registers, small business systems, personal computers, microelectronic components, item processing, and automated teller machines.

NCR's favorable balance sheet is a major source of strength in its turnaround effort. The company is maintaining tight cost controls with lower inventories and receivables, is building cash levels, and has little debt. Given this healthy balance sheet and low fixed costs, any significant upturn in orders and revenues will result in rapid earnings improvement.

Nonetheless, the metamorphosis now occurring at NCR is unfortunately not a total panacea for the company's past malaise. NCR is still committed to selling retail and financial terminals (it enjoyed great success with them in the 1960s and 1970s), even though prospects for growth in those areas are slim. The retail market is cyclical and increasingly competitive, especially in light of Japanese entrants. There has been almost no growth in NCR's retail terminal business in 5 years. The financial market is dominated by IBM's computer mainframe presence and the deep thrusts of such specialty companies as Diebold and ISC Systems, and it is subject to the capital spending vagaries of banks and savings and loans. NCR's sales of financial terminals have expanded only about 10% annually over the past 5 years. Finally, even though it is lucky not to have gotten heavily into mainframes, NCR's meager base of large corporate customers presents a frustrating hurdle blocking the company's expansion plans. Using industry standard software operating systems, NCR hopes to penetrate large users for the first time, but its chances are poor and it has hedged its bets with an "alternative plan if it is unable to obtain Fortune 500 customers . . . We won't abandon outside marketing channels."

While an important part of the strategy is IBM compatibility, NCR does not seem to have recognized the degree to which systems integration will be a major requirement in the computer industry in the years to come. NCR's products are not compatible with one another to the degree necessary to meld them into an integrated system for office automation. Thus, NCR is bucking the trend toward the creation of large internal corporate networks. Although they are aimed at such specialty areas as word processing, they are general-purpose, stand-alone products. NCR has adopted an approach similar to IBM. Its products are not aimed at specific industry segments. IBM can get away with this, but who knows about NCR. NCR may find a niche, but zigging when the rest of the industry is zagging is always risky.

In the long term, the question remains as to whether NCR can successfully change its course to fuel order and revenue growth.

Achieving high growth represents a huge challenge for all the non-IBM, general-purpose computer companies. NCR's progress in this regard is promising, but not convincing. Because the company has strong financial resources and effective top management, and was the first of the BUNCH to radically alter its strategies, it has the best chance among the five companies to regain lost momentum. In today's environment, though, once a lead is lost it is almost impossible to catch up again. Things are just moving too fast. But NCR is moving heaven and earth trying.

CONTROL DATA:
TOO MANY FINGERS, TOO MANY PIES

Control Data's chairman and founder, William C. Norris, epitomizes both the strengths and weaknesses of the company. Norris is both a sociologist and a seer. He is a man who is able to look at the hard, practical, everyday realities of the present and yet at the same time think both creatively and idealistically about the future. He is a man of diverse interests and convictions, and has the willingness to gamble on those convictions. This pioneer is patient. If it takes 10 or 20 years to turn a business profitable, fine. At 72 years of age, Norris works from 8:30 to 4:00 every day, swims each morning before work, and watches his diet.

Norris realized early—15 years ago, in fact—that a computer company committed to a mainframe product line was an architect of its own doom. Today, mainframes account for only one-fifth of Control Data's revenues. Peripherals and data services together account for the vast majority of the firm's income both through products Control Data builds itself and through the joint ventures it has with such other firms as Computer Peripherals Inc. and its semi-custom-integrated circuit design center with NCR. Control Data is the leading supplier of tape drives, disk storage devices, and printers to the minicomputer industry. In data services, Control Data's activities range from its Cybernet time-sharing service, to its Arbitron radio audience rating service, to its Plato computer-based education service.

Computers, peripherals, and data services are not the only activities. Norris's humane social and international interests have taken the company far afield into hydroponics (the science of growing plants in solutions, containing the necessary minerals, instead of in soil), Indian reservation health maintenance, day-care centers, Rumanian manufacturing plants, small-farm financing, and executive health clinics. Control Data is really like several government agencies: the Health and Human Services Department, the Education Department, the Small Business Administration, the Bureau of Indian Affairs, the State Department, and the Department of Agriculture—except that Control Data is trying to make a little money at the same time. Often that's what it fails to do to the degree that it should or could.

But Norris seems unconcerned. He is absolutely convinced that the ultimate business over the long term is to address basic social needs. He has dedicated his existence at Control Data to developing data processing, education, health, and agricultural services. Although these endeavors are long-range propositions and internal pressure is building to weed out the hemorrhaging start-ups and run the company on a shorter term business basis, Norris believes his strategy will ultimately prove triumphant. "There will be an education market explosion in three or four years," he maintains, and Control Data wants to be ready for it.

Because of Norris Control Data is a survivor. It is not caught in the vise that the rest of the BUNCH find themselves in. But it is making a massive bet on social service businesses that may not develop fast enough or be profitable enough, soon enough, to take up the slack for maturing mainframe and peripheral businesses. Control Data's extreme degree of specialization in so many different aspects of the computer business, combined with its broad community service and humanitarian endeavors, have overtaxed management and led to poor execution, low profit margins, and an inadequate return on equity (annual percentage return on net worth) and return on assets (the return on total assets). Control Data's numerous operations are all reasonably sound, healthy businesses, but they are not flourishing or fast growing. With its fingers in every pie, Control Data has gone too far in specialization; it is in too many pies.

Control Data is a relative newcomer compared to the rest of the BUNCH, starting out in 1957 and developing a large-scale mainframe computer for engineering and scientific applications. In the mid-1960s, the company entered peripherals, tape drives, and printers. A short time later, the company started its time-sharing business, the Cybernet network, aimed at the same engineering and scientific customers that used its mainframes. In 1968, its mainframe business in financial trouble, Control Data acquired Commercial Credit, to provide financial stability and computer lease financing.

That same year, Control Data filed an antitrust suit against IBM, charging that the newly announced IBM 360/90 computer was a paper or phantom computer aimed at Control Data's already existing 6600 computer. It was a lonely battle for Norris, who was adamantly opposed by his associates. By January 1973, IBM had seen enough of the computerized index approach Control Data was using to prepare for the antitrust suit and settled on exceptionally favorable terms to Control Data. As a part of the settlement, Control Data purchased IBM's Service Bureau Corporation time-sharing data services operation inexpensively. Thus by 1973, the company had arrived. All four legs of the stool were formed: mainframes, peripherals, financing, and data services. Control Data was no longer solely dependent on mainframes in its computer business and in fact began touting itself as a data services company.

Peripherals

Peripherals is where Control Data shines. The company may call itself a service firm, but it is today mainly a manufacturer of peripheral equipment for other computer companies. Its major peripheral market is the minicomputer industry, where it offers tape drives, disk storage devices, and printers. Peripherals represent 40% of the company's total computer business, almost $1.5 billion in revenues, and have expanded more than 20% annually for many years. (In the 1981–1982 recession, peripherals proved sensitive to the cyclical downturn in minicomputers and growth flattened. Orders began to surge back sharply by mid-1983.) Now it seems that the company has reached a crossroads in peripherals. Growth has shifted to smaller disk drives, tape drives, and printers associated with microcomputers. Control Data finds itself behind in this market. Its new thin film technology microdisk drives, made to address this sector, ran into technological problems and had to be aborted before the first shipment. Heavy capital investment will be required to render the peripherals operation more competitive now that demand has shifted away from minicomputer manufacturers, Control Data's traditional strength.

Control Data's strategy in peripherals, like computer services, has been a shotgun approach, a widely scattered effort. Peripherals are manufactured internally as well as with six other firms: Magnetic Peripherals (67% owned, jointly held by Sperry, Honeywell, and Cii HB in France); Computer Peripherals (60% owned, jointly held by NCR and ICL in England); Centronics Data Computer (35% owned, the remainder public); Disk Media (40% owned, jointly held by Burroughs/Memorex); Peripheral Components (60% owned by Magnetic Peripherals, jointly held by Burroughs/Memorex); and Optical Peripheral Laboratories (52% owned by Magnetic Peripherals, jointly held by Philips).

Control Data had the foresight to go outside for help, gaining expertise and reducing financial risks. But once again it took this approach to the extreme. It is one thing to purchase products or technology outside; it is another matter to develop products by committee, especially if most committee members (i.e., Sperry, Honeywell, NCR, and Centronics) have been notably unsuccessful in their own right in peripherals. It has to be impossible to manage and coordinate peripheral equipment development and production by all these sources, but Norris thinks he has the answer: Put one manager in charge to make decisions, have one partner more equal than others.

Data Services

Nowhere is Control Data's proliferation of businesses more evident than in computer services. Like peripherals, services account for 40% of all computer operations, approaching $1.5 billion in revenues. And as in peripherals, Control Data's Computer Services group represents an overly broad array of maturing, low-profit pursuits that protect the company from the industry squeeze in mainframes, but are far from the vanguard of the data services industry. At last count, there were 13 different services being offered by Control Data, including an executive health clinic. The others include the Cybernet time-sharing network, the Service Bureau Network, engineering consulting services, Control Data Institute (education courses), Plato (computer-based education), Ticketron (ticket issuing), Arbitron (radio audience rating service), Worldtech (technology database), the Source (database for personal computers), Brokerage Transaction Services, CDC Software, and Magnacom Systems (services for cable TV). In traditional computer data services (which is only half of this entire group), Control Data is among the largest entrants in the industry, at about the same size as Automatic Data Processing, Computer Sciences, and Electronic Data Systems. However, it is far from being the most profitable or fastest growing. In fact, it is closer to the bottom in these categories, expanding in single-figure percentage terms in recent years. The time-sharing network business is characterized by minimal growth and considerable cyclicality. Most competitors offer similar commodity-like software packages or databases, and many potential or former customers have taken this service in house onto personal computers or internal time-sharing networks.

Control Data's education services are highlighted by the controversial, perhaps $200 million investment in Plato, a computer- and terminal-based set of courses that have been in development for close to 20 years. Plato's first full year in the black will be 1984, but it may be another 10 years before the investment is paid back. Questions arise as to its ultimate potential, probably good in the vocational job-training market, but not so hot in the mainstream education market because it's too expensive. It is a unique service, more a reflection of Norris's drive to better society than a business so far. No one can dispute the need for improved training and education or the profit Control Data can derive from certain courses in such areas as statistical quality control. But the overall payoff of Plato is anybody's guess.

Mainframes

This is where the company got its start, but since it diversified extensively into peripherals and services, mainframes have diminished to 20% of the total, an $800 to $900 million business. Growth has been at a steady 10 to 15% pace over several years, even during recessions. Control Data's mainframes are scientific and engineering oriented, and as such, even here the company is entrenched as a niche or specialty entrant, largely protected from IBM. The company was once the undisputed leader in large-scale number-crunching mainframes for such customers as the Atomic Energy Commission and the Weather Bureau. It lost that lead to Cray Research after Seymour Cray, the pioneer of Control Data's original supercomputer, the 6600, departed in 1973 to start up his own company. Control Data virtually dropped out of the supercomputer market for much of the 1970s, but subsequently it reentered with the Cyber 205 once it saw that commercial corporations had an interest in such huge machines. In 1983, it spun off its supercomputer development operation into a separate independent entity, an enlightened approach to keeping up in this specialty niche, but also an indication that the company may not want or be able to fund the $60 million or more R&D investment required there during 1984–86. Because Control Data has a long-established, loyal customer base, is not directly confronting IBM, and generates only a small portion of its profits from mainframes, the company is not caught in the same bind as Burroughs, Sperry, and Honeywell, whose mainframes compete directly with IBM.

But Control Data has paid a price for its survival. Profit margins before tax, under 7% for over a decade, are the lowest of the BUNCH. Its presence in so many nooks and crannies of the computer and data services industry has given the company a frazzled quality. Top management reflects this overextension. There is a chairman of the corporation, a deputy chairman, a chairman of commercial credit, and three other vice chairmen. That's a lot of chairmen. IBM has only one chairman, and it is eight times bigger than Control Data.

Even now, with his ship launched and stabilized against any storm, Norris never tires of taking it on a cruise down yet another river, without regard to the investment of time required or how minimal the payoff prospects may eventually be. The latest such move is the establishment of small business centers (through Commercial Credit) to sell computer products and services to small businesses (it will also provide financing and education). The creation of the small business centers will require a $100 million commitment and will incur major losses for some years before becoming a viable business.

Control Data is a survivor, but it will never be a leader. The company could have channeled its huge investments in Plato or its current financial commitments to retail business centers into selected peripherals or data services offering higher growth and better profit opportunities sooner. That way Control Data could have become more focused, more profitable, and an industry leader instead of the safe but unexciting and somewhat confusing company it is today. Winds of change, though, may be in the air. Management, particularly the president and heir apparent, Robert M. Price, may be gradually beginning to run the company more like a business. Certain loss leaders, such as property casualty insurance, may be weeded out. Some small business centers will be closed; much of Commercial Credit no longer serves a purpose at Control Data (the company doesn't need it to finance its computers anymore). While divestitures or closings were once unheard of, there will be more in the future. Norris, the prairie pioneer who lives in an earth-sheltered conservation house with a windmill to heat the pool, is proving more flexible with age. This company still has some potential left, but the changes are ever so slow in coming, and before too much longer it may be too late.

BURROUGHS: THE LONG ROAD BACK GETS LONGER

Burroughs was the premier BUNCH company of the 1970s. Not as big, or as powerful, or as financially successful as IBM, Burroughs had something almost as good: A reputation for quality and technological leadership. From the mid-1960s until 1979, when things began to fall apart, Burroughs's presence in the industry was characterized by brilliant mainframe design, superior software operating systems, and such leading-edge technology as virtual storage and intelligent terminals. Customer loyalty was high because of the products. While an IBM computer was compared to a Buick, a Burroughs computer was likened to a Porsche. The company emphasized growth and steady earnings expansion to keep the Wall

Street financial community enamored and the stock price rising. Revenues expanded annually by 11 to 19% (except during the recession year of 1971), and profits grew even faster.

Suddenly, the ground began to shift beneath the company's feet. Burroughs is the classic BUNCH company in its response to the slowing of the mainframe market: It tried to deny that it was occurring. To keep its record going in the face of slowing sales, Burroughs starved customer support, systems engineering, and maintenance budgets. R&D was short changed. Selling became aggressive to compensate for ill-conceived products, such as the ill-fated B-80 small business computer.

By 1979, the results of this disastrous policy were becoming clear. Market share was declining dramatically in mainframes, word processors, small business computers, and bank teller terminals—all areas where Burroughs was once a leader or a pioneer.

Aspects of the company that before were considered minor failings now loomed as major liabilities. Manufacturing plants were scattered all over and each specialized in only one product. The sales force was not specialized; all salespeople sold numerous products. International presence was limited. Personnel was bloated. Asset management was poor, and return ratios low. The most embarrassing debacle was the B-80, the stand-alone small business computer Burroughs marketed in the late 1970s. Instead of getting a Porsche, the customers who bought this product found themselves with an honest to goodness lemon. The numerous lawsuits that proliferated from the nonperformance or overselling of the B-80 created a public black eye and severely cramped marketing efforts.

To get out of the mess, Burroughs turned to W. Michael Blumenthal, former secretary of the treasury and before that in the brake business at Bendix. Blumenthal came in as chairman in 1980 (replacing Ray W. MacDonald), bringing with him a high profile and a well-known reputation. Long neglect and a certain degree of ostrich-like behavior preceded his arrival. A turnaround, which Blumenthal expected to accomplish in 2 years and MacDonald had said might take as many as 3, is taking longer and longer. Blumenthal and his lieutenant, Paul G. Stern, a former IBMer brought over from Rockwell International, "began to turn over one rock after another and found the landscape unattractive." When asked recently if the Burroughs turnaround is more laborious and massive than originally perceived, Blumenthal answered, "unqualified yes."

The key to Burroughs's industry position in the future is its long-term strategy, which it began formulating in 1983, late in comparison to NCR but still ahead of Honeywell and Sperry. The strategy represents a practical response to Burroughs's past history and the current predicament it now finds itself in. But in its conception and execution to date, the strategy has shown itself to be fraught with hazards. The first element of the strategy calls for Burroughs to concentrate on mainframes and attempt once again to be an innovator. Burroughs really has no other choice in view of its commitment to that market. Of all the BUNCH companies, Burroughs was the most successful in competing against IBM at its own game. Unfortunately, however, to regain its success in mainframes it still has to compete with IBM, and that's a tall order. It can never match IBM's marketing, maintenance, low manufacturing costs, and software. Moreover, its market is the medium-scale mainframe business, where market growth has slowed to a snail's pace.

A second part of the strategy calls for Burroughs to make hay in the add-on memory and storage products market via Memorex, which Burroughs acquired in 1981 along with Systems Development Corporation. This is a fast-growing business formerly dominated by Storage Technology and Memorex, but now captured by IBM and several innovative specialty companies, such as Tandon, Seagate, and Masstor. By attempting to reemphasize this market through Memorex, Burroughs may have made a bad choice. All three of the established companies in large storage devices—Memorex, Storage Technology, and Control Data—have lost their cutting edge and are in a malaise. Memorex is a $1 billion IBM plug-compatible tape and disk storage peripheral company that nearly went bankrupt in the mid-1970s. Profits remain miniscule. IBM has severely damaged the plug-compatible companies' profit outlook with its renewed technological push and pricing schemes. These companies cannot keep up anymore. Memorex's laboratory technology and product development may be all right, but its marketing lags. Burroughs sees Memorex as a key new strategic market and technology opportunity. I have grave concerns, however, that all plug-compatible mainframe and peripheral companies may be in trouble and that Memorex could prove to be an Achilles' heel for Burroughs.

Another element in the strategy, as formulated to date, calls for Burroughs to pursue certain niche markets, such as document processing, software, and small business computers. Specialty niches are the way of the industry today and if approached correctly (through autonomous business units having ample freedom) can be lucrative opportunities, as IBM has discovered in personal computers. Burroughs, however, is not giving niche markets the narrowness of focus required and is staking out too many of them to keep concentration pointed. Its small business computer based on Convergent Technologies' processor is a step in the right direction, but it is risky to stake such an important aspect of the product line on someone else's technology.

Other strategies are still in their formative stages, which is something of a liability at this increasingly late date. Communications will have a role, but what that role may be has not as yet been spelled out clearly. Systems integration figures to be important, but Burroughs is behind in communications and local area networks, so its capability here is uncertain. A Japanese connection (for help in products and manufacturing) is expected. Burroughs's OFIS 1 office automation system is off to a slow start, and it is unlikely that at this late date Burroughs will be able to play a major role in that area.

Burroughs is making progress, but it's a long road. Maintenance and service, although light-years above the level of 5 years ago, are still subpar. Current generation high-end B 7900 mainframes and B 4900 midrange computers are in shipment now, but they are over a year behind IBM's equivalent products. Applications software is still lagging. Many of the early turnaround moves put into motion by Blumenthal were significant, if familiar: write-offs of obsolete inventory, new management (17 of top 25), personnel reductions, and manufacturing plant consolidation and closings (14 plants have been shut down). Financial controls are better than they were, but the database and reporting procedures still need more upgrading. Since Blumenthal arrived debt is down from 37% to 24% of capitalization, inventory turnover is up from 1.3 to 2.3 times per year, and return on investment is up to 9.3% from 4.0%, but still lackluster.

Unlike NCR, Burroughs's goals are not growth per se. Objectives are primarily return on equity, assets, and investment, and profitable market share in its strategic areas of concentration. Big emphasis is on asset management. Blumenthal claims that once these objectives are met, growth and earnings will follow as night follows day. Blumenthal may well be right. And Burroughs may very well survive as a result of these turnaround moves, but it will not regain its industry position or flourish as the leader it once was until it arrives at a long-term strategy that is a little more original or ahead of the market than the one it has now.

Amid the great upheaval and sharp transformation that characterize the computer industry in this decade, any company that finds itself having to turn itself around financially suffers from an overwhelming disadvantage in trying to keep up with IBM, Digital Equipment, Wang Laboratories, Electronic Data Systems, and other leaders. On top of that, if a company must revamp all its critical market and product strategies and start over almost from scratch, it is even more difficult to become a contender once again. Markets and competition are not standing still waiting for the laggards to catch up. Burroughs is not without resources. It has a chance. But so do a lot of companies, and it is late. Blumenthal's attempt to bring Burroughs through a metamorphosis is equivalent to a secretary of the treasury balancing the budget: It is possible, but the road is long and hard, and time is running short.

HONEYWELL: A GRACEFUL EXIT FROM COMPUTERS?

If it were not in the computer business, Honeywell today might be considered a premier company. As it is, computers are dragging the company down, draining its resources, stifling profits, and diverting concentration away from Honeywell's bread-and-butter business: controls and defense. Honeywell derives only 30% of its overall revenues and less than 20% of its profits from computers. Yet management spends the overwhelming portion of its time seeking ways to get the computer operation moving again. If management is not careful, the rest of the company may begin to suffer.

Moreover, despite the efforts by management, Honeywell is lost in the computer business. It remains unrepentant in its desire to relive the 1960s and 1970s, when it was possible for a company to compete against IBM as a broad, wide-ranging, mainframe generalist. Because it can no longer emulate IBM, Honeywell is lost. It seems to have little notion of how to latch on to any of today's specialty markets. Company officials are frank in admitting their frustration, but they have little idea of how to extricate themselves from the situation.

My discussion with Honeywell's chairman, Edson W. Spencer, reflected the frustrating, harassed ordeal the company is confronted with in computers. Spencer was tight for time and hurried that day, even though my visit was scheduled well in advance. He was not well briefed on who I was or why I was there. Answers were quick and short: an immediate response but little reflection. His strategies and ideas are not bold or creative; they are practical and obvious. Actually, there are no major new strategies yet in computers. The refocusing effort is still on the drawing boards. The chairman seems more like a division vice-president involved in day-to-day operations than a grand strategist or philosophical leader. And "computers" was the answer that recurred several times in response to my inquiries of the most frustrating business problem or where most work has yet to be done.

Appearances to the contrary, the Honeywell computer operation is not without certain strengths. It has a sizable customer base (its own, plus GE and Xerox computer customers); a stake in semiconductors through Synertek, which it acquired in 1978; and one-fourth of its overall revenues coming from services. Nonetheless, these strengths alone are not enough to make Honeywell computers viable. Synertek's semiconductor business plummeted into the red in 1983 after the electronic games and personal computer business at Atari, its largest customer, hit the skids. Honeywell needs a long-term strategy in computers, but it has barely begun the task of formulating one. Rather than attempt a turnaround in what is possibly a lost cause, Honeywell might do well to fold up its tent in the computer business over the course of this decade. The company is laboring under some extreme disadvantages that will not be easily overcome. A quiet, graceful departure from computers might be far more profitable and prudent than an investment in an expensive turnaround that may well be doomed before it gets off the ground.

Honeywell's problems stem from the fact that its mainframe line was fractured into three separate and incompatible product lines. Honeywell was already a reasonably successful BUNCH company when in 1970 it purchased GE's computer business. GE computers had a superb software operating system, GCOS, that today is still considered one of the best in the business. Moreover, the acquisition (for $234 million plus stock) made Honeywell the No. 2 computer company. Of all the BUNCH companies, Honeywell was trying the hardest to beat IBM at its own game. And for a time, it seemed to succeed.

In 1975, Honeywell added to its mainframe presence by assuming responsibility for service and support of Xerox's customer base. Honeywell's French connection, originally a 47% ownership position in the French-based Cii Honeywell Bull, also developed as a result of the GE acquisition.

Despite unexpected expenses associated with the GE acquisition and the development of a new product line, Honeywell generally flourished in the 1970s. A move into minicomputers was successful. Incoterm was acquired in 1978, putting the company into on-line terminals. Overall computer profits climbed steadily as a portion of the total company, from 15% in the early part of the decade to 35% by 1980. Operating profit margins got up to more than 11%.

Starting in 1981, however, the computer operation hit the skids. By 1983, computer profit margins were under 5% and profits were down 60% from the 1980 peak. The cost of maintaining three separate model lines, requiring separate software operating systems and support, began to take a heavy toll, as did the head-to-head competition against IBM.

As a result of its commitment, Honeywell was wedded to mainframes and a broad-line approach to computers in general, while the industry was fragmenting into specialty markets. Mainframes matured and slowed in growth. Honeywell slipped technologically. New large-scale models were delayed or cancelled. Many customers hesitated, and some switched over to IBM computers. Honeywell lost market share. Along the way, its foray into minicomputers went sour. That sector shifted, requiring more applications software and direct end-user systems rather than pure hardware. Honeywell did not change with the times. The minicomputer operation went into the red. The computer marketing effort remained systems oriented and was not specialized by product or niche market. No individual piece (peripherals, software, the mainframe itself) stood alone as a competitive piece of equipment.

Honeywell did not sell, it accepted orders. Computer management was disorganized and ineffective. Clancy Spangle, the president of Honeywell Information Systems who orchestrated the smooth acquisition of the GE and Xerox customer base, departed for Memorex in 1980. Stephen G. Jerritts, his successor, was replaced by James J. Renier in 1982. Numerous vice-presidents revolved out of Honeywell's computer business during 1978–1982. Spencer, in praising his overall management team, is quick to note, "It's tough to find good management in computers. We've brought in people from elsewhere."

Bureaucracy and slow reaction time set in. Honeywell was not in close touch with its markets—or its customers. The results are beginning to show. GE, an important Honeywell customer, is now trying a Nippon Electric Company (NEC) mainframe as a hedge to its Honeywell machines. The company needs to make a major strategic change. It is losing the battle in mainframes, but it does not know where to turn.

In 1983, consultants were called in to evaluate and decide upon a new computer strategy. Honeywell's new theme line, used in advertising, is "Together, we can find the answers." This seems particularly pertinent in computers, where Honeywell obviously does not have all the answers itself. Employment was slashed by 2900 in 1982, 5 to 10% of the work force. The 47% interest in the French operation, Cii Honeywell Bull, was reduced to 19.9% in the same year, producing a fat $150 million in proceeds and a capital gain of $30 million, and was cut again to under 10% by the end of 1983. Honeywell also sold its 16% share of GE Information Services (GEISCO) for a $36 million capital gain. Organizational changes are evident with separate profit-and-loss responsibility in office systems, manufacturing, and various end-user application markets. Hardware sales to OEMs are now separated from the end-user systems business. A renewed concentration on existing customers is evident. New and different products, such as the low-end microSystem 6/10 desk-top microcomputer, are being offered to these customers. Cooperative agreements or joint ventures are being sought with Magnetic Peripherals, Inc., for peripherals; Ericsson in Sweden for voice and data communications products; and NEC in Japan for mainframe manufacturing and technology. Vertical market niches are being addressed in minicomputers, terminals, and mainframes, yet the record of success in the bank and airline terminal business, for example, has been lackluster.

Honeywell's original mainframe strategy, similar technology yet lower price than IBM, no longer works. This approach must be altered, but the how and when have yet to be determined. The emergence of specialty markets throughout the industry was not realized by Honeywell until recently. Now Honeywell must participate, but so far its product offerings and moves to decentralize its operating units to encourage such specialization have been meager. Finding niches where Honeywell can be a leader is not easy. The future strategy seems to be (1) to protect and defend the existing mainframe business, perhaps by emphasizing such features as database management or UNIX operating systems; and (2) to sell small machine solutions or microprocessor systems in the personal computer, military, or control systems markets. The company will need to do a lot more than this to survive in computers. Perhaps its outside consultants will point the way. But advising is easy; timely execution is another matter.

In light of the situation, we have our own unsolicited advice to offer. The company has already sold a chunk of its mainframes to the French and its interest in data services to GE. Why not cut back on the capital investment and R&D in computers, shrink the size and overhead so as to make it profitable again, sell off certain business lines or portions of the customer base, and streamline the entire operation? Later in the decade, when its computer business is smaller and more profitable, the whole thing could be sold. Proceeds could be reinvested in Honeywell's healthier controls and defense sectors, where it is a leader. The Achilles' heel would be gone. Management could concentrate on the areas it knows best. After all, the chairman and vice chairman are both steeped in the controls systems business, but currently the overwhelming portion of their time is involved in computers, only 30% of the company. Meanwhile, some cracks are surfacing in the controls business. Microswitch, Honeywell's line of industrial switches and components, suffers from a Japanese competitive pricing blitz in switches, and technology mishaps in the membrane sensitive keyboards it produces.

For Honeywell to flourish again, it must be out of computers or at least narrowly specialized, so it can concentrate on its mainstream business. The company, of course, can never admit that one good alternative is to wind down and out of the computer business. But it is the only alternative.

SPERRY: A QUESTION OF SURVIVAL

In the 1950s, the words Univac and computer were synonymous in the minds of most people, like Kleenex and tissue paper. Remington Rand had the computer business by the tail in 1951. The Univac 1, delivered to the Census Bureau in June of that year, was far ahead of any computer other companies at that time could even dream of producing. Nonetheless, Remington Rand and Sperry, which merged in 1955, let this early lead evaporate. An aggressive, cutthroat IBM had a lot to do with it. But the managements of the companies shoulder a great deal of the blame also: They did not move quickly enough and allowed a substantial lead to slip away.

The same might be said of Sperry today. Sperry's management, like that of most of the BUNCH mainframers, is bewildered by the change occurring all around it. No longer able to compete against IBM, it is trying to find a place for itself. Unfortunately, Sperry is slower than even the other members of the BUNCH in trying to formulate a new strategy. The rate of change at Sperry is typified by its chairman, Gerald G. Probst, whose personality and office reflect the reserved, low-key management style he has adopted. Probst, who has a computer engineering background, is not a shaker and a mover. But unfortunately, that is exactly what Sperry needs.

Unlike Honeywell, Sperry does not have the luxury of relying on its other businesses to carry it along. Except for defense, which accounts for 24% of revenues and is doing quite nicely in the Reagan era, its other businesses, farm equipment and hydraulic machinery, have been taking a beating. Sperry, even more than the other BUNCH companies, *must* succeed in computers. Its survivability is indeed at stake.

The 1970s were golden days for Sperry. The mainframe was king, and Sperry was right there with the premier and still widely respected Univac line. Elsewhere in the company, things were just as good. High levels of capital spending fueled a demand for Sperry's Vickers heavy hydraulic equipment, while a farm machinery boom took off through an unusual and unforgettable set of circumstances—heavy buying by the Saudis, large purchases of U.S. wheat by the Russians, and year after year of high crops prices—spurring demand for Sperry's New Holland farm equipment.

Such a set of favorable circumstances for Sperry may never occur again. The Vickers hydraulic business faced a major and expensive undertaking to take its equipment out of the hydraulic era of the past and into electromechanical technology. Demand plummeted in 1982 and 1983, and the division lost money. It was sold in early 1984 for close to $300 million, a smart move on Sperry's part. New Holland farm equipment is in a market that was similarly depressed in 1981–1983. Though Sperry sold off its retail shaver and typewriter businesses, it is still a confirmed conglomerate, a multiheaded hydra that has diffused its resources and taken on cyclical characteristics. I expect New Holland will eventually also be sold off, in the major reallocation of resources that Sperry is undertaking.

Leading up to 1983, finances became overly leveraged, ladened with debt. The computer and farm equipment divisions had a lot to do with the financial problems, but they were not the only factors. A major selling advantage of Sperry computers was long-term, low-interest, fixed-rate leases. Sperry borrowed short to finance long, which contributed to earnings when interest rates were low but became a millstone once interest rates surged into double digits. Sperry also became a bank to its farm equipment dealers. Debt climbed to close to 50% of capitalization. The balance sheet was bloated. Asset turnover was slow, once per year. "We didn't watch the store closely enough," in the opinion of Probst.

However, Sperry's most egregious shortfall in strategy and execution took place in computers. Like most BUNCH companies, Sperry continued to emphasize mainframes, until it was too late. But Sperry, at least, had some justification for its tunnel vision. In two attempted forays into smaller products—the Varian minicomputer acquisition and the internal BC-7 thrust into small business computers—Sperry was burned badly. Red ink gushed. In later years, Sperry was reticent to enter other new specialty markets. Sperry's computer customers went to other vendors, such as Digital, Wang, and Hewlett-Packard, for these items. While Sperry attempted to retain its mainframe base, other companies took away the specialty product growth opportunities. Sperry not only missed these markets, it also began to slip technologically in mainframes and disk drives. The large-scale 1100/90 computer was delivered a year late. As at Honeywell, it was the acquisition of another incompatible product line from a manufacturer leaving the business that eventually led to Sperry's downfall. Sperry took over the RCA base in 1971, and since then, it has had to duplicate all development, software, and support costs, putting a major strain on the budget and diminishing profitability. A single, unified product and software line was not possible with two separate mainframe computer lines, the Univac 1100 and RCA Series 90. The Series 90 customer had little product upgrade alternatives from Sperry without going over to the 1100, a burdensome software conversion cost. Many customers reasoned that, if a major software conversion effort were necessary, why not move to IBM? This indeed began to happen. The RCA base is diminishing, although dual support costs continue. Overall, Sperry computer customer loyalty has ebbed, perception has tended to be negative, and market share has eroded.

As a corporation, Sperry has begun to shift gears, to do things differently, to recast itself. It will reorganize into two separate parts—electronics (computers, defense, and flight systems) and machinery (farm equipment)—rather than five as in the past. Once these are separate entities, divestiture of the machinery portion is easier and that course seems prudent. The emphasis and investment will be on the electronics side. Sperry will attempt to leverage its strong position in defense to catapult it into broader commercial electronics markets, as the Harris Corporation has been so successful in accomplishing (see Chapter 15).

Management is also changing. In the past, its background was engineering and finance. Now marketing expertise is surfacing, particularly at Computer Systems. The former chairman and chief financial officer have retired. A new chief financial officer, Vincent R. McLean, has been added from NL Industries, the first new face from outside in the ranks of top management in a long time. The makeup of the board is also changing: the chairman of the Computer Science Department of Stanford University and McLean have been added, while the Group Executive of the Machinery Division and an outsider, the former chairman of Inspiration Consolidated Copper, have both retired. Additional changes are expected.

Major efforts to improve finances are under way. Overhead costs have been cut by a net $150 million, and personnel is down to 77,000 from 98,000. Financial hemorrhaging has been stemmed. Sperry is out of the leasing business now; Citibank and GE Credit have taken over such customer financing. Debt is declining, currently about 30% of capitalization, and refinancing is under way. Sperry sold 6 million shares of stock in mid-1983, raising $225 million. The goal is to get debt down to 25% of total capital. Other financial objectives are to achieve return on equity and assets of 15 to 20%, and better profit margins compared to the historical 7 to 10% pretax level. In recent years, profit margins have been half that level. Toward these ends, the company has cut inventories and accounts receivable, short- and long-term debt, and interest expenses. It is a start in the right direction, but more financial progress is still needed.

In computers, new directions and strategies are only in formative stages, having been reassessed by outside consultants in 1983. Sperry is at about the same preliminary stage in recasting its computer business as Honeywell is. The company is going outside for help: Mitsubishi mainframe technology, an equity investment in Trilogy Systems semiconductor technology, and, in peripherals, melding its solid disk operation into Magnetic Peripherals, Inc. It will make other acquisitions and joint venture agreements, such as the one it has with Northern Telecom for PBX voice and data switching systems. Sperry will attempt to participate in computer markets outside of mainframes and, in McLean's terms, "will not remain solely mainframe junkies." Sperry's leading specialty market thrust is in office automation, with its Sperrylink product line, integrating word and data processing, personal computing, and electronic mail and voice services. (Sperry's personal computer is so compatible to IBM's it will not run Sperry's own software.) Unfortunately, a sound product alone does not guarantee success. The company has its mainframe sales force in charge of this specialty product line, but to date it has had precious little experience or entry in the office market as compared to the computer center. To make it big in office automation, Sperry must sell to new customers who do not use its computers, a difficult task. In mainframe computers, the company must eliminate the costly RCA line and meld it into the Univac model line. It must also get back to leading-edge technology, which Trilogy Systems might provide if it is successful with its wafer scale, integrated, superchip semiconductor development—a big if.

In computers, Sperry seems to have some good ideas, but it has not yet completely decided how to execute them. In reformulating its strategies, Sperry knows some changes are necessary, but exactly what it must do is not readily forthcoming from in-house sources. Like Honeywell, Sperry is letting consultants show it how. But unlike Honeywell, Sperry does not have the luxury of relying on other businesses, except for defense, to carry the company. It must succeed in computers. Such an obligation may bring dedication and commitment. Sperry has resources, customers, maintenance and service, and a sales force, but no more than any other non-IBM mainframe company, and it is starting out late to reposition itself. Sperry computers may still be a factor in the industry by 1990, although they will play a diminished role. Sperry will be a defense electronics company in the future and its computer business may be more closely tied to the defense business. If computers are not a factor, Sperry may be facing a very tough time: a fight for its survival.

6

Can They Survive in the Office of the Future: Xerox and the Office Products Industry

Conventional office equipment has lost a good deal of the pizzazz it once enjoyed. Copiers, dictating machines, electronic typewriters, postage meters, even stand-alone word processors, are no longer hot selling items. They are old hat. Each new product generation differs only slightly from the one that preceded it or from the competition. The market is still large and important— $10 billion a year—but it is harder than ever to make a decent profit in it. Conventional office products are now price-sensitive commodities aimed at saturated, cyclical markets. Average annual growth rates are 10%. In 1981 and 1982, copiers (which dominate the market) and dictating machines saw no growth whatsoever. The economic upswing stimulated a mild recovery in 1983, but the maturity phase definitely has arrived.

Back in the 1960s when it was becoming a household name, Xerox made the conventional office equipment market exciting. Now the only companies doing well are the Japanese. Because it is a market where technological change is slow and growth is modest, the market for conventional office equipment is ideal for our friends from across the Pacific. It gives them the time they need to perfect a product, secure a foothold, compete on price, and gain market share. Already a roaring success in copiers, the Japanese are now poised for similar moves in stand-alone word processing machines and electronic typewriters. When Japanese companies are doing so well, it is time for American companies to read the handwriting on the wall and find other vistas to pursue. For Xerox, Pitney-Bowes, and Lanier, the current leaders in the conventional office market, it is time to make the big move toward the frontier of tomorrow: the all-electronic Office of the Future.

Desk-top computers, work stations, shared word processing systems, electronic printers (printers that use laser or ink-jet technology), computerized office switchboards (known commonly as PBXs, private branch exchanges) that can carry both voice and computerized data—these are the hot growth items of the 1980s and 1990s. Although the market for such equipment is currently only half of what it is for conventional equipment, it is growing explosively. And who is in a better position than Xerox to bring the corporate offices of America into the electronic age?

Unfortunately, life in the electronic era is not so simple. Although it seems a logical (if not simple) progression to go from conventional equipment to electronic computerized devices, it does not work that way in practice. For one thing, it is no easy task to take a sales force that sells copiers and get it to market computers with the same verve. No way! It's been tried by plenty of people, including IBM, and it does not work.

And even if you could get these salespeople to sell computers, that is not enough. To make it in the automated office market involves more than just selling computers. To be successful, a company has to sell systems. Software and integration are the name of the game today. And if you think it is hard to get a copier sales force to sell computers, try to get it involved in selling systems. It won't happen.

Not only the sales force, but the whole company has to change to a systems point of view. It requires a metamorphosis that is greater than the one that IBM and the BUNCH mainframe companies are going through. At least they have the benefit of 20 to 30 years in computers. Xerox, Pitney-Bowes, and Lanier are relative newcomers. Instead of being a high-growth and high-profit avenue, the Office of the Future could very well be a dead end for these entrants.

The bellwether company here is Xerox. It is the biggest and the best. If it can make it into the Office of the Future, the others have a chance. But as we shall see, the early moves by Xerox are not encouraging. (Lanier will be discussed in Chapter 15 with Harris.)

XEROX: SO NEAR AND YET SO FAR

The most go-go of all the 1960s go-go companies, Xerox fell off its high growth track in the early 1970s and never found its way back. For about 15 years, however, it enjoyed a stretch of growth that is usually called "dizzying" and success that is best referred to as "astounding." It began in 1959. Known then as the Haloid Company, it came out with the first office copier that relied on xerography, the now familiar dry duplicating process that uses ordinary, untreated paper. Up until then, office copiers used a wet process that required specially treated paper. The 914 copier was an immediate smashing success. From 1959 to 1974, Xerox's net income rose from $3 million to $348 million. It reached No. 40 on the Fortune 500 listing, and its stock peaked at $172.

Then things began to go sour. Xerox tumbled from its high growth track as abruptly as it originally got on. Today, profits increase in single-digit percentage figures, and its stock sells for less than a third of what it used to. Xerox would gladly trade away some of its old magic for just a little piece of whatever it is that is enabling such companies as Wang, ROLM, and even IBM to be taking over in an industry where Xerox should be ruling the roost.

It won't be easy to get back on top. Xerox's first mistake was to believe its own press clippings and watch idly as the Japanese cut its share of the copier market from 80 to 40%. The Japanese companies now have one-third of the U.S. copier market and are still gaining. Almost all the share gains came from Xerox. The Japanese began at the low end of the copier market, where growth opportunities were not pursued by Xerox. Successful there, they are now poised to move into mid- and high-speed copiers.

At the same time as it was handing over its copier business to the Japanese, Xerox was also pursuing acquisitions in computers that ranged from the merely lackluster to the absolutely disastrous. Xerox was looking for a company that could establish it in the commercial computer market and even considered a purchase of Digital Equipment. In 1969 it purchased Max Palevsky's minicomputer company, Scientific Data Systems (SDS). Xerox either didn't realize or thought it could easily change the fact that SDS supplied computers largely for scientific and technical applications. The whole thing was a disaster, and Xerox bailed out in 1975, writing off the company at a cost of $84 million (it cost $1 billion in stock to buy). Xerox was acting smartly when it picked up Diablo Systems (daisy wheel printers), Shugart Associates (microcomputer floppy disk drives), Versatec (electrostatic printers and plotters), and Daconics (shared logic word processing), but not much came of these purchases. Once leaders in their fields, Shugart and Diablo are now just one of the pack, and Diablo really never did make much money. As late as 1979, Xerox was still looking for a good acquisition. Western Union International was merged into Xerox that year, but it never took and was sold two years later to MCI.

Over the years, Xerox has come up with some good ideas in office automation, but poor product planning and marketing have killed its chances for any major successes. The Xerox 810 Star Workstation is the standard in the field, but it was overpriced, ahead of its time, and not IBM compatible. The Xerox 820 personal computer is a fine 8-bit computer, but it appeared just when the move in the industry was toward 16-bit. This in and of itself would not have done the microcomputer in if Xerox had not adopted the ill-conceived strategy of selling it only through dedicated Xerox stores. Another major product, an XTEN nationwide digital microwave data communications network, was an overly ambitious scheme to compete head to head against AT&T and the U.S. Postal Service. XTEN was subsequently scrubbed after tens of millions of dollars in investment.

Xerox shows some signs of waking up. David T. Kearns, president and chief executive officer, admits that in copiers his company "did not understand the cost structure of Japanese manufacturing that led to the surprising intensity of pricing pressure. We did not predict the speed at which the Japanese were continuing to improve. We lacked effective development, having research, but accepted American standards in development." Xerox's partner in Japan, Fuji, is helping it to emulate the Japanese in development and manufacturing. The new Series 10 line of copiers was developed to be more cost competitive. No matter how successful these efforts to regain lost market share are, the copier business still offers little growth prospect. A turnaround there is a necessary but by no means sufficient prerequisite for future success.

In office automation Xerox has seen a few successes. Certain products, such as memory typewriters and electronic printing equipment, are winners. Ethernet, a local area network to connect office devices from varying vendors, is established as one of the industry standards at this early stage. Digital Equipment, Intel, and a multitude of other computer and office systems manufacturers have adopted the Ethernet architecture, although users still only number in the hundreds. A Palo Alto research center has a heavyweight team of scientists focusing on office systems. The ball game is by no means over.

Overall, however, the Xerox strategy for the future is wanting. The company is still attempting to be a generalist in office automation, when the winning formula is to specialize à la Wang Laboratories. And it is still selling computers, as stand-alone boxes, not as systems. Xerox's annual office automation sales of over $1 billion are spread out over a wide range of unassociated products, ranging from memory typewriters to daisy wheel printers.

Kearns admits that his company's greatest weakness is the lack of a systems strategy. Yet, incredibly enough, Xerox seems to occupy the worst of both worlds, because its pricing is based on a systems orientation. As stand-alone items, Xerox products are overpriced. People don't buy them. The only advantage to the customer is to buy them in quantity and hook them together as a system. But this rarely happens, because the products are not designed with a systems orientation.

To survive, Xerox must undergo a metamorphosis. The entire company, from the sales force on up, has to be transformed from the stand-alone orientation of the copier business to the systems orientation that the office automation market requires. This will be no easy task. Teaching an old salesperson new tricks is almost impossible. The trick was never accomplished at IBM's Office Products Division or at Pitney-Bowes either.

Moreover, this metamorphosis must occur despite a debt-leveraged financial condition and the major move into the property casualty insurance business with the acquisition of Crum & Forster for $1.6 billion in 1982. Insurance earnings may account for half of total corporate profits in the future, substantially diversifying the company away from the office automation market. In 1983 Xerox purchased Van Kampen Merritt, a municipal and tax exempt bond investment banking firm for $150 million plus as much as $68 million more over three years. This widened the company's financial service stake. Kearns states he was "the last one over the hurdle" on the Crum & Forster acquisition, done as an "anchor to windward," to reduce future financial risk. The question raised by this sweeping move away from the company's traditional business is its commitment to the office automation market. Xerox remains dedicated to that sector all right—it has to be—but the insurance acquisition reveals Xerox's uncertainty about the prospects for future profits and returns in that business. The company needs other profit sources. The Crum & Forster acquisition was a defensive move and a huge investment. Maybe it was done to avoid the possibility of an unfriendly takeover of Xerox itself. In any case, it makes a statement of Xerox's lack of confidence in its ability to ever earn adequate profits in office automation.

The addition of the insurance business as a backstop inevitably will drain away some of the intensity and resolve that were evident when Xerox had to make it in the office, or else. Xerox may be willing to fight now, but what about 5 years from now if office systems are still in the red, insurance earnings expand to two-thirds of the total company, and the company is being squeezed between IBM and AT&T? There is no way Xerox can hope to avoid these two in the office automation market. It may become a question not of whether Xerox can do it but of how long Xerox will stick it out.

Xerox is fortunate in the fact that few chief executive officers seem better prepared for a long, drawn-out ordeal than Kearns. A long-distance runner, he finished the 1978 New York City Marathon in under 4 hours. Kearns is on his feet all the time, at a stand-up desk in his office and in the field. He is a leader with charisma, who is dedicated and talks fast. He is a man in a hurry. If he could whip Xerox into the same shape he is in and if Xerox stays the course in office automation as he did in the marathon, the company could be a winner again by the time of his retirement in 1990. The problem is that the office automation race is not a marathon, it's more like a mile run. There is less time to catch up.

The race is by no means over, however. The runners have not yet completed the first lap. Even though it is still at the starting block, tying its running shoes, Xerox has shown before how it can burn rubber. And after all, this is Xerox's race. It has ownership rights in the office automation business like no one else. But the move into insurance raises unsettling and confidence-shaking questions. It leaves the impression that Xerox is making other preparations as a hedge against losing the race.

PITNEY-BOWES: ABSOLUTELY, POSITIVELY . . . IN MAILING EQUIPMENT, THAT IS

Pitney-Bowes is No. 235 on the Fortune 500. If it were in the computer industry, it would rank ninth in size in the business. As it stands now, Pitney is a conventional office products company whose name is synonymous with postage meters. It has 1.1 million installations, 94% of the U.S. market. The business might be a little dull, but it certainly is profitable. The meters are all on lease (by law), so the revenues recur almost forever, an annuity of the best kind. The meters last 20 years but are depreciated in 7. Unlike for copiers, prices for meters are rising. Meter profits are three-quarters of the total company earnings. Gross margins are over 90%. But any way it's sliced, mailing equipment, like other aspects of the conventional office equipment business, is not an exciting growth area. Office automation is.

In 1980, Pitney turned its attention toward office automation, moving into word processing by acquiring Artec International for $10 million. Sales were $50 million in 1983 and unprofitable. Chairman George B. Harvey admitted that he was open to learning. By late 1983, however, it was all over. The word processing business, Pitney's stab at office automation, was terminated at a cost of $23 million.

Everyone makes mistakes. The company has done much better leveraging its one million customer base and 7000-member maintenance service force by providing Japanese copiers and facsimile machines. It terminated its own copier manufacturing and now markets the Ricoh line. The mailing equipment salespeople do not market the copiers or facsimile machines. Pitney has smartly employed a dedicated sales force for both the Ricoh line and the dictation equipment it now sells after acquiring Dictaphone in 1979.

Pitney will do all right avoiding the Office of the Future and sticking to conventional office equipment and postage meters. Although revenue growth and profits over the last decade were not the best, the long-term outlook, while not dynamic, is decidedly healthy. By 1985, over 125 billion pieces of U.S. mail will be sent annually. Mail continues to expand faster than the GNP. At 20 cents per letter, mail is cheaper in the United States than in any other country. (Sweden is the most expensive, at 30 cents per letter.) Business-to-home mail, over half of all mail, outstrips all other types, expanding 15 to 20% annually. Television, radio, telegraph, and telephones never made a dent in such mail, and this is the type of mail most likely to be run through postage meters and mailing machines. Pitney ships some 100,000 such meters each year. The company is also seeking new markets for existing mailing machine products and has discovered the U.S. Postal Service to be a lucrative one. A $112 million contract for sorters was completed in 1983. Meter and stamp-issuing business, potentially worth $300 million over 3 to 6 years, is being bid in the PRISM contract. This project will automate several thousand post office windows; the contract is to be awarded in 1984. Pitney is a subcontractor to Electronic Data Systems. Leasing was found to be another effective means by which Pitney-Bowes could take advantage of its customer base and service force while not diluting sales force efforts. Leasing is a highly profitable and easy business, since most of the company's customers prefer to lease Pitney products directly from the company anyway rather than through third parties.

Pitney's financially oriented management expresses goals of improving margins and return on equity each year. Postage and mailing machine profits are being reinvested into other conventional office products to stimulate growth. Pitney will do reasonably well, although grow only modestly, by staying with simple, conventional products that can be sold to existing customers and serviced by the existing maintenance force. A measure of economic sensitivity will always be present, but higher margins are likely. Sophisticated office automation products are probably not suitable for Pitney. But if Pitney sticks to its conventional business, the future looks encouraging.

7

Nothing to Fear but . . . . : Japan, Inc.

Americans once viewed the Japanese economic enterprise with disdain (recall the ridicule that greeted an item labeled "Made in Japan"), which turned to anger and astonishment (the shock over Japanese triumphs in steel and automobiles) and lately has been softened by attempts at emulation (the spate of books, articles, and seminars now available to tell American business how to copy the Japanese success story).

Computers are about to add another chapter to this troubled and deeply competitive relationship, but it will not be the story that most Americans expect or even want to hear. The Japanese are not about to enjoy another stunning conquest at America's expense, nor will they retreat to their shores a vanquished enemy. If it is not already evident, the Japanese have no magic formula for success in computers. Although they have rightly identified information technologies as the key to their future, the computer industry lacks the characteristics that will make a Japanese triumph easy.

First of all, the computer industry is not the mature, stable environment (as in steel, cars, televisions, or even copiers) in which the Japanese can exercise their skills of adaptation. The industry is moving much too fast for the Japanese, as indeed it is for many American companies. And while they possess some unique strengths as a nation that are conducive to the growth of high-technology industries—a literate and information-oriented population, government assistance and planning, a financial structure that encourages flexibility and freedom—in many other ways, the Japanese are terribly deficient. They are years behind us in software. The intense concentration of their computer industry in a handful of large companies makes it almost impossible for them to specialize in high-growth market niches, and they lack the network of sales, service, and support that is the prerequisite for making it big in the American market.

To make up for these deficiencies, the Japanese have only one option: to form alliances with American companies, either through joint-venture agreements or as original equipment manufacturers (OEMs). The Japanese will supply the low-cost manufacturing, while the American firm will carve out the market niche and supply the marketing, software, service, and support. It is virtually the only strategy open to the Japanese, but it is one filled with potential hazards and built-in limitations. For one thing, these alliances demand a certain delicacy from both parties that is enormously difficult to sustain over long periods of time (witness the strains in the relationship between Amdahl and Fujitsu). While being an OEM might provide the Japanese with desperately needed exports and ease of entry to the American market, at the same time it denies them the control they would like to have. Nonetheless, through this strategy, by 1985 the Japanese will reach their goal of $1.7 billion in exports, 15 to 20% of their domestic computer production. This is enough to earn Japan, Inc. a ranking among the largest computer competitors but immaterial compared to the $110 billion sales by American computer companies in 1983. They will still be stuck selling through American companies. Japan will not be a real competitor until it is able to sell directly, and that will not occur for quite some time.

The Japanese have come quite a long way in computers in a very short time. Starting in the mid-1960s, later and in a smaller way than the Europeans, Japan's computer market today is second in size only to that of the United States. Domestic production in 1983 stood at more than $10 billion.

The Japanese industry is highly concentrated among IBM Japan and six domestic manufacturers: Fujitsu, Hitachi, and the Nippon Electric Company (NEC), followed by Toshiba, Mitsubishi, and OKI, which have much smaller computer businesses. Together, these six domestic companies control 60% of the market and IBM Japan another 25%. In 1980, Fujitsu became the largest computer company in Japan, its sales outstripping those of IBM Japan for the first time. IBM Japan, however, remains a major presence in the market, accounting for 50% of Japan's computer exports and 28% of the installed base of equipment. The performance of IBM Japan is the standard by which all Japanese computer companies measure themselves.

Fujitsu had close to $3 billion in 1983 revenues, which still makes it smaller than Digital Equipment or any of the American mainframe computer companies. Computers represent two-thirds of Fujitsu's business, a much higher portion than for any of the other major computer companies in Japan. Hitachi is No. 2, with $1.8 billion in computer revenues—about the same size as Wang Laboratories. But computers account for only 10% of Hitachi's overall business. NEC ranks third, with $1.5 billion in 1983 revenues. Computers account for just over one-fourth of the company's business.

In the international market, Japan is still quite weak. Fujitsu generates about 20% of its sales abroad. For Hitachi, only about 10% of its computer business is from exports, largely the IBM-compatible mainframes it sells in the United States and Europe. NEC's mainframes are not IBM-compatible, which has largely foreclosed it from international markets. IBM, of course, dominates the international scene, controlling more than 50% of the world computer market. Several other American computer companies individually have as large a position in the non-Japanese international markets as all the Japanese companies combined. It is in semiconductors that Japan has scored its biggest coup. Japanese companies have stolen the lead from Americans in sales of the 64K random access memory (RAM) chip and are poised to repeat the triumph in the next generation of 256K chips.

The domestic success of the Japanese computer industry owes a great deal to the efforts of the Japanese government. Through the

Ministry of International Trade and Industry (MITI), more than $500 million was funneled to selected Japanese companies during the 1970s to foster progress in computers. It is this close cooperation between private industry and government that gave rise to the term *Japan, Inc.*

Government assistance is only part of the story behind Japan's remarkable progress in computers. Japanese culture and the country's industrial infrastructure possess characteristics that make it ideally suited to the new age of information. As Robert C. Christopher notes in his book, *The Japanese Mind:*

> *Even when it serves no immediate purpose, the Japanese collect information with the compulsiveness of a magpie hoarding brightly colored objects. . . . There are few statistics about Japan so esoteric that someone has not ferreted them out, and sooner or later almost all of these data are put to use: no Japanese Government agency or major corporation would dream of undertaking a new venture until it has acquired mountains of information on every facet of the matter. . . .*

Partly because of this intense dedication to data, the advent of the computer and the proliferation of radically new communication technologies have played right into Japan's hand.*

The Japanese are, by and large, exceptionally well educated. While estimates of functional illiteracy in the United States run as high as 20%, in Japan, with its notoriously difficult language, estimates are closer to 1%. Critics might attribute this to educational cramming—an emphasis on rote learning—but studies have shown that this is not necessarily the case. In a 1970 study sponsored by the United Nations, Japanese youngsters outscored those of other nations largely because of their ability to understand and apply the information they possessed.

All this and more creates an environment highly conducive to computers, while the Japanese economy and financial structure provide the reason and wherewithal to make it grow. Japan's lack of raw materials and energy resources is reason enough for the country to hasten its efforts to leave the industrial age behind. Its style of business is also uniquely suited to the high-technology era.

---

* Robert C. Christopher, *The Japanese Mind: The Goliath Explained* (New York: Simon & Schuster, 1983), p. 207.

Japanese traditions of lifelong employment and worker involvement in management have helped make it possible for Japanese companies to achieve high levels of productivity and quality—key factors behind its success in semiconductors. The Japanese financial structure, which essentially permits a much higher degree of debt financing than is permissible in the United States, gives Japanese companies greater flexibility and freedom from the bottom-line, quarterly profit results mentality of American management. It also helps give the Japanese a built-in pricing advantage: Japanese companies can sell their products for 20% less than their American counterparts and still get the same return on equity.

Above all, Japan has a lengthy track record in successfully and profitably adapting itself to the leading technologies of the day. It happened with thirteenth-century ceramic pottery from Asia and in the fifteenth century, when Japan acquired the ability to make firearms from the Portuguese. And it has happened again in the twentieth century, with steel, shipbuilding, automobiles, and consumer electronics. The Japanese, while quite inventive at what they do, have not been pioneers. They have been best at adapting, cultivating, and refining the creative discoveries made by others.

It is this skill in adaptation, however, that may well be Japan's Achilles' heel in computers—for the time being at least. Adaptation works only when an industry is stable and mature, not when it is exploding, fragmenting, and transforming. Because the Japanese computer industry is concentrated in a handful of companies—by design, so it can achieve maximum economies of scale—Japan is almost completely unable to pursue the specialty niche markets where all the big growth is occurring in the U.S. market. There are few (if any) entrepreneurial, venture capital start-ups in Japan, spawning creative new ideas and products. The traditions of large corporate structures, lifetime employment, and cooperative group effort all serve to inhibit Japan's entry into the era of computer specialization. The business, the technology, the markets are all racing ahead too fast.

Software may prove to be the greatest barrier to the Japanese. Programs written in Japan are virtually impossible to export. And because Japanese customers have preferred custom software for a long time, there is no large body of standard software packages.

The Japanese are trying. They are building software factories and employing thousands of programmers. But that approach seems to lack the creative dimension that software development requires. Japan's skills of adaption seem to be of little help when it comes to software. In addition, the real importance of software has not been recognized to the extent that it should have been by now. The big Japanese computer producers are still not spending as high a portion of their R&D funds on software as are American computer companies.

Japan will have to wait until the computer industry matures and stabilizes before it can make a move. That could be a long wait. As the industry continues to take on more of a commodity nature— ideally suited to Japan's manufacturing abilities and its skills at adaptation—most of the profits will come from specialty devices, software, systems integration, and services. Even though Japan benefits from the trend toward smaller, dispersed computers, it may have to wait until computers are hooked into networks routinely, as general-purpose, mundane, compatible equipment, before it can make a serious dent in the American market. For the time being, the Japanese must remain content to allow existing American computer firms to do their bidding for them. By shipping products to U.S. computer vendors on an OEM basis, the Japanese are able to skirt their deficiencies in the areas of software development, marketing, and maintenance support.

As suppliers of low-cost, quality, mundane computer equipment, the Japanese have export needs that meet in a happy convergence with those of certain American firms. Inevitably over the next few years, several U.S. computer companies (most notably some of the BUNCH companies) will find themselves stretched too thin or behind in products and technology. To get ahead, they will look to the Japanese. This OEM purchasing will not be in advanced specialty areas, but for stable and mature products. In mainframes, Sperry, Burroughs, and Honeywell will be looking for help, while in microprocessors, IBM, NCR, and Sperry have already established relationships with Japan. I expect to see more products such as personal computers, terminals, disk and tape drives manufactured by Japanese firms for resale by U.S. computer companies.

Such OEM relationships almost never go smoothly. Fujitsu supplies IBM-compatible mainframe assemblies to Amdahl and owns 49.5% of the company, but the relationship is tense. Fujitsu's tie-in prevented Amdahl from merging with Storage Technology in 1981. Fujitsu's joint-venture agreement with TRW to market small computers, terminals, and automated teller machines (ATMs) went sour after only a couple of years (though Fujitsu may be making another ATM thrust into the U.S. market on its own now). Hitachi discovered how difficult an OEM relationship can be after its first partner, Itel, went bankrupt in 1979. In the future, plug-compatible OEM relationships will be even more difficult for the Japanese. IBM's successful trade secret suit against Hitachi is one way of making life more difficult for the plug-compatible companies, and IBM's move to microcode more of its operating system software will make copying even more difficult.

In the meantime, MITI is still pursuing its drive to bring the Japanese computer industry on a par technologically with the U.S. industry. MITI has received a great deal of publicity over its effort to develop a so-called Fifth Generation computer that uses the principles of artificial intelligence, enabling it to reason and inform, rather than just calculate and store data. The Fifth Generation project, however, has been received with mixed enthusiasm by Japanese companies, and there is reason to view the whole project as containing a fair amount of blue smoke and mirrors. Although ostensibly aimed at creating a new kind of computer, it is as much an effort by Japan to close the 2- or 3-year U.S. lead in software and systems. If Japan is going to become a leading factor in computers in the 1990s, it has to take more risks and become more innovative, individualistic, and creative in software development—something that will not come easily for the Japanese. Although the Fifth Generation project may help, MITI's $94 million subsidization stretched over 10 years is not a lot of money.

There may be more near-term merit in the $96 million that MITI has allocated toward the development of a high-speed, high-powered supercomputer. However, supercomputers, although of strategic importance, are a limited, maturing market, and it appears unlikely the Japanese can come up with anything that could unseat Cray Research in that market niche. MITI's total electronics-related research budget for the year ended March 1984 was just $113 million. Some of the major pieces: $11.3 million for the Fifth Generation computer project, $6.5 million for the supercomputer, $200,000 for smart robots, $21 million for all software. These numbers are underwhelming by any measure. By comparison NASA spent about $7 billion in 1983, the Department of Defense research budget topped $20 billion, the National Science Foundations over $1 billion. There is just no way the U.S. can view the Japanese technology subsidization as an unfair advantage or serious threat in and of itself.

Japan, Inc. may be eyeing the possibility of selling brand name computers, particularly supercomputers, directly in international markets beyond Australia, the Philippines, and the Pacific Basin by the last half of the 1980s. Such a goal appears ambitious and is unlikely to be achieved in the next 10 years (if it can be done at all) in view of the sales and service buildup required and the software lag that will take several years to close. The computer market is not going to mature enough in 5 years to enable the Japanese to use their adaptive skills. Eventually, as Japan mounts direct marketing abroad, its focus is likely to be largely in the IBM plug-compatible area. If so, the primary American targets would be such OEM and plug-compatible equipment manufacturers as Control Data, Memorex (Burroughs), Dataproducts, Amdahl, and Storage Technology.

When (and if) the invasion comes, the U.S. computer industry is not likely to stand by idly and make a Japanese incursion easy. IBM has already become aggressive in price, technology, and cost as a preemptory move. And the U.S. computer industry is learning how to play the low-cost, automated manufacturing and quality games. Moreover, American computer customers will for a long time undoubtedly have serious reservations about buying vital computer products from a source 6000 miles away. Also, specialty niche computer markets will predominate for years to come; software will be an increasingly higher portion of the business; and systems integration will be a vital value-added service. I do not expect Japanese parity in these areas during the next decade.

8

A Cautious Baby Elephant: AT&T

The telephone company is in the computer business now. Ma Bell, I mean AT&T (as part of its reorganization, AT&T was forced to relinquish use of the name Bell), made its formal bow in the computer and office automation race in 1983. Given all the excitement surrounding its deregulation and divestiture, AT&T's debut was surprisingly low key. But don't let that early slow form mislead you. AT&T is going to make some waves. It is already being more raucous in 1984, and the thunder will intensify in years to come. Some 30 new products are expected to be announced during the 1984–85 period.

First, a bit of history. As it is now clear to anyone who owns a telephone, AT&T has undergone one of the most massive reorganizations any business has ever undertaken. The factors that brought about this reorganization include the various regulatory decisions (primarily the Federal Communications Commission ruling known as Computer Inquiry No. II) that cleared the way for AT&T to enter the computer business, and the settlement of the government antitrust suit in which AT&T agreed to divest itself of the 22 operating companies that provide local telephone service.

The new AT&T is a lot smaller. After the reorganization it was left with the long distance business, its Western Electric manufacturing facility, Bell Labs, and AT&T International. Total assets are $34 billion compared to $148 billion before the reorganization. Revenues are expected to be $56.5 billion in 1984. AT&T may be smaller, but it still ranks No. 4 on the Fortune 500 list. Debt is high at 40%, twice what it is for most technology companies.

The new AT&T is divided into two sectors, AT&T Communications and AT&T Technologies.

AT&T Communications is essentially an expanded version of the Long Lines Division of the old AT&T. It is a regulated entity, supplying long distance communications services to some 66 million residence and business customers. Because it is separate and apart from the computer and office automation markets that are discussed in this book, a discussion of AT&T Communications is not included here. However, it should be noted that it will account for some 60% of AT&T's total revenues.

AT&T Technologies is an umbrella group, organized along a line-of-business structure, and is responsible for all of the equipment that AT&T will sell to the computer and telecommunications market, from the simplest rotary dial telephone for the homeowner to the most elaborate communications switching systems and computers. AT&T Technologies consists of Western Electric, Bell Labs, AT&T Network Systems, AT&T Consumer Products, AT&T Technology Systems, AT&T International, and AT&T Information Systems, the new deregulated marketing organization that will spearhead AT&T's foray into computers and office automation.

While Bell Labs remains intact (although significantly pared down) Western Electric no longer exists as a whole entity, being functionally dispersed. Its brand name will still be retained for AT&T products. Western's manufacturing resources will be dispersed across three divisions of AT&T Technologies.

AT&T Network Systems. Manufactures and sells telecommunications equipment. With anticipated revenues of $8 billion in 1984, this will be AT&T's second biggest line of business, selling switching equipment, transmissions systems, cable and wire, and so on, primarily to the operating companies, other AT&T divisions, independent telephone companies, and very large businesses.

AT&T Consumer Products. Manufactures and sells communications products for homes and small businesses. Marketing will be done through the Information Systems division and third-party retailers, such as Sears and J.C. Penney. 1984 revenues from this division are estimated to be in the $500 million range.

AT&T Technology Systems. This is a large grouping that consists of three subdivisions:

1. **Components and Electronic Systems.** Produces telecommunications components and semiconductor devices and other products. Leading edge products include the 256K random access memory chip and a 32-bit microprocessor chip, the WE 32000 and newer WE 32100. 1984 revenues are expected to be around $2 billion.

2. **Processor and Software Systems.** Manufactures and sells computer systems for use in communications and for general purpose. Leading products from this division include the UNIX operating system and the 3B line of 32-bit superminicomputers. 1984 revenues are expected to be about $1 billion.

3. **Government.** Manufactures and sells systems primarily to the Department of Defense. 1984 revenues are expected to be about $4.5 billion.

The two other divisions that make-up AT&T Technologies are:

AT&T International. Sells the products of AT&T Technologies abroad. This division took a major step forward in 1983 when AT&T purchased a 24% stake in Olivetti. 1984 revenues are expected to be around $1 billion.

AT&T Information Systems. Sells computers and office automation devices, and home communications products (supplied by the Consumer Products division). Anticipated 1984 revenues are expected to be in the neighborhood of $5 billion, with the bulk of that coming from leasing and sales of telephones.

Altogether, AT&T Technologies will generate revenues of $22 billion (compared to expected revenues of $34.5 billion for AT&T Communications).

AT&T Information Systems

This is the division that will play the most critical role in AT&T's effort in computers and office automation. AT&T Information Systems (ATTIS) is primarily a marketing operation, and actually is precluded (by Computer Inquiry No. II) from having its own R&D and manufacturing facilities. That means it will be at the mercy of Bell Labs and the other AT&T Technologies divisions for those capabilities, creating lengthy and complicated product development pipelines that could prove to be a possible source of vulnerability.

But ATTIS has significant resources, including a 3,500-member sales force and an extensive customer base. As part of the reorganization, ATTIS assumed responsibility for all the equipment already installed by AT&T and the operating companies at customer sites. This amounts to billions of dollars worth of equipment (including some 147 million telephones alone). ATTIS also has a $4 billion line of credit from AT&T.

ATTIS has its work cut out for it. Its top priority is to reestablish AT&T's market position in PBXs. Although AT&T once had the PBX market all to itself, its share has fallen to under 25% in the past few years, compared to more than 50% throughout most of the 1970s. A number of competitors, led by ROLM (which is benefitting from its IBM connection) and Northern Telecom, have snatched up huge chunks of this market:

Company	Small PBXs (under 100 lines)		Medium PBXs (100–400 lines)		Large PBXs (over 400 lines)	
	1980	1982	1980	1982	1980	1982
AT&T	25	7	51	33	60	29
Northern Telecom	6	4	5	13	14	23
ROLM	8	11	17	20	5	9
Mitel	21	36	1	2	0	0
Siemans	9	10	3	4	0	0
Fujitsu	5	6	3	6	0	0

	Small PBXs (under 100 lines)		Medium PBXs (100–400 lines)		Large PBXs (over 400 lines)	
Company	1980	1982	1980	1982	1980	1982
United Technologies	0	0	1	1	2	9
ITT	1	4	0	0	0	0
NEC	3	5	2	3	3	8
All Others	22	17	17	18	16	22
Total	100	100	100	100	100	100

Reprinted with permission of Northern Business Information, Inc., New York.

Others, such as ITT, L.M. Ericsson of Sweden, and even Japan's Nippon Electric Company (NEC), are waiting in the wings.

A turnaround in the PBX market is essential if AT&T is going to be a major presence in office automation. If it can accomplish that, and there is good reason to believe it can—after all, AT&T sales representatives have been selling these things for years—then there is a good chance that ATTIS can be operating in the black by 1985 (by 1984 if leased telephone equipment revenues are included) and perhaps realizing over $2 billion in annual computer related revenues by 1986.

If AT&T can do that it will be one of the Top 10 computer companies. Such an achievement would not be a sure-fire guarantee of long-term success, but it would at least preclude a premature also ran status. AT&T was not a flashy company before, and it isn't about to become one now. But the company will surprise anyone who still views it as the slowpoke that it used to be in its regulated days. AT&T will dazzle, but it will dazzle gradually.

PRODUCTS

AT&T has adopted a three-pronged approach to the computer market: Business customers will be sold enhanced computer and office automation devices to be used with existing communication equipment; residential customers will be provided with a personal computer/telephone device to be used as a home information terminal; and AT&T will strive to be the master communication systems integrator, hooking together all computers, desktop devices, and communications equipment into a common network.

The centerpiece for AT&T's turnaround effort in PBXs, and the key product in its foray as an office automation company, is the System 85 PBX. First announced in 1983, it is AT&T's first digital PBX, designed to compete with the offerings of ROLM and Northern Telecom.

All of the 30 or so products that AT&T is expected to introduce during the next two years will be designed to communicate with each other through the Dimension System 85. These products include word processors, electronic document processors, work station terminals, and even a desktop computer, in addition to the printer and data terminals that AT&T already offers for sale. Teletype sells $500 million in terminals annually.

ATTIS has signed a five-year agreement with Convergent Technologies for a version of the NGen work station product, with an integrated telephone capability that will run the UNIX operating system. This may rival ROLM's Cypress telephone-terminal product. The value of the product purchase is believed to be $200 million at a minimum. AT&T also has a deal with Wang Laboratories for design and development of communication interfaces between AT&T's System 85 PBX and Wang's computers and terminals. This will eventually lead to more product arrangements between the two, similar to the Convergent agreement. We expect to see AT&T buy more computer products for resale from other manufacturers in the future. This method gets AT&T into the market faster. (For more on AT&T's entry into office automation, see Chapter 15, pages 297-299.)

A local area network will be introduced in 1984, highly centralized in design and closely tied to the System 85. Then there is the 3B series of 32-bit superminicomputers. AT&T has been using these computers internally since 1980.

On top of everything else, there is the UNIX operating system. UNIX allows easier communication among computers and offers greater capability for computers to operate in parallel, key features in the coming era of integration. UNIX, which was developed at

Bell Labs, is now sweeping the personal computer sector as the industrywide standard for 32-bit desktop computers. AT&T has made its license fees cheap for any vendor that wants to adopt UNIX for its computer products. The line-up of licensees is impressive: Digital Equipment, Data General, Hewlett-Packard, NCR, and soon even IBM in its new personal computer, the PC XT, and probably a 32-bit work station in the near future.

The fees AT&T collects from these licensing agreements could be substantial. More important than the revenues, UNIX gives AT&T an immediate presence in the office automation market. IBM may dominate the office automation market with its hardware, but AT&T has the software. And that gives it a powerful wedge. AT&T undoubtedly will come out with its own line of computer products using UNIX and it may also put UNIX into a proprietary semiconductor chip that the rest of the industry may have to buy if they want to use UNIX.

AT&T is also tackling the computer market with an offering in data services: the Net 1000 wide area computer network, the successor to the Advanced Communications Service that never got off the ground. Net 1000 is a data network that stores, processes, and transmits both voice and data and is designed to be compatible with all kinds of computer equipment. It got off to a halting start in 1983 and is deep in the red, but it is expected to be available in seven cities by the end of 1984.

THE CHALLENGE

AT&T's debut in the computer business was not smooth. ATTIS lost $750 million in 1983. Within the company there was widespread confusion over the company's decision to divest. Even though it was a smart move, sparing the company what would have been years of trials and appeals, many employees were confused by the decision.

So were the customers. Stories abounded in 1983 of problems caused by product delays, shuffling of marketing responsibilities, and other organizational chaos. Software is lacking for some of the new products, particularly the System 85 PBX.

Friction between the new entities within AT&T was apparent.

Acrimony between the manufacturing divisions and Archie McGill, the president of ATTIS, was a key factor leading to McGill's abrupt departure from his position in mid-1983.

ATTIS may well benefit in the long run by McGill's departure. A marketing genius and a catalyst for change, McGill almost single-handedly made ATTIS look like a winner and sound like it knew what it was doing in computers and office automation. But he tended to treat manufacturing and Bell Labs as if they were subsidiaries under his direction, promising products and features that were not necessarily immediately forthcoming. Because ATTIS really has no direct control over Bell Labs, though certain lines, of business do have budgetary power over work done at the Labs, it must maintain good relations with the other divisions in order to get the products it needs.

It will take more than diplomacy to bring Bell Labs and the old Western Electric manufacturing facilities into the new competitive world of computers. Before the reorganization, both Western Electric and Bell Labs were highly respected organizations. Western Electric was known for high-quality manufacturing at correspondingly high prices. Most of its products, such as telephones, still rely on electromechanical technology, which it produces in volume, keeping production costs low. Its market used to be a highly captive one; 90% of its sales went to AT&T and its operating companies. Little marketing and maintenance capability were required.

Now everything has changed. The computer and office automation devices that AT&T will manufacture are electronic and do not offer the same production economies of scale as electromechanical equipment. Intense price competition will necessitate a change in Western's tradition of high quality at a high price. It goes without saying that AT&T no longer has a captive market. AT&T is going to have to fight to keep the operating companies as customers.

Bell Labs will also be changing its ways. Although it is a national resource, responsible for major breakthroughs such as the development of the transistor, it will have to become more sensitive to the needs of commercial markets. In the past, development cycles were 5 to 6 years long, too slow for the computer industry. As part of the reorganization, Bell Labs's budget is being reduced by at least

25% to $1.5 billion and its staff is being reduced even further. Still, such R&D expenditures dwarf that of any other company in the computer business except IBM.

Once the manufacturing and product development cycles are improved, the essential challenge to the future of ATTIS may remain: with no research and manufacturing facilities of its own, can it bring to market a product fast enough to keep pace with IBM, Wang Laboratories, or Digital Equipment, all vertically integrated?

The sales force will be making a transition from phones, PBXs, and terminals to the business of selling computer systems, word processors and local area networks. And the sales force will have to reverse some long-ingrained attitudes and habits and learn to sell aggressively. AT&T has to sell, sell, sell in order to make it big in computers.

Over the long haul, I am optimistic about AT&T's chance of becoming a major competitor in office automation and computers. If nothing else it has a huge customer base, and that counts for quite a bit in this business. It is going to take AT&T a few years to iron out its strategy and coordinate the pieces. And time is of the essence. Nothing stands still in this business. If its divestiture had occurred in 1980, instead of four years later, AT&T would have had an even better chance. It is going to have to play a game of catch-up, but I believe it will do it.

One of the pleasures to be gained by having AT&T in the computer business is that for the first time there is a company that can stand toe to toe with IBM, on the basis of size at least. The whole world will be watching while these two titans battle it out over the future in the information business. It will be quite a while before anyone will be able to call this one with any certainty.

Oddly enough, the battle is already being fought on the most ethereal of levels: the architectural design of the two buildings IBM and AT&T have constructed across the street from each other in midtown Manhattan. The design of the two new buildings, one of which serves as AT&T's headquarters, could not be more different. The 43-story rose granite structure of AT&T resembles nothing so much as a grandfather clock. Its base is a series of Roman arches while its most distinguishing and controversial feature is its top: a

30-foot-high pediment split at its apex. AT&T calls it an "obicular." Because it harks back to the rococo style found in eighteenth-century furniture, other people have dubbed it AT&T's "Chippendale Top."

The 36-story IBM building, by contrast, is dark, sleek, and modernistic, much closer to the International style that has dominated office building design over the past 40 years. Its facade is a dark gray granite marked by a repetition of horizontal lines. It is pentagonal in shape so that, as IBM spokesmen tell you, "it shows a different aspect when viewed from different directions."

Is there a clue here to the outcome of the coming battle between these two information giants? On the one hand, compared to IBM, AT&T seems stodgy and old-fashioned. One can already imagine an advertisement showing a picture of both buildings with a voice asking, "Which would you ask to help bring you into the twenty-first century of data communications?"

On the other hand, the AT&T building actually is far more daring aesthetically than IBM's. It is now New York's best-known architectural example of postmodernism, a broad-based movement in the arts distinguished by its propensity to borrow openly from other styles and periods, creating a pastiche that makes its statement as much by irony as anything else. In addition to its Chippendale Top and Roman arches, the AT&T building contains other recognizable architectural touches from here and there. The overall effect is a building design that, as *Datamation* magazine noted, "is as American as the 'A' in AT&T." These are conservative times we live in. Perhaps AT&T has scored a tidy, subtle, artistic coup that will serve it well in years ahead. Perhaps its entrance into computers and office automation will be similar. Then again, perhaps postmodernism is the passing fad its critics accuse it of being. AT&T could be stuck with an embarrassment. And then again . . .

The permutations are endless. Art, though often subservient to commerce, is nonetheless an unreliable guide to it.

Part 3

The Middleweights at Midlife

People follow some predictable patterns as they make their way from youth to maturity. One such pattern involves the apparently unavoidable midlife crisis. Somewhere between the ages of 35 and 45 men and women make the sudden, inevitable, and unoriginal observation that half of their life is over and time is running short. Some spend the rest of their days cursing themselves for the things they failed to accomplish. You know the type. For others, it is a time of searching and renewal. They begin to do their best work. Life for them begins at 40.

The world of business is no different, except that the age of a company is not a reliable guide to detecting the onset of a midlife crisis. It can strike at any time. Size is a more accurate barometer. When a company reaches the $500 million to $1 billion size range, something happens. Imperceptibly at first, things become less interesting. The company does not seem as exciting anymore. It is more bureaucratic, less entrepreneurial in spirit. New products and services are slower in coming. When they do come, they seem less dramatic, less unique. They are often refinements upon refinements of previous successes.

Company founders become less active or move on to start other new companies. Often a company tries to sustain the growth it saw in its youth by broadening into other markets, but this rarely works. The company loses its character as a specialist and becomes a generalist. Other young specialty insurgents begin to emerge, finding high-growth niches that were overlooked.

Balance sheets are fine—in some cases, better than ever because there is less need for heavy capital expenditures. Slower growth results in a good cash flow. Equity financing, raising money by selling new stock, is still readily available because investors may still perceive the company as being youthful, not yet at midlife. Often, slower growth rates are attributed to the effects of the economy or a product cycle transition. No one likes to admit to being at midlife. Some companies would do well to hire Gail Sheehy for consultation.

The three most notable sectors of the computer industry at midlife are data services, minicomputers, and the plug-compatible manufacturers (PCMs). Some are doing better than others, but for the most part, the companies in these three sectors are confronting painful midlife transitions. In the case of the minicomputer companies, it is a midlife crisis of almost classic dimensions. The wunderkinder of the 1970s, they have seen their thunder stolen by the microcomputer companies. To survive, they will have to pay more than just lip service to these oung upstarts. For data services firms, the situation is different. They too have been hurt by the advent of cheaper hardware. Because more companies can afford their own computers, there is less need to go outside for services. But the data services firms are also ideally positioned to take advantage of the growing emphasis on software and services. For those data services companies that play their cards right, life will begin at 40. The outlook is bleakest for the PCMs. They rose to stardom fast by taking advantage of the weak spots in IBM's suit of armor. Now IBM has decided to get tough. Those who live by the sword, die by the sword. Midlife crisis and all, for some PCMs it may be a short life indeed.

9

Going All the Way:
Data Services

Things have been quiet of late in the data services business, but this placid situation may be about to change. The services industry generates some $15 billion annually (not including software) through thousands of companies that range in size from local mom-and-pop operations to the handful of independent industry leaders—Automatic Data Processing, Electronic Data Systems, and Computer Sciences—each approaching $1 billion in revenues.

In many ways, Automatic Data Processing (ADP), currently the biggest data services firm (though not for much longer), sets the tone for the industry. After 35 years, ADP still makes a handsome living by processing payrolls for thousands of companies across the country. No one expects much in the way of excitement from a payroll processor—just reliability. That has been the calling card of the data services industry right from the start. In a world that is increasingly dependent on computers, the data services firms offer a reliable leading-edge source of computer capability to companies that lack the resources to develop their own.

But things are changing. The data services companies—the successful ones at least—may no longer have to play second fiddle to the hardware manufacturers. Instead of serving simply as alternatives for companies that do not want to buy their own computers, certain capabilities offered by data services companies—software and systems integration capability—in the long run will prove more valuable than hardware. The data services firms are in the catbird seat for the coming era of systems integration. The quiet period is over. The fun, really, has just begun.

First, however, the data services firms must finish successfully navigating their way through a fairly treacherous period—so treacherous, in fact, that some may not make it. Cheaper hardware has made it possible for most companies to buy their own computers. As software becomes more user-friendly and hardware easier to use, the need for companies to go outside for computer services will continue to diminish. Moreover, because such traditional data processing activities as accounting and financial analysis are easily available using small computers, even those companies that continue to go outside are no longer seeking such mundane services, which in years past have been the backbone of the services industry. As a result, companies that sell traditional time-sharing services, such as Tymshare, Comshare, Computer Sciences (through its Infonet operations), ADP (through its Network Services Division), and Control Data's Service Bureau and Cybernet, all suffered sharp contractions and profit pressures in 1982–1983. In contrast, companies that concentrate on offering specialized services to particular market niches, such as Shared Medical Systems (hospitals) and Quotron (brokerage data services), are flourishing like nobody's business.

For those companies willing to think big, opportunities are much greater than to become simply a supplier of services to a specialized market niche. The data services industry is in a strategic position—smack dab in the center of the information business (see Figure 9.1), occupying the middle ground between conduit and content, between the medium and the message. Unlike the rest of the computer industry, computer services companies have always sold information, not equipment. Because of that background, they are ideally positioned to take advantage of the major trends that are changing the face of computing: the move to software and systems integration as the key areas of profitability. In the future, the data

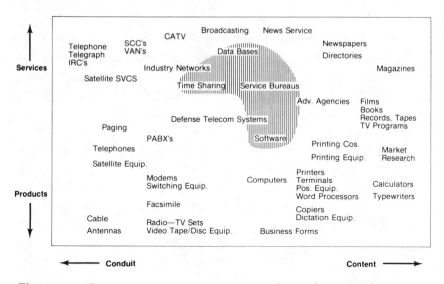

Figure 9.1. Data services occupy centerground in information business. Reprinted with permission of Harvard University, Program of Information Resources Policy, McLaughlin and Biryini, as adapted by Salomon Brothers Inc.

services firms will get business that used to go to the big hardware companies. This is already happening with federal government systems integration contracts—the new megacontracts—as we shall see in our discussion of Electronic Data Systems, a future leader of the data services industry. Possibly several leaders will emerge from the ranks of the data services industry. But companies that are now experiencing trouble, such as Tymshare and Computer Sciences, may have problems making it to the systems integration era.

Because it occupies a middle ground, the data services industry is ripe for challenges from the various sectors that surround it—computer manufacturers on one side; publishing, media, and other service firms on the other. Many of the recent takeovers in the industry exemplify this situation: National CSS was taken over by Dun and Bradstreet (both a publishing and a financial service firm); Data Resources was acquired by McGraw-Hill, Systems Development by Burroughs, and On-Line Systems by United Telecom whose data service busines in turn was acquired by Control Data.

The industry is also becoming more competitive within. In years past, it was one of the few industry sectors where IBM was not a factor. Now that is no longer the case. Both IBM (after a 10-year hiatus, as per its agreement settling the antitrust suit brought by Control Data) and AT&T have entered the data services business. Citibank is another newcomer, while several captive operations, General Electric Information Services (GEISCO), McDonnell Douglas Automation (MCAUTO), and Control Data, are flexing their muscles.

In 1970, data services revenues accounted for $1 billion, under 5% of the computer industry. No single company came close to revenues of $100 million. Today, the $15 billion generated by data services is well over 10% of total industry revenues, and this is not including the software sector. There are hundreds of data services companies in the $50 to $100 million range, and the three leaders are each approaching $1 billion in sales. And this is only the beginning. The computer services industry at midlife is poised for a take-off. It is ready to go all the way.

ELECTRONIC DATA SYSTEMS: ON THE WINGS OF MEGACONTRACTS

For sheer controversy, few businesses anywhere can match the record of Electronic Data Systems (EDS) and its founder, H. Ross Perot. Whether he is at the doors of the North Vietnamese embassy in Laos demanding the release of American POWs, leading a commando raid to Teheran to rescue EDS employees imprisoned there,* or at home in the United States competing for one of the many megacontracts that are the backbone of his company's business, Perot is likely to kick up some dust before he is through.

His Texas-style, rock 'em, sock 'em approach to business has won EDS and Perot (the two are basically inseparable) a slew of detractors and supporters. To be sure, no one who comes in contact with either the man or the company walks away without an opinion one way or the other. In the 1960s, EDS was a cause for celebration. Founded in 1961, the company was one of the genuine high fliers

---

* One of the most notable corporate adventures of all time, celebrated in the first nonfiction book by the best-selling author Ken Follett, *On Wings of Eagles* (New York: William Morrow & Co., 1983).

of the period, growing at 100% a year. Perot stole center stage when a skyrocketing stock market in 1969 made him a billionaire on paper. Even though his right-wing political views were out of step with the highly charged politics of the time, EDS was one of the meteoric go-go companies that gave the economy of that period its wild and unforgettable character.

In the 1970s, however, the star that shone over EDS and Perot seemed to go into eclipse. Perot's political views remained out of step with the "me decade" atmosphere, and on the business side, things weren't going so hot either.

The rapid growth of the 1960s overtaxed the company's centralized management structure (a polite way of saying that all things had to go through Perot). And the company, heavily dependent on a handful of large contracts, suffered when it lost a few of them and had no new contracts to take their place. The real debacle of the period, however, was Perot's costly venture on Wall Street. The failed effort to prop up the duPont Walston & Co. brokerage house put a big black mark on Perot's then flawless business record. This cost him and his associates an estimated $80 million and cost EDS a pair of large customers. Both duPont Glore Foran and Walston & Co. were customers of EDS before Perot arranged for their merger, hoping it would improve the fortunes of duPont Glore Foran. It didn't. After the merger went sour, the bankruptcy trustee filed suit, charging that Perot had been misleading about certain key aspects of the affair. An out-of-court settlement was reached in 1979, with Perot and his coconfidants paying $6.7 million (but not admitting guilt to any of the allegations). Moreover, while Perot and EDS management were devoting time to duPont Walston, EDS was taking a beating. Instead of the high growth it was accustomed to, between 1974 and 1976 earnings actually declined.

Today, however, all that seems part of a distant past. To say that business is booming would be to put it mildly. EDS is now riding a surge of growth that not only will make it the largest data services company but by the end of the decade will enable it to reach the echelon of Top 10 computer companies, the first data services firm to get to that level. EDS, on the strength of the enormous megacontracts being let by Washington, is on its way toward becoming the premier company in the era of systems integration. As IBM was to the 1950s and 1960s and Digital Equipment was to the 1970s, EDS will be to the 1980s. And, if nothing else, the political climate of the Reagan era is one that H. Ross Perot can feel right at home in.

The renaissance at EDS actually began in the late 1970s, and much of the credit for it has to go to Morton H. Meyerson, one of the key players in the EDS-duPont Walston affair. After it was over, he returned to EDS and became president in 1979, taking over the reins for day-to-day operations from Perot. Meyerson had stunned the organization by leading it on a whirlwind campaign to obtain new medical claims processing contracts (EDS had not sold any big new medical claims business in some 3 years) and then, upon becoming president, pushing the company into new areas, including government, defense, banking, and financial markets.

As almost everything connected with EDS, this resurgence generated controversy. EDS was accused of reaping excessive profits in its California medicaid claims processing. Competitors in various states claimed that EDS was awarded contracts unfairly. The most celebrated controversy occurred when EDS itself claimed that it had been unfairly passed over for a contract. When the Human Resources Board in Perot's own state of Texas awarded the Medicaid contract to New York-based Bradford National, Perot cried foul and eventually prevailed upon the Texas board to reverse its decision.

Nonetheless, this aggressive resurgence—call it the "Meyerson Miracle"—produced definite results for EDS. The customer base more than doubled, from 47 customers in 1974 to 122 in 1980. Actual contracts increased from 55 to 140. Revenue growth, which averaged 6% in the 1974–1976 period, has stayed at 25% ever since. It is this momentum that will take EDS to the top of the data services market within the next few years.

EDS's business resembles a layer cake (see Figure 9.2). Its data services contracts are long term, stretching from 3 to 10 years. Rarely are contracts lost after the initial term expires, and those few that do go to the competition when up for rebidding are usually offset by add-ons to other contracts. New business is layered onto the base each year. Revenues are retained over time, like an annuity. The contracts signed in 1978 contributed as much revenue in 1983

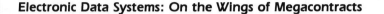

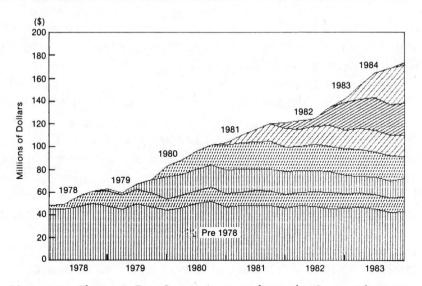

Figure 9.2. Electronic Data Systems' revenue layercake. *Source:* Electronic Data Systems Corporation.

as in 1978. This repetitive nature of the business lends a high degree of predictability and certainty to the future stream of profits.

Insurance and medical claims processing services is where EDS got its start. In the 1960s it established itself as the leading company in this area. Today, EDS alone processes more than 10% of all Medicaid claims. Medical claims processing and insurance together account for just under 40% of the company's revenues. But this is a maturing area and intensely competitive in recent years, growing just 10 to 15% annually.

Far more dynamic is the commercial sector, such as services to banks, credit unions, and automated clearing houses, as well as to some large commercial corporations, such as AT&T and Bank of America. EDS is the largest processor of credit union accounts, recently surpassing Control Data's Service Bureau. The commercial sector contributes 33% of total revenues and is expanding 30% a year.

The key to EDS's future is its business with the federal government. In 1983, this was the smallest revenue contributor, just 25% of annual revenues, but this area is exploding in growth at 50% a year. EDS has scored major victories here, and there will be more. The federal government is now at the beginning of a period that will see it award huge contracts for the overhaul of the government's information systems, from the Postal Service to the Social Security Administration to the military to . . . .

These contracts are so large and run over such long periods that they have come to be known as *megacontracts*. The megacontracts are the contemporary equivalents of the massive government projects of years past: the construction of bridges, tunnels, highways, dams, and government buildings. Those were the megacontracts of the days when the country was still young and growing. Millions of dollars in work were generated; thousands of men and women were employed; and the economies of various regions were transformed overnight. Moreover, huge fortunes were made by those firms that obtained the contracts.

But the country isn't growing anymore. The westward expansion and the rise of the cities have ended. We are imploding, not exploding. Instead of a network of highways, we are now seeing the creation of a network of information. An attempt to fathom the implications of this would require another book—and indeed many undoubtedly will be written. What concerns us here are the companies that will make their fortunes in the new megacontract era. And EDS has a good chance of being the most successful of them all. As Perot himself told *Fortune* in 1983, "This is the too-good-to-be-true-era of EDS." *

EDS has already scored major victories. In 1983, it won a $400 million contract to establish an inventory control system for the Navy during the next 8 years, renewable for 16 years beyond that. From the U.S. Postal Service, it won a $200 million, 7-year contract to create an airmail sorting system. The initial breakthrough, however, occurred in 1982, when EDS scored a stunning victory and the first real coup of the megacontract era: Project VIABLE, a $656 million 10-year contract to overhaul the computer systems at the 47 Army bases around the country. This is a job that a few years ago might have gone to IBM, Burroughs, Sperry, or Honeywell, all computer hardware manufacturers. By winning it, EDS became the first data services company to become a prime contractor on a major federal computer systems integration. Even if EDS had not won the

* *Fortune*, Oct. 31, 1983, p. 124.

contract, it was still likely to have gone to a data services rather than a hardware company. The favored competitor was Computer Sciences, for years deeply involved in government software development, with IBM as a subcontractor. Not often does an upstart beat out IBM.

The contract is mega in every sense. All Army base administrative functions had been run on long since obsolete IBM 360 mainframe computers and terminals. EDS is building a system consisting of regional data centers located near five bases, tied to IBM 4300 medium-sized mainframes at each base, hooked to over 20,000 terminals. By August 1982, ahead of schedule, EDS had the first regional data center up and running. It contains two Amdahl mainframes (Amdahl is a subcontractor on the job), 80 disk drives, 19 tape drives, and 4 printers. Before EDS finishes the job, add-ons and extras could almost double the initial size of the business to over $1 billion. The company will train 60,000 Army personnel as part of the job.

There will be more megacontracts. Other potential new business pertains to some $1 billion in work to upgrade the Social Security Administration's outmoded computer system, a systems integration project for the Federal Aviation Administration, a U.S. Army Reserve contract, U.S. Navy Stockpoints, the Defense Logistics Agency, and more business with AT&T Information Systems and possibly even Bank of America.

EDS could easily handle some of these contracts, but too many might overstrain its resources. Although they represent a continuous stream of revenue, profit margins on government contracts are not high, especially if they are hardware oriented. And if they involve a lot of software, other problems can arise. Software development is subject to numerous bottlenecks that EDS has had only modest success in improving. It even tried paying for software on a piecework basis—per line of code. No breakthrough appears to be forthcoming.

The main danger to EDS is that its personnel resources might become overstrained. EDS has always invested heavily in training new systems engineers and programmers, at a cost of $40,000 each in their first year on board. Such extensive training takes time and makes the company vulnerable to competitive hiring. To thwart that, EDS now has its new trainees sign a contract—an innovative first in the industry. More importantly, EDS's top 10% of technical personnel are paid 25% higher than the average market salary and are given stock vesting over a 7-year period. Turnover for this top echelon is under 6%. By taking on too much work, EDS could quickly overstrain its resources and risk not performing well on one of these key contracts. Government work has high visibility (as EDS already knows well), and when a company gets egg on its face, it is hard to get it off. Over the years, EDS has sometimes operated on an almost boom-and-bust cycle. It goes out and does a lot of selling, and once it has won a number of contracts, it settles down and works on them. This is fine, provided the timing stays right and the company does not oversell itself and take on more than it can handle.

EDS also faces possible problems if it does not keep a narrow focus on its mainstream markets. A substantial financial war chest and a lofty stock price are often inducements that make a company want to go on an acquisition binge. Although the company traditionally was shy of such moves, in the late 1970s it did become involved in a number of other areas, including turnkey minicomputer systems, a venture to sell "home of the future" electronic gear (personal computers, video recorders, etc.), microcomputer software, airline reservations, and various other odds and ends. All of these sideshows have now been terminated. But coming as they did after the duPont Walston fiasco reveals a potentially troublesome weak spot at EDS when it comes to acquisitions or side ventures. Even acquisitions elsewhere in the data services business merely to increase size could be risky for EDS. Discipline is the key here in the future.

To prepare for an onrush of business, EDS reorganized its top management structure in late 1983, transferring the head of the federal government group over to be in charge of all megacontract marketing; switching the commercial group manager to training and recruiting, and reserving his talents to handle a potential super-megacontract if awarded; and giving the former insurance group manager responsibility to operate and execute all existing business and marketing for routine new business. This new setup will ensure current business is not given short shrift, will put even more emphasis on the pursuit of both commercial and government systems integration megacontracts, and will give added attention to developing the systems engineering talent required for future business. EDS will about double its annual training program from 500 new recruits each year to over 1000.

It is unlikely, however, that anyone will ever discipline Ross Perot's propensity for translating his views into action on the important matters of the day, be it drugs, politics, or the education system in the state of Texas. Perot has made it clear that he is a man of the grand statement and the flamboyant gesture, and that he is always prepared to back his words with actions. Had Perot entered politics, he might have enjoyed a brief career in the limelight and then found himself out of favor and out of office. Fortunately for them, businesspeople are not as dependent on the fickleness of public opinion.

Far from being just an eccentricity, Perot's showmanship is actually an effective managerial device. It encourages a certain elan at a company, or what is often referred to in management books as "corporate culture." At EDS, the corporate culture is, as you might expect it to be, much like H. Ross Perot himself: dedicated, persistent, loyal, patriotic, family oriented, and determined to succeed. EDS can rival IBM in white shirts and outdistance it in American flags. When such values are out of style, it does not necessarily work against a company. On the contrary, it encourages spirit. And when it is in step with the times, nothing works better. But more than just corporate culture is at work here. The Dallas symphony plays on the EDS lawn during the summer. Mort Meyerson led the effort to construct a new symphony hall in Dallas.

Corporate culture does not in and of itself make a company succeed. Business has to be good. No amount of "ever onward employee gung ho-ism" can alter the result of a disastrous marketing policy or make a bad acquisition better. If business is bad, everything falls apart. But EDS doesn't have to worry about that now. It is right in step with the political climate of the 1980s. And business, already good, very good in fact, will only get better.

AUTOMATIC DATA PROCESSING: RECAPTURING
THAT OLD FORM

Anyone who has ever held a paying job probably is familiar with Automatic Data Processing (ADP). ADP just about invented the concept of data services. In 1949, before any computers were even available for commercial purposes, ADP prepared the first payroll for one of its customers in a storefront in Clifton, N.J. Today it does the paychecks for almost 100,000 companies, some of which are the most sophisticated computer users in the country. ADP is the largest independent data services firm in the industry, approaching $800 million in revenues in 1983. The company's profit record is absolutely flawless: never a quarterly decline since it went public in 1961. Its customers obviously hold it in high regard. Although they sign no contracts and are entitled to walk away on a moment's notice, most customers who use ADP's payroll and commercial services stay with the company an average of 7 years.

The vast majority of ADP's customers are small. They use ADP for the classic reasons that companies have always gone to data services firms: They are either unwilling or unable to commit the resources needed to develop their own in-house computer expertise. Many of these customers are absolutely dependent on ADP, leading ADP's president, Josh Weston, to refer to ADP's customer base not as a market, but as a "psychological niche."

In the future, however, this psychological niche could prove to be a serious weakness. It will be a strain for ADP to get the same growth out of this market that it has been accustomed to in the past. Although ADP sells direct and, according to Weston, its 1000-member sales force "plumbs hundreds of thousands of prospects through the sieve each year," ADP has been combing the same markets for a long time. Although there are some 3.2 million corporations out there, it is getting harder to locate enough prime candidates to keep the payroll business expanding at a fast rate. In recent years, ADP's revenue growth has slipped well below the 20% rate it was accustomed to in the 1970s.

ADP, of course, has not stood still. It has moved into a number of other areas. For stock brokerage firms it provides back-office trade processing services as well as a front-office stock quotation service.

It also provides data services for a number of other niche markets, including accountants and automobile dealers. And it operates a time-sharing network. In recent years it has embarked on several smaller pursuits, such as a network of automated teller machines (called Exchange), an automobile collision damage estimating service, and interactive accounting services.

These other services have helped keep ADP's growth rate respectable, but profits have continued to suffer. Profits, which expanded 28% a year in the 1970s, are now growing at only 13% a year. Profit margins actually have declined for seven years in a row.

The reviving economy will help to boost ADP's prospects somewhat. The average number of paychecks per account, having bottomed out at 66 in December 1982, was back to 70 as of the beginning of 1984. More important, however, are the internal changes that ADP has instituted. As the result of a major reorganization of its commercial sales force, sales representatives are now specialized by account (national, major, or small) and by type service (payroll or accounting). This new organization has led to a higher rate of new business which indicates that ADP's recent higher revenue growth from payroll services may continue for a few years, and is not solely dependent on the economic recovery.

Other areas are also experiencing significant improvement. Because of the heavier trading volume on the New York Stock Exchange in 1983, ADP's back-office brokerage processing business resurged. ADP significantly expanded its Wall Street computer facility, so the increased volume is needed to carry that overhead. If trading volume continues to increase, as is occurring from the new AT&T issues, this business will grow more profitable. A profit swing is occurring in the 18,000 terminal brokerage quotation service which was acquired from GT&E in August 1983. Automatic Data is also developing an in-house quotation system exclusively for Prudential-Bache that will lead to considerable revenues over the next three years. This system will consist of some 215 minicomputers and 3,600 micros (IBM and Convergent Technologies are supplying the hardware) and will generate some $20 to $40 million in revenues over the next three years, not counting the additional service business. The Comtrend commodity quotation service is also growing at 40% a year.

Some 1,000 dealers of International Harvester farm equipment will be added to the auto dealer data service business during 1984 and most of 1985, adding another $10 million in recurring revenues (helping to sustain a 20% growth rate). ADP has done well with its collision estimating service and because this market is so lightly penetrated, it should be able to expand at a 30% annual rate for a long time.

The interactive accounting services (accounts receivable/payable, general ledger), which are offered over a microcomputer or terminal at the customer site, are expanding at 40% a year. As personal computers flood the market, small businesses need help in putting their accounting onto the computer and automating this function.

Even in time-sharing services, ADP has been able to come up with a formula that is superior to the rest of that industry. While this business was severely hit by both the recession and the inroads made by small computers, ADP shifted some of its own services, such as collision estimating, and brokerage quotation services onto the ATM network. As a result, ADP is able to sustain a profit margin, albeit in the low teens, while the networks of most of its competitors are operating in the red.

ADP has worked hard to get itself out of the doldrums, and its efforts are paying off. I estimate its prospects for revenue growth over the next five years to be 16%. That's below the 20% rate that ADP was once accustomed to, but it's better than the 11% rate that the company fell to in 1983. But what's really significant about this recovery is the fact that ADP will be able to keep it going.

The various internal moves that this company has made, such as the marketing reorganization in commercial services and the effective utilization of its timesharing services, are smart moves that will benefit ADP in both good times and bad. Although the company has diversified quite a bit in the past—payroll and commercial services now account for 55% of its total revenues—it seems aware of the danger of becoming a generalist. ADP recently sold its pension accounting and tax preparation services, encouraging signs that the company knows how to focus its efforts.

But the years ahead are not going to be a cakewalk. There are still major areas of uncertainty. Payroll processing is still an economically sensitive business. Brokerage trading volume is unpredictable. The quotation system being developed for Prudential-Bache may not be marketable elsewhere. The ATM network may have limited potential because large banks seem to prefer joining other bank ATM networks instead. An encore to the large International Harvester contract may be difficult to find. Although there is a lot of room for growth in collision damage estimating, its a fact that the largest auto collision firms have already been signed. That means future increments will result in lesser growth.

In a way, ADP's business is too assured, too repetitive. New sales activity in any one year does not have much of an impact on the company's overall growth rate. While Electronic Data Systems, in contrast, adds huge megacontracts that can boost its growth rate sharply, Automatic Data does not have that kind of potential in its base of small business customers. Attempts by ADP to enter new markets seem to follow a pattern: They start small, develop nicely over time, but rarely become a big business. Few of them become large enough to be major contributors and many fall by the wayside in time.

This is not to say that ADP does not do things right. It requires first rate execution and constant quality of service to perform the way Automatic has for the past 30 years. In 13 years on Wall Street, with two different firms, ADP prepared every check this author ever received, with only one mistake: it under-withheld federal tax one time. It requires tremendous effort to sustain that level of performance, especially when a company is growing 15 to 20% a year.

If ADP is going to remain a leader in the highly volatile data services market it has to be something more than just old reliable. ADP needs to take a bold step into a big, new data services sector. It needs to make a big splash, shake up the routine, and give itself a chance to accelerate its growth back to 20% or higher on a susainable basis. The company needs to develop a creative new strategy for the future, instead of refining and adding to existing services. ADP traditionally has been acquisition-shy, but the company recently has indicated that it may be willing to change that stance and make a big acquisition, if the circumstances are right. That's a good sign.

The bottom line at Automatic Data Processing has always been quality, consistency, and integrity. These qualities were instilled into the company by the former chairman, and now U.S. Senator from New Jersey, Frank R. Lautenberg. They are still there under the current tough, no-nonsense president, Josh Weston. ADP has shown that it has what it takes to remain a leader in data services.

COMPUTER SCIENCES: DOES IT HAVE THE "RIGHT STUFF"?

On the surface, Computer Sciences appears to be a company with a great future. It is No. 2 in data services. Its special expertise is in the development of complicated custom software and computer systems integration projects. Moreover, its main customer is the federal government, a lucrative source of revenue today and one that will be an even greater source of business in the coming era of systems integration megacontracts. Computer Sciences is a company in the right place, at the right time, with the right resources.

Unfortunately, something is missing. Instead of acting like a young, aggressive software and services company, Computer Sciences seems moribund. Profits fell 26% in 1981 and remained flat in 1982 and 1983. Return on equity fell from a peak of 36% in 1980 to 14% in 1983. Although Computer Sciences is one of the top three data services companies in terms of revenues, its net income is only a fraction of what EDS and ADP make.

The causes of the malaise are not hard to identify. Over the years, its biggest customer has been NASA. (The space agency actually provided Computer Sciences with one-third of its revenues.) Today, however, the only excitement generated by the space program was in the movie *The Right Stuff* and as a backdrop to John Glenn's ill-fated presidential race. We aren't going to the moon anymore or trying particularly hard to beat the Russians. Space shuttle launchings, while exciting for a while, have become something of a routine. Computer Sciences needs to find another big customer to replace NASA.

For a couple of years, it appeared that business with Saudi Arabia and California Medicaid would lead to a resurgence. But this business along with NASA's have been winding down, and an effort to crack the traditional data services market has done little to pick up the slack. A group of West Coast data centers, acquired from

Itel in 1979, never got out of the red (they perform such services as payroll) and were sold to ADP in late 1983. Computer Sciences' time-sharing network, called Infonet, has also suffered from the major structural changes that have dramatically reduced the value of time sharing. Infonet was also hurt when it lost a large proprietary federal franchise in the late 1970s. Overall, profits from commercial data services peaked in 1980 and are now less than a quarter of that previous level.

Computer Sciences has been frustrated at almost every turn. A huge contract with California Medicaid (MediCal)—a keystone to its medical claims processing business, generating $35 million annually in revenues—was renewed in 1983, but only after a blistering competition that Computer Sciences won on an extremely low-profit (perhaps no-profit) basis. A $221 million, 5-year contract with Saudi Arabia to create a data communications network there is coming to an end and will be a difficult act to follow. In 1982, Tennessee Medicaid terminated in midstream a $4 million-a-year contract. In mid-1983, the company suffered another serious and unexpected setback. After more than a year spent developing software and establishing a dedicated data center to process payroll for the corporate clients of Security Pacific Bank, Computer Sciences lost the business when the two companies could not reach agreement on a continuation of the contract into the operational phase. This was to have been an important part of the company's commercial data services business.

There are some bright spots to the picture at Computer Sciences. Its cash flow is positive. Management is intact. Its position in the government contract market is still strong (especially now that a fraud and false claims suit has been settled). Although the NASA business is no longer growing, the Army, Navy, and Air Force together represent almost as large a portion of revenues, and this is expanding upwards of 20% a year. Computer Sciences has not secured any of the big megacontracts (although it was favored to win Army VIABLE), but it has secured a few in the $15 to $25 million-a-year range, and it bid on some three-quarters of a billion dollars in new government contracts during the first half of 1984.

To get ahead, Computer Sciences needs to shake off the sluggishness that has made it seem less like a computer company and more like a government agency. One important step would be to dispose of its commercial data services business, such as its consumer credit reporting, pharmacy data services, and Infonet. Unless a major turnaround can be accomplished (highly unlikely), keeping this business around will only dissipate the energies that Computer Sciences needs to secure some of the government megacontracts that are beginning to proliferate.

To play the megacontract game successfully, the company may have to start gambling a little more than it does now. Like a government bureaucracy, Computer Sciences tries to play things a bit on the safe side. More than three-quarters of its business is priced on a cost or time and material basis. This greatly reduces risk and gives the company security against major losses stemming from cost overruns on fixed-price contracts. But it also bars Computer Sciences from earning the higher profit margins that are possible with fixed-price contracts.

The era of the megacontract is a high-stakes era. To compete in this market, Computer Sciences needs to summon the courage to be a high-stakes gambler, and it needs a more vigorous, win-or-die attitude. This indeed may be the missing ingredient that has made the company seem so dull these past few years. Computer Sciences needs some of the vaunted "right stuff" that put the seven Mercury astronauts into space and launched both NASA and Computer Sciences on their way to fame and fortune. Without it, Computer Sciences will become just another data services company, growing a modest 10% a year and ripe for a takeover by someone else.

TYMSHARE: A MERGER OF LAST RESORT?

Once a leader in the data services market, Tymshare has fallen far off the winning pace. The market for the financial data services it offers to businesses, has been seriously eroded by the advent of small computers. At the same time, an unfocused business strategy has kept the company from capitalizing on markets where there is a potential for growth. Divisions have not been well integrated, and many of Tymshare's smaller operations run as totally unrelated profit centers.

Tymshare's crown jewel is its Tymnet data communications network, which is growing by leaps and bounds. Unfortunately, efforts to move into other segments of data communications (as opposed to providing data services) have not fared as well and do not have anything like Tymnet's robust outlook. As a result, Tymshare is suffering. Profits have fallen from a lofty peak of $19 million in 1980 to well under $10 million in 1982 and an almost $2 million loss in 1983. In March 1984 a preliminary agreement was reached for McDonnell Douglas Automation to acquire Tymshare. Only time will tell how this marriage willwork out.

Tymshare started out in 1966 as a supplier of interactive time-sharing services for engineering and scientific applications, then successfully transformed itself in the mid-1970s into a supplier of data services for business and management. Today, it is a $300 million company with three main revenue sources: its remote time-sharing network services for business and management (Information Network Services Division), which generates over $100 million; Tymnet, which serves over 200 cities and is the nation's largest packet-switched data communications network, contributing another $100 million annually; and Tymshare's tax processing services, which top $60 million. Everything else—and there is quite a bit else—adds up to peanuts.

It is in the traditional business, time-sharing, that Tymshare is being hurt the most. Companies can now obtain such services by buying their own personal computers or establishing in-house networks. Tymshare is attempting to deal with the problem by offering a complete customer system solution, involving applications and database management software, its own computer mainframes and data network, coupled with personal computers and work stations at the customer site. This new direction is ambitious, and complicated, and may be difficult to sell. It will be at least a year or two before Tymshare has any such integrated capability, if ever. There recently have been significant personnel changes in this division. More are needed.

Tax processing is a lackluster business, growing at little more than a 10% annual rate and slowing. It is seasonal and not an integral part of Tymshare's network and time-sharing data services offerings.

As for the rest of the company, several of the smaller data services—including credit card processing, hospital data services, and a shared automated teller machine network—have been disappointing and have been sold off or have folded. International data services are not growing, and management service for travel agents is in the red.

The future does have some silver linings. Tymshare has made several key acquisitions in the area of the electronic funds transfer that should serve it well in the future world of electronic banking and retailing. These include the purchase of Validata from TRW (credit authorization) and the acquisition of Telecheck (point-of-sale data services). Nonetheless, the real key to Tymshare is its Tymnet data communications service. For companies that regularly send computer data over phone lines, but not enough to justify having their own dedicated data line, Tymnet is an economical alternative. It offers service to nearly all large, urban areas, and also to many remote locations. Its only competition in terms of size is GTE's Telenet. Three years ago, things were so good for Tymshare that, even when Tymnet was growing at 50% a year, it still represented only 10% of the company's overall revenues. Today, its growth has fallen off slightly to 40%, but it now looms as Tymshare's single largest revenue contributor.

The enormous success of Tymnet has led Tymshare to pursue other areas of data communications. The acquisition of Microband gives Tymshare a set of local microwave transmission stations in some 45 U.S. cities for the distribution of pay television programming. Tymshare also further entrenched its position in electronic mail through the acquisition of FTC Communications, an international record carrier providing telex, telegram, and leased line communications.

Riding herd over this vast array of services is Thomas J. O'Rourke, Tymshare's chairman and founder. There is no more sincere, hardworking pioneer in the business (and there are few who appreciate California wine better than he does, a fact that I can attest to from enjoying many relaxed dinners with him over the years, discussing Tymshare's prospects).

Tymshare possesses some valuable building blocks from which

it could possibly shape a future. Its data communications network capability and expertise are considerable and will serve Tymshare well in building private data networks for commercial corporations. Its stake in electronic funds transfer should lead to growth as that market develops. Check authorization, credit card authorization, and point-of-sale data services have favorable growth prospects. Valuable software (such as MAGNUM and EXPRESS) and databases have been developed that might be used in new total systems offerings. Tymshare's broad customer base includes Fortune 1000 corporations, accounting firms, banks, and telephone companies. The balance sheet is healthy; debt comprises less than 10% of capitalization.

Tymshare has a schizophrenic strategy toward growth, emphasizing computing services one day and communications the next. In 1983, the company announced a shift from "communications-enhanced computation" to "computer-enhanced communications." But in communications, except for Tymnet, it is outclassed. The integration of computer services with the company's far-flung communications resources has always been elusive. And despite Tymnet's leadership position, the communications business is no piece of cake. Tymnet is being technically upgraded and geographically expanded, necessitating a major investment. And it is no longer so alone in its field. In addition to GTE's Telenet, there are now AT&T's Net 1000, IBM, United Computing, and Infonet as competitors. The acquisition of FTC puts Tymshare into direct competition with ITT, RCA, and possibly AT&T.

Tymshare has too many irons in the fire. And that, in a way, is its biggest problem. All these communications possibilities spark the hope of future sizzle but contribute little in the way of current profits. There are too many tomorrows and not enough todays at Tymshare.

Tymshare needs to channel its resources and concentrate its efforts on data services, especially those where it has a niche, such as credit and check authorization, tax preparation, and the proprietary aspects of its time-sharing computer services. These, along with Tymnet, are winners. Tymshare is still running in too many directions at once, especially off on communications tangents. Bold, creative new thrusts are needed in carefully selected, related data services segments. And, with Chairman O'Rourke nearing 60 years of age, there is a question as to how long he will remain at the helm. Other top management changes are occurring. Tymshare has some favorable attributes that make it an excellent fit with McDonnell Douglas Automation. The question is whether McDonnell Douglas can take advantage of these attibutes and establish a more focused strategy for Tymshare.

COMDISCO: THE LUCRATIVE LIFE OF A MIDDLEMAN

Comdisco has never assembled a piece of hardware or churned out a line of programming code. In an industry filled with highly specialized market niches, Comdisco has carved out one of the most unique niches of all: It is the industry's largest and most successful middleman. Comdisco leases new equipment, resells used equipment, and packages leases for sales to outside investors. Customers include 70% of the Fortune 500 and 49 of the top 50 largest corporations in the country. Comdisco's customer base is growing by 30% a year and now totals over 4000 clients. About two-thirds of its revenue is from repeat business.

Founded in 1969 as a computer broker and dealer (remarketer), Comdisco is currently the leader of this niche. In 1976, the company expanded into IBM equipment leasing, and today it is the leading independent computer leasing company. About one-half of Comdisco's revenues are from direct leasing, one-quarter from remarketing of used IBM computers, and one-quarter from packaging leases for outside investors. That portion of the computer leasing that involves investor tax shelter programs, however, has proven to be an Achilles' heel. It represents a disproportionately high contribution to earnings as the fees are recorded up front at the outset of the sale. Moreover, the Internal Revenue Service scrutinized the entire tax shelter investment business, encompassing any number of companies, beginning in early 1984, effectively disrupting the sale of such computer lease programs temporarily. This impacted overall profits, which subsequently declined modestly in late 1983, continuing in 1984.

IBM is deemphasizing and discouraging direct short-term rentals. This is good for the entire third-party leasing industry. The amount of third-party long-term leasing, the service provided by Comdisco, is expanding threefold to replace the rentals. Also, as mainframe computer product cycles shorten and used equipment becomes available more quickly, there is a greater need for Comdisco's remarketing services. Revenues have expanded close to 30% and earnings per share by over 45% annually during the past 5 years. In net income, Comdisco ranks third in the data services industry, behind only Electronic Data Systems and Automatic Data Processing.

More than anything, Comdisco has compiled an exceedingly good track record in a difficult business. Over the years, third-party computer leasing has led many companies to ruin. History is replete with such disasters as Itel, O.P.M. Leasing, Leasco, Data Processing F&G, Management Assistance, Booth, Greyhound, and Levin-Townsend. Like the others, Comdisco is exposed to obsolescence or price/value degradation in its leases as a result of IBM price changes and product introductions. The number of leasing and remarketing opportunities available in any particular year is influenced by IBM's computer product cycle and product shipments. When customers sit awaiting introduction of new IBM products, it slows down Comdisco's business activity. IBM, for its part, is becoming more aggressive in offering more long-term leases directly through its financial subsidiary. It is even compensating its sales force for channeling lease business to IBM Credit Corporation, so IBM may gain market share and make it less profitable for other third-party lessors. These are all major risks. One risk never suspected was the press. In October 1983, *Barron's* published a scathing article criticizing the company's accounting. The stock dropped like a rock, and the doubts raised not only impacted sales of tax shelter leases but also drew to the industry the attention of the Internal Revenue Service. A series of setbacks occurred following the article, including the departure of the senior vice president of marketing.

Comdisco has minimized the risks by emphasizing peripherals rather than mainframes. Some 70% of its leases are peripherals.

Peripherals represent a lower financial risk, have a longer life span, and retain value longer. Comdisco also provides an effective re-marketing service for a computer user's old equipment, which it will package together with a customer's lease on any new computer equipment, a service that IBM will not provide. This is a key support advantage when marketing leases.

Lease exposure is minimal, because less than 2% of the lease portfolio is in operating leases. In other words, if all the computer leases expire and become worthless at the end of the initial term, only 2% of the value of the base would have to be written off. Almost all computer leases are full payout or close to full payout—that is, fully depreciated over the period of initial lease. Residual value assumptions on peripherals are conservative. Comdisco retains the rights to any rental revenue or value after the lease expires. And now that the lease base is sizable, approaching $1 billion, any single year's activity or additions to the base are not as meaningful as in earlier periods, such as in 1980, when IBM customer hesitancy in waiting for new mainframe introductions caused an earnings decline at Comdisco. The company's lease base is now maturing and beginning to generate higher profits from expiring leases put back out for release or sale. Such earn out or profits from its lease base will bulge over the next couple of years, diminishing the dependence on sales of tax shelter computer leases. Comdisco has proved its viability, having come through the turbulent 1979–1980 period with flying colors, when Itel and others went bankrupt. It is seasoned. Its approach to leasing is conservative.

Over the long term, I expect Comdisco to continue to expand. A broad sales force, highly stimulated by commission-based compensation, is the key strength. There is a saying on Wall Street that a stockbroker's dream of heaven is to die and reappear as a Comdisco salesperson. Because Comdisco is primarily a marketing company, it has the image of being too smooth, too polished, and too aggressive. But it has a sound balance sheet. If anything, it has too much cash, possibly burning a hole in its pocket following a $250 million convertible debt offering in 1983. Cash flow is positive. The net worth of this company is over $200 million, but is actually understated by perhaps $150 million. Considerable equipment out on lease, and generating profits and has been fully depreciated or written off. Also the real market residual value of the peripherals on lease, which is assumed by the company to be only 15% of cost, is highly likely to be much more substantial than that.

Comdisco may begin to alter the mix of its business in future years, providing other types of computer or financial services. Acquisitions are likely. This raises the risk that the company may bite off more than it can chew or make a bad acquisition. Comdisco knows its current leasing and remarketing business cold, and the future there is sound, though more intense competition by IBM is certain. If the company pursues more distant ventures, it could stumble. Comdisco's challenge will be to keep its eye on a straight and narrow path. Middlemen should not diversify, lest they risk becoming outsiders.

SHARED MEDICAL SYSTEMS: THE PROGNOSIS IS GOOD

R. James Macaleer sold IBM computers to hospitals in the 1960s. It was then that he came up with the idea of creating a computerized financial management system that hospitals could share over a computer network. On that idea, Shared Medical Systems, the company Macaleer founded, became the premier hospital data services company, the only real alternative at the time to creating an in-house hospital computer system. Business surged. Revenues grew almost 30% annually from 1978 to 1983, to over $210 million. Financial data processing systems for patient billing, payroll, and internal accounting were the first services Shared Medical Systems offered to hospitals. Subsequently, a patient care system was developed to computerize and track actual medical services rendered and monitor the status of hospital patients. Still another service combines financial and patient care into an integrated hospital information system. The era of systems integration has arrived in the hospitals, and SMS, as it is now officially called, is the leader in providing this capability.

Information is critical at hospitals. Some 40% of an acute care hospital's budget is devoted to processing information. The need to automate is overwhelming. Currently, SMS generates $2 to $3 per bed daily in revenues from the 600 hospitals it serves, and that figure will double by the end of the decade. The big market opportunity for the company is to sell additional data services to existing hospital clients. One influence that will stimulate considerable new business is federal legislation changing the basis for hospital Medicare reimbursement. Hospitals must now determine the cost to treat each type of patient and will be reimbursed a predetermined amount regardless of the cost of treatment. This will inevitably make hospitals more profit-and-loss conscious and in need of better financial and patient care information systems.

The hospital computing market is undergoing considerable change. Instead of obtaining data services from a shared data center or a broad-based data network, many hospitals are buying their own dedicated computer systems and minicomputers. SMS is already providing such systems and wisely changed its name to deemphasize the "shared" aspect. In another more ominous trend a number of hospital management companies are acquiring hospitals and installing computer systems that they have created, potentially foreclosing to SMS a significant portion of the market. It remains to be seen just how many hospitals might be merged this way and whether SMS can crack into the hospital management chain computing business.

Still, long-term prospects are good. SMS is the dominant leader in a specialized data services market niche, and as a specialist, it should continue to flourish, subject to hospital management company competition. Its growth is controlled and consistent. The hospital market potential remains favorable, as hospitals are now required to be more cost conscious by federal medical reimbursement programs. There are innumerable related markets to exploit, such as physician group practices, retail pharmacies, and federal government hospitals. SMS's growth should average about 25% over the long term. As long as Macaleer, the no-nonsense, tough, pragmatic, hands-on founder of the company is involved, SMS will remain healthy.

QUOTRON SYSTEMS: WALL STREET IS ONLY SO BIG

Quotron has a vertical niche market (I'm a member of it). The company has a 57% share of the electronic stock price quotation market. Revenues are $154 million. There are some 60,000 Quotron terminals installed at over 5000 customer sites, in 1100 cities and towns, connected to 10 computer centers. All terminals are provided free. Quotron makes money from the $150 to $200 monthly fee it charges for the various financial quotation and database services it offers. It has only a dozen or so salespeople. This is the ultimate in narrow market specialization and penetration. It's a monopoly, or as Chairman Milton E. Mohr prefers to describe it, "it's big enough to be damned interesting and small enough to avoid attracting major competition"—at least until now. Quotron was founded in 1957 and was almost bankrupt in 1970, when Mohr arrived. But in the next 10 years, Quotron blossomed. Revenue expanded almost 30% annually during 1978 to 1983. Stockbrokers' customers may not own yachts—and until the 1982–1983 bull market on Wall Street, neither did the brokers—but Quotron has earned enough profits from the brokerage market to buy a fleet.

Unfortunately for Mohr, Quotron's future may be less interesting than its past. The company has saturated so much of the existing market, the question looms: Where does it go from here? Already at customer sites there is one terminal for every one and a half persons. After this reaches one user per terminal—which it soon will—there is little market potential left. Half the company's revenues already stem from terminal services other than stock price quotation, such as financial databases. Future growth depends on banks and other financial institutions entering the stock brokerage business and requiring Quotron's services. The company is also betting on its new QUOT-1000 Financial Office Services computer system. This system will provide brokers with word processing, electronic mail, computerized filing, and a host of other automated office functions. Such a comprehensive computer system is a big leap from existing quotation services and puts Quotron in direct competition with IBM, Data General, Automatic Data Processing (using Convergent Technologies hardware), Monchik-Webber/Merrill Lynch, and other brokerage in-house computer systems. And competition is also finally beginning to surface in the basic stock quotation business. Automatic Data acquired GTE's stock quotation business in 1983, and its contract to develop a $20 million internal quote system for Prudential-Bache may lead to other business eventually. Merrill-Lynch is teaming up with none other than IBM to first go in-house with its own system, displacing Quotron (Merrill is 25% of its business) and eventually compete for other brokers quote business.

Over the longer term, Quotron may sell more services and terminals to existing customers and gain business from new entrants to the brokerage field, but these sources will not sustain much growth. Efforts in other markets, such as insurance agents and transportation/air freight, are inconsequential, and the QUOT-1000 system may not change the outlook significantly. Quotron's entrenched position in the brokerage quotation data services market is threatened by large brokers developing their own internal systems. It's a nice niche, but it won't take Quotron too much further.

NATIONAL DATA: WATCH IT GROW

The world of electronic banking and retailing is inevitable, and no data services company is in a better position to capitalize on this trend than National Data. The company already performs one-third of all Visa and MasterCard credit authorizations. When stores switch over from voice authorization systems to electronic on-line terminals supplied by National Data, the number of authorizations increases sixfold. The reason is that, because the service is so much quicker, even very small credit charges are checked. Already the company has installed over 50,000 such terminals, accounting for half its credit authorizations. This is a service that is a valuable and vital component of the coming cashless society.

National is also solidly entrenched in corporate cash financial services. In cash management, National Data does balance reporting for over 5000 corporations through 1500 banks. In deposit report-

ing, over 2500 clients (mostly retail) report their various outlets'
deposits through 180 major banks. This market has great potential.
Currently only half of all corporations practice electronic cash management. The opportunity to address smaller customers—the 85,000
secondary businesses just below the 10,000 largest corporations—
now appears substantial.

Credit authorization and cash management together account for
some 60% of National Data's revenues. By concentrating on such
a specialized financial industry niche, National Data overcame a
difficult start and diffused strategy in the early 1970s and has pro-
gressed from $30 million in revenues in 1977 to some $130 million
by early 1984. Actually, National Data was once a hodgepodge of
varying data services, from hotel reservations to mail forwarding.
Over the past decade, Whit Whitney, who became president after
coming over from Burroughs, streamlined operations, combining
the two major financial services with a computer data network,
supplemented by the acquisition of Rapidata, a time-sharing network. Large banks are now interested in extending cash management services to small businesses. For that market, National Data
offers a turnkey bank computer system, NETS, to supplement its
own network as an electronic funds reporting mechanism, hooked
to IBM personal computers or electronic cash registers located at
stores and small business sites.

Two other contributors are small now but have the potential to
be big: telephone and catalog merchandising (telemarketing), and
retail pharmacy data services. Both are expanding at over 40%, and
both fit snugly with the company's credit authorization and network capabilities. Future services in these areas will involve active
solicitation, rather than just taking retail orders over the phone,
and electronic Yellow Pages. Advertisers can list a National Data
number in the Yellow Pages for customers to call for a nearby store
location and other information. In pharmacy services, the state of
New Jersey is commencing an automated, electronic Medicare eligibility system for pharmacy customers. All pharmacies will likely
be required to have the National Data system. This could be the tip
of the iceberg, as health care eligibility authorization goes electronic, the same route as credit authorization.

Despite its healthy long-term outlook, National Data went through a difficult period in 1983. Its profits temporarily flattened as it experienced a number of adverse crosscurrents: the incorporation of the newly acquired Rapidata time-sharing operation; a cyclical downturn in credit card authorization; the loss of a large New York bank customer cash management system that went in-house; and Atlantic Richfield's termination of its credit cards, which National Data processed. Although these adverse factors have subsided, the company still faces the challenges of achieving growth in its Rapidata time-sharing business; reaching smaller customers in cash management services now that the large business market is saturated; and competing against such banks as Citibank and Chemical, which may increasingly provide electronic funds and cash management services directly to customers. Down the road, there will be the home banking market, but it has not yet developed to the stage where it is a business. However, Chemical Bank is already out of the starting gate with its Pronto home banking system.

On the whole, National Data appears to be headed for a profitable future. By the end of the decade, it will be a sizable, broad-based, leading vendor of financial data services. Its bank and corporate customer list is impressive. Other data services can be sold to these customers, such as software to help customers interpret financial data and manage assets better. National Data is strong in marketing. Its chairman, Whit Whitney, is a consummate marketer, eminently likable, smooth, and low keyed. As the record shows, this small company has signed a laundry list of big-name customers. The possibilities in leveraging the sales capability and customer base are tremendous. The greatest uncertainty is Whitney's future role. He is 61 years of age, even though he appears 50, and is a critical element in the future of this company. After his retirement in another few years, he will be difficult to replace. National Data could end up merging into a larger financial services company if an effective management leader to succeed Whitney is not found.

10

Old and Gray before Their Time: Minicomputers

Before there was such a thing as a desk-top microcomputer, there was that other breed of small computer known as the minicomputer. When it first appeared in the 1960s, the minicomputer seemed like a revolutionary development. At a time when businesses were accustomed to spending over a million dollars and filling a whole room with a computer, the first minis, produced by Kenneth H. Olsen at Digital Equipment, sold for $120,000 and took up little more space than a large filing cabinet. In a few years, the minis were even smaller and so was their price: under $20,000 for some of them.

But the mini was not radical simply because it was smaller and cheaper; it also gave people the freedom to think about information processing in new and different ways. The minicomputer established the novel idea of applying one computer to one job no matter where that job happened to be. Computers began popping up in laboratories, in engineering design rooms, and on the factory floor. They could even fit into airplanes. At large universities, there could be one to a building, and in business, ultimately, one to a branch office. The minicomputer gave rise to the concept of distributed data processing: the idea that individual computers linked in a network could bear the brunt of a company's data processing needs, without relying on one central computer facility. The minicomputer was the first computer to be sold outright, rather than rented. And it produced the industry's first major wholesale market: the thousands of small firms, the systems houses and OEMs, that buy minis direct from the manufacturers and equip them with extra hardware and software to make them appeal to different markets.

Anyone who doubts the fortitude required to bring about all this change must keep in mind the rather closed atmosphere that prevailed in the early days of the industry. When Ken Olsen and an associate were searching around in the late 1950s for the venture capital to start Digital Equipment, they approached American Research and Development (ARD), the venture capital firm headed by General Georges Doriot. Doriot was receptive to Olsen's ideas but advised him against coming on too strong to the other members of the ARD board.

"We told Ken not to emphasize computers," Doriot recalled later. "Here were IBM, Burroughs, RCA in that business. To have two young men come to older men and talk of competing with them didn't sound quite modest. A lot of companies needed circuit modules for testing their equipment . . . so we settled on that for the first product, and the proposal mentioned that the company eventually planned to make computers." * On such tag lines are revolutions made.

For better or worse, however, instead of being appreciated as a radical departure in computing, the minicomputer may only be remembered as the opening gun in the hardware race that culminated in today's micros. The minicomputers launched the explosion of devices we are now seeing all around us. The minis inaugurated the period of shorter product cycles, product leapfrogging, and heavy price/performance competitiveness. They were in the vanguard, but at the same time, the companies that made them kept one foot firmly planted in the mainframe era. Like the mainframe companies that preceded them, each minicomputer manufacturer developed its own custom processors and software.

* Katherine Davis Fishman, *The Computer Establishment* (New York: Harper & Row, 1981), p. 212. The strategy worked; ARD gave Olsen $70,000 to start Digital Equipment.

There was no compatibility with what other manufacturers were doing. When customers bought a mini they were hooked for life, unless they were willing to undergo a painful and costly transition. The microcomputer manufacturers, on the other hand, use mass-produced microprocessors and invite anyone who is interested to write software for them. Thus, micros are much cheaper to make and have much more software written for them. The rest is history. The microcomputer companies have been killing the minicomputer industry. The market for minicomputers was expected to be favorable at least until the beginning of the 1990s. But when the micros came in and stole the show, mini market growth turned out to be less than half of what was expected. Those minicomputer companies that have built up sizable reputations and customer bases may adapt to this changed environment—the jury is still out—but it will be tough.

Most of the leaders in minicomputers—particularly Digital Equipment, Data General, Prime Computer, and Datapoint—have slowed markedly, showing cracks and even large crevices in their operations and incurring major financial setbacks during 1981–1983. The list of minicomputer businesses on the wane is long: Texas Instruments, McDonnell Douglas's Microdata, General Automation, Motorola's Four-Phase, Honeywell, Computer Automation, Sperry's Varian Data Machines, Modcomp, Perkin-Elmer's Interdata, and on and on.

The traditional 8-bit and 16-bit minis are no longer growing in sales. The industry is fragmenting into specialty niches, such as superminicomputers (Prime) and fault-tolerant computers (Tandem). Traditional minis are being squeezed from below by the microcomputer companies and also from the top as IBM gets more aggressive. Although traditional minis were a $6 billion market in 1983, they were superseded by the $13 billion market for personal computers, small business computers, and microprocessors.

It's the same old story. Just as the mainframe companies failed to capitalize on minicomputers, the minicomputer companies missed the major specialty niche where they should have been leaders—microcomputers. The minicomputer companies, acting old, gray, and protective, were caught asleep. Only a few years ago, they were the industry's young turks. That's how fast things move.

Almost all the minicomputer industry growth is in the market for the superminicomputers. These are computers that use 32-bit processors and pack mainframe power at a minicomputer price. They support 16 to 128 terminals, have 1 to 16 megabytes of main memory, can address far more memory faster, are more accurate, and are easier to program. Superminicomputers are swamping the rest of the market. Digital Equipment owns some 40% of the business (even though it was late into the game). Wang Laboratories, Prime Computer, and Perkin-Elmer's Interdata are also major players, while Hewlett-Packard lags in this higher growth sector. But even though the superminicomputer market is growing at 30% a year and totaling almost $3 billion in sales, that is not enough to offset the malaise in the rest of the minicomputer business. Competition in superminicomputers has intensified. They have become widespread and commonplace, almost a commodity, and some of the early pioneers, such as Prime Computer and Perkin-Elmer's Interdata, have topped out and are running out of steam.

Office automation is another high-potential market, but traditional minicomputer vendors are at a distinct disadvantage in penetrating this area. Because minicomputers have been sold through OEMs for the most part and only to a lesser degree directly to the end user, the minicomputer companies lack the experienced, direct sales forces that are needed to tackle the office market. In this respect minicomputer companies are even worse off than Xerox and some of the mainframe companies. The minicomputer companies have the technology and the products, but they lack the presence in the office market to begin with (remember, many of the mainframe companies started out as office equipment companies). Thus, they are unlikely to play a big role. The office automation market will not be the salvation for most minicomputer companies.

Nonetheless, the minicomputer companies are trying. Many of them are attempting to supplement their OEM sales outlets with direct sales forces that go right to the end user. This is a painful and costly transition, as both Datapoint and Data General have discovered. There has been much management turnover in the industry. Both Prime and Data General have turned to former IBM managers in hopes of getting some of whatever it is that enables a company to survive over the long haul.

There are no easy or clear answers. Of the companies we analyze here, Digital Equipment and Hewlett-Packard emerge as the two with the best chances of survival. Ironically, these two stalwarts have adopted strategies that are diametrically opposed to each other.

DIGITAL EQUIPMENT: NO. 2 MUST TRY HARDER TO RETAIN POSITION

Digital Equipment is the most incredible success story in the computer industry, after IBM. It has had the kind of growth that other companies dream about. The company took off with a running start in the 1960s and soared like a bird in the 1970s, never looking down or back. It defied everyone's expectations and proved that a company could become progressively richer by selling computers that were progressively less expensive. Sales went from $25 million in 1966 (a year after Digital introduced the PDP-8, the first mass-produced minicomputer, with a price tag under $20,000) to $1 billion in 1977. Revenues grew at an annual rate of 86% in the 1970s, as Digital disproved the axiom that says a company slows down after reaching the $1 billion mark. Digital kept right on going and hit the $4 billion mark in 1982. When Fortune magazine charted the growth of the 20 companies that, like Digital, achieved the $1 billion mark in 1977, it confirmed what many might have suspected: Digital was growing twice as fast as the group average and faster than any of the other 19 (except for one firm that had made an acquisition).

Digital was ready to steamroll its way through the 1980s when suddenly history caught up with it. The company ran out of steam. Profits began to decline. The recession took its toll. A new line of high-performance superminicomputers was still not out of the factory—24 months behind schedule. While the growth in the industry was gravitating toward microcomputers, Digital remained focused on minis—as it will continue to do for quite a while, a key decision of its founder, Kenneth H. Olsen, that will have a major bearing on the company's future.

Digital was as surprised by the sudden change in the weather as everyone else. The company expected to keep on growing as fast as it had in the past. And it did not anticipate that, when the slowdown came, it would be quite so abrupt. The company was placed in the unusual position in 1983 of defending itself before the outside world—investors, customers, and the press. It clammed up. Aside from the usual expressions of confidence that things would get better, Digital was not forthcoming about what was happening inside the company. Considerable management turmoil was evident.

Obviously, as a $4 billion company, Digital is not about to roll over and play dead. The company has significant resources at its disposal, including a highly automated, high-volume manufacturing capability and a broad array of engineering, sales, and service resources. But it is by no means clear that the company is sure what to do with them.

Not surprisingly, the key to Digital's future is in the hands of Ken Olsen. Digital is the largest computer company in which the original founder is active in day-to-day management, a distinction the company may retain into the 1990s. Olsen built Digital from the ground up: no acquisitions, all outright sales, strong finances. An original who combines a touch of homespun Americana with sharp-minded views on the future of the computer industry, he works out of the old Civil War blanket mill where he located Digital when he founded the company in 1957. His office is filled with beaver and duck models, wood beams, and brick, giving it a log cabin appearance.

Unlike many of his counterparts in the industry, Olsen manages a company, not a stock. The focus is on the basics: customer needs, product capabilities, engineering, and manufacturing. When those things are done right, in Olsen's view, the profit and financial picture will take care of itself. Olsen thinks long term. Unfortunately, in recent years he may have been caught thinking a little too long term.

Digital did not come out with a superminicomputer until 1977, well after Prime and Perkin-Elmer had already staked out the market. Because Digital was committed to the service and support needed for its line of 8- and 16-bit minis it was slow to recognize the potential in making the jump to the 32-bit superminicomputers. It was a costly error, but Digital made up ground fast. When it finally came out with the VAX line of superminicomputers, it effectively utilized its large customer base and sales force to garner 40% of the market. On the strength of the VAX line of superminis, Digital went from $1 billion in sales in 1977 to $4 billion by 1983.

Digital was late again in tackling the microcomputer market. This time Lady Luck turned a deaf ear. By the time Digital came out with its line of personal computers in 1983, IBM had already stolen all the thunder. The tardiness already looms as a costly mistake. Digital's personal computer, designed for business, had a limited software selection, a closed architecture, and (perhaps the worst sin of all) was not compatible with the IBM PC. Digital can't be faulted entirely. The enormous success of the IBM PC took everyone by surprise. Digital also may have been a little overcautious, holding back in deference to the new line of 32-bit VAX computers it was about to introduce, which included a desk-top microcomputer. The bottom line, however, is that Olsen really isn't very committed to personal computers and doesn't believe that his customers or corporations in general will be either.

"Businesses don't want a computer on a table to run the business," claims Olsen. "They want a real computer and disk drive that stand on the floor, not an Apple that looks like an amateur machine. Businesses can only afford the very best. They only buy the best equipment with the best service."

Olsen sees personal computers as "too limited, eliminating freedoms. They are easier to use, but they have no potential for upgrade. People were misled into thinking a PC would solve problems and are now learning that it won't. Personal computers stole the show," claims Olsen, "because [Digital] didn't sell minis aggressively like it should have."

The question is: Can Digital sell anything aggressively? Digital's marketing efforts were once taken lightly by the industry. The story was that you had to go bang on the company's door before they would come and sell you one of their computers. This was fine in years past when a minicomputer company could be engineering oriented and still be successful, when a great leading-edge product sold itself to sophisticated customers. Salespeople merely visited customers; they did not sell. But times have changed. Digital is making some progress in direct marketing in the office market, where it's needed most, but it is slow. Its sales force, which has always operated on salary, traditionally was specialized by product class, addressing all customers. Now the sales force is specialized by customer type. Sales representatives sell the full range of Digital products to only a select few customers.

Digital will have to do better than this if it hopes to be a force in office automation. It has a weak reputation in white-collar offices. This is a market that does not buy price/performance characteristics. Office automation customers want easy-to-use solutions to their computing problems. Digital claims to be No. 3 in office automation, behind IBM and Wang (Hewlett-Packard makes the same claim), but this is mostly due to its early lead in the newspaper market, where Digital is the dominant force with computerized word processing, editing, typesetting, and composing systems. Unless the Digital sales force learns to sell aggressively, Digital will never crack the Fortune 1000 office automation market.

Digital must also get more competitive again in product development. Its late arrival in superminicomputers and microcomputers cannot be repeated if it wants to retain its position as an industry leader. Digital must learn to react quickly to the competition, or better yet, preempt it.

To meet the new competitive environment in the industry, Digital is attempting an internal reorganization. The company rode to over $4 billion in sales on a matrix management structure where each element—manufacturing, R&D, and sales—was equal and independent. Many managers reported to several bosses. As the pace of industry product competition accelerated, this matrix management structure proved unwieldy and a source of problems. Digital could not make decisions fast enough or coordinate functions closely enough to get the proper product to market fast. A more pyramidal organization is now being formed, while at the same time the company is being broken into more pieces to allow freedom and flexibility. As size expands, the tendency at any company is to lose lower-level freedom and creativity. Olsen is trying to keep the pieces small to preserve the entrepreneurial spirit, much of which may have already seeped out of Digital. Olsen knows the danger of running Digital like one big company. The pieces must be allowed to run and perhaps fail on their own if Digital is to remain in the forefront in the industry. This managerial feat will be tough to bring off.

The transition has been wrenching, causing chaos and confusion. There have been several high-level management departures, including C. Gordon Bell, vice-president of engineering, Andrew C. Knowles III, a senior vice-president and group manager, and Julius L. Marcus, a group manager-engineering, all had been at the company seemingly forever.

The company is also learning that its financial controls are in need of major improvement. Digital never paid enough attention to such things as financial reporting, forecasting plans, inventory, and receivables management. Financing was always readily available from Wall Street investors, so there was no need to optimize returns. This inadequacy came to haunt the company in 1982 and 1983, when profits suddenly collapsed. At one point in fall 1983 Digital couldn't even match up orders with production and shipment schedules properly, causing a drastic eclipse in profits. The company needs to tighten up its financial reporting and controlling procedures considerably.

For the next couple of years, Digital has a lot going for it. The company is about to introduce a new line of VAX 32-bit computers, a product line that will stretch from the smallest microprocessor to a high-end mainframe (all compatible with each other), which should stimulate strong bookings. Although Digital is behind schedule with this product line, given the complexity of the design and the incredible denseness of the circuitry, that is not surprising. After a slow start, the company's new personal computers and disk drive products may also eventually help sales growth.

No doubt the company will solve its reorganization problems with Olsen at the helm over the next decade, though the weak marketing and cyclical nature of the company will remain. These are almost congenital defects that the company is going to have to live with.

Looking long range, Digital, by virtue of its size, is a de facto generalist in this era of specialty niche companies. Although the company is giving a new emphasis to marketing, it is not willing to give up its character as a technology-driven company. Ken Olsen's goal is to tackle only the hard jobs in the industry, leaving the easy products for others to sell. He wants products to do all jobs, "in quantities so huge, that specialty companies won't be able to touch us." Digital is striving to be more technological, not less. Managers running the company are still more engineering oriented than is common throughout the rest of the computer industry. This technological emphasis was further confirmed when Digital made the unprecedented move of acquiring a 9% equity stake in Trilogy Systems (for $26 million) in return for the right to license that company's future semiconductor wafer technology.

The effort to remain a technological leader reveals the bold, risk-taking side of Ken Olsen. He is not afraid of zigging when the rest of the industry is zagging. Nonetheless, this is a risky strategy, especially at a time when the company should be concentrating on its weaknesses in marketing. Technology leads, once attained, are tenuous and hard to keep for very long.

Digital faces many severe challenges over the next few years:

1. The company will suffer the self-impact on orders for old products during 1984 as new products loom but are not yet ready for volume production.
2. Competition is shifting. Digital must now confront IBM head to head in virtually every computer market, rather than enjoying its comfortable niche in the scientific, engineering, education, and industrial minicomputer markets.
3. Digital must succeed in the office automation market—a tall order given its small presence there and IBM's renewed aggressiveness.
4. The company's personnel level is bloated.
5. The personal computer effort is subpar.
6. Product development seems to have slipped.
7. Financial and administrative controls are inadequate.
8. The minicomputer market is maturing.
9. Management changes and turnover have added to internal turmoil.

Digital has many strengths that, if leveraged properly, will help it regain its position as a dominant competitor in the industry.

Perhaps Digital's greatest advantage is its huge and loyal customer base. Moreover, the company has financial, R&D, and field service resources that surpass most other companies in the business. However, a major transformation effort, such as the shift in gears accomplished at IBM in the late 1970s and early 1980s, is required to put Digital into a more competitive stance. The sweeping corporate restructuring that is currently in progress is a step in the right direction, though this effort temporarily added to the confusion in 1983 and early 1984. More changes are necessary, including: productive R&D and state-of-the-art technological products; a more motivated, incentive-driven sales force to penetrate the office market; much tighter financial controls and reporting procedures; and some new top management and new members of the board from the outside.

It appears Digital should be able to make these changes and that it will come away from its recent adversities a stronger competitor. The transition will take time and money, however. Profit margins may never again reach prior record levels. So, while overall profits will eventually recover, Digital may not meet the high expectations that many observers once had. The company's No. 2 status is no longer totally secure. Digital will have to fight hard to retain it.

HEWLETT-PACKARD: COMPUTER INDUSTRY BRONZE MEDALIST

Like most of the established computer companies, Hewlett-Packard viewed the beginnings of the personal computer revolution from afar—but not anymore. Hewlett-Packard is pinning its hopes of becoming the industry's No. 3 company on the strength of its effort in personal computers. In a striking contrast to Digital Equipment, Hewlett-Packard has personal computer religion.

"In the past, if you were not a minicomputer supplier, you are now obsolete," states Paul C. Ely, Jr., the executive vice-president of Hewlett-Packard's Electronic Data Products group. "In the future it will be the same with personal computers." In 1983, Hewlett-Packard made its presence felt in the personal computer market with the Hewlett-Packard 150, a personal computer that utilizes touch screen technology, IBM mainframe communications, and impressive graphics. The HP-150 is compatible with the IBM PC—a key marketing stroke.

Hewlett-Packard has also shown it is not content just to put a product on the market and watch what happens. It plans to sell, sell, sell. In an unprecedented move, the company has gone outside to obtain mass marketing from such places as Heublein. The number of retail stores carrying Hewlett-Packard computers was doubled to 600 in 1983, and the number of stores that Hewlett-Packard itself operates was expanded to 60, from 26.

You know Ely is serious when he says that he views the personal computer market as a "necessity, not just an incremental opportunity. . . . It will be the center of attention for years to come."

Hewlett-Packard brings a number of key assets to this new effort. In almost every way, it is a first-class company. When it sets out to accomplish a business goal, it succeeds. Products are high quality all around, and innovation is a byword. Hewlett-Packard customer service is superior to all other minicomputer companies. Along with IBM, it regularly ranks at the top of the *Fortune* listing of firms with best reputations.

Hewlett-Packard's skills lie in both computers and its first business, instrumentation. Until 1975, the company had considerable difficulty in developing a viable commercial computer business. Once it regrouped under new management and exploited semiconductor memory technology (as competitors remained dependent on core memory), the business took off and quickly became over half of all revenues. In 1983, total sales—including minicomputers, graphic plotters, terminals, and several personal computer models—topped $2.4 billion. The five-year compounded growth has been 26%. During the recession, Hewlett-Packard made major gains, while Data General and Digital Equipment suffered.

Hewlett-Packard also has the financial strength and discipline to go the distance. It has financed all its growth internally, compared to the constant external financings at Digital, Wang, and even IBM in recent years. The company has consistently achieved higher profit margin levels, meeting goals that it set several years ago. As a company, Hewlett-Packard's total revenues (including those from instrumentation) are comparable to those of Digital, yet operating profits are substantially higher. And Hewlett-Packard is able to sustain this level of profit even though it is the third largest R&D spender in the electronics industry (behind only AT&T and IBM). Hewlett-Packard is a leader in factory automation and presents a stiff challenge to IBM in that area. It also claims that it, not Digital Equipment, is No. 3 in office automation.

Does the company have any drawbacks? A few. One would have even more confidence in Hewlett-Packard's prospects if it had positioned itself in the 32-bit superminicomputer market. Hewlett-Packard never even came out with a supermini. It is only now offering a 32-bit engineering work station. In its own defense, the company points out that its Model 3000 family of 16-bit commercial minicomputer has not been impaired by its smaller word length. Moreover, Hewlett has been a leader in database management software, a key in carving out an enviable market share in office applications. A more significant drawback stems from the fact that Hewlett-Packard's minicomputer line is actually seven different families of computers—all of them incompatible—and that is too many. Ely claims that the job of making these seven lines compatible is a mere technical problem. But that's what they all say! Shades of Honeywell and Sperry. Moreover, Hewlett-Packard has not really shined in the office automation market. Although it already sells over $550 million in desk-top computers, two-thirds of these sales are for the terminals, engineering work stations, and programmable calculators it sells to its engineering and scientific markets.

Hewlett-Packard's strategy is to push personal computers in the commercial market, concentrate on the huge factory automation market in minicomputers, and offer no large computer systems priced over $350,000. Long term the company's objective is to expand its computer business at a 25 to 35% rate, and eventually have computers comprise at least three-quarters of total sales. It wants to be No. 2 in personal computers and No. 3 in the computer industry overall.

The company has an excellent chance of attaining these goals. But it won't be easy for a minicomputer company to transform into a personal computer company, especially after starting out a couple of years late. The mainframe companies never transformed into minicomputer companies, and only IBM has made a mark in micro-computers—but that's IBM. And funny things can happen on the way to a new market. The market may not last long, may shift in emphasis, or may not be as big as anticipated. In personal computers, a profitless boom may ensue for everyone. Give Hewlett-Packard the benefit of the doubt. Management is effective, hard hitting, business-like, and humble. No fat cats here. Ely's office was the only open-air, partitioned cubicle of all the 40 or more chief executive officers' I interviewed for this book. His surroundings were comparable to those of a low-level software programmer: no airs. Of course, the founders and pioneers, David Packard and William R. Hewlett, are phasing out, close to full retirement. Professional management is taking over. Overall management is still predominantly engineering oriented. Nonetheless, this company is for real. It is a powerhouse. It will be a big factor in the computer business.

DATA GENERAL: THE SOUL OF A COMPANY PLAYING CATCH-UP

Data General is No. 3 of the big three minicomputer companies, and the only computer company to date that has been the subject of a best-selling book—a Pulitzer prize winner to boot. *The Soul of a New Machine* made folk heroes of the engineers and programmers who set out hell bent for leather so that Data General could make up lost ground in the superminicomputer race. Unfortunately, what Data General did for the publishing industry, it has been unable to do for itself. The company hasn't had anything like a best-seller in its product line in years. Even the MV-8000, the "machine" of *The Soul of a New Machine*, fell far short of expectations.

It was in 1980 that things began to go wrong at Data General. Sales growth came to a halt; profits began a steady plummet. In retrospect, it is not hard to see why things went sour: Data General had no position in either superminicomputers or microcomputers, the two specialty sectors that were stealing all the growth from the traditional 8- and 16-bit minis. (Digital Equipment, at least, got into superminicomputers soon enough to grab a big chunk of the market.) At the time, however, Data General was coming off a 5-year period in which sales increased annually at a 40% clip and profit margins were 20%. It was lean and happy, ready to wait out the recession for the favorable conditions to reappear, when it could once again sell its computer processors to its traditional OEM customers and not worry about software, maintenance, or systems engineering support. Those days didn't return. They never will. And when Data General woke up and realized that, it began to recognize how much time it had lost and the awesome task that confronted it.

A malaise overcame the company. Edson D. de Castro, the president and founder, had an autocratic style —he often tracked details down to the smallest expense account—that was soon overwhelmed by the complexity of the transition task. It was impossible for him to make all the decisions anymore, yet other managers were not used to acting on their own. The company set out to make the necessary changes: installing new management, reasserting product and technology leadership, building a sales force, reorienting the company toward the end user, strengthening the service and maintenance organization, and bolstering software development. But the recession impact grew worse, and earnings caved in. A tumultuous reorganization and upheaval commenced, lasting over 3 years.

While de Castro still rules the roost at Data General, he is trying to decentralize and share some power. A major shake-up has taken place. Only half of the company's 20 top managers have been there 10 years. Seven have been there less than five. Most significantly, six of the company's top executives are from IBM, a conscious effort by de Castro to graft a little of IBM's vaunted organizational expertise onto the loose seat-of-the-pants style that has prevailed at Data General. But it is not easy to tame a wild bronco. And once too tame, the small-company atmosphere—the creative, rewarding environment described in *The Soul of a New Machine*—will be gone.

If Data General can't get its act together, it will be a shame. The industry will be poorer for it. While the company has always been characterized by a brash style and aggressiveness toward competitors (and even customers), it hasn't just been blowing a lot of hot air. Data General has come up with imaginative, high-quality products. Its current superminicomputer, the MV-10000 (the successor to the "machine"), is capable of 2.2 MIPS and has temporarily hurdled all the computers in its class. Data General's new line of microcomputer work stations designed for the office is equally impressive.

Data General's main problem is that it still suffers from its traditional OEM orientation. It believes good products will sell themselves. Its salespeople still sell hardware price/performance characteristics that appeal to technical OEMs. But Data General is trying, and some results are beginning to show from its efforts. OEM hardware customers now contribute only a third of the company's revenues, from two-thirds 5 years ago. Service has grown to 27% of revenues and is profitable. The company's customer service ratings have risen. E. F. Hutton awarded the company a $40 million contract to install in 300 to 400 branches an information processing system using Data General's office automation software. The U.S. Forest Service gave it a $70 million contract to create a network of 900 computers at some 800 locations.* These aren't the huge megacontracts that the industry is beginning to see, but they will do nicely for Data General. In addition to large office automation users, Data General is targeting a number of other specialty areas: small businesses, factory automation, medical, scientific, and government markets.

Another major uncertainty is management. While de Castro still rules the roost, he is trying to decentralize, share power, and allow the management style of some of his new IBM recruits to flourish. A visitor at Data General does notice more coats and ties these days and fewer jeans and polo shirts. De Castro has even become a little laid back, with a nice tan. The day we interviewed him, he was reading *The Electronic News* (during office hours!), when we ex-

---

* For this contract, Data General beat out AT&T's Western Electric in AT&T's first bid in the computer processor market.

pected him to be scurrying about, managing everything he could get his hands on.

Data General's long-range objective is to be a survivor of both the explosive fragmentation occurring in the industry today and the implosion that may come about as early as the 1990s. De Castro thinks the industry will go the way of the automobile and steel industries in 20 years and that there won't be more than 10 companies left by that time. He wants to be one of them. To be a survivor in 20 years, the company is seeking to be as broad-based as possible as fast as possible, with a broad array of products, marketing approaches, manufacturing, and service. De Castro sees specialty niche wars developing that will kill off the participants, and he observes that specialty niche companies often have trouble coming up with an encore. He wants to be in some niches, but not dependent on only one or two. In de Castro's opinion, only two other companies besides his own, IBM and Digital, have a start in all the areas—semiconductors, peripherals, software, offshore manufacturing, field service, and products—that will enable them to survive over the long haul.

It seems somewhat fanciful, however, to speak about Data General in the same breath as Digital Equipment and IBM. Data General comes up very short in a key area that de Castro failed to mention: size. Data General is less than one-fourth the size of Digital Equipment and one-fortieth the size of IBM. It will take more than a half-dozen ex-IBMers to overcome that deficit. Companies six times the size of Data General, such as Burroughs and NCR, tried and failed to be successful generalists and are now seeking specialty niches. Considerable outside help in the form of joint efforts will be necessary if Data General wants to be a generalist. Even IBM has gone that route, but Data General has not yet pursued such alliances. Moreover, the attempt to be a generalist may be doomed before it begins if the market keeps on fragmenting the way it is now.

Data General is reversing its 1980–1983 slide and should enjoy some good years ahead, but making it back into the Top 10 rankings is another matter. De Castro is right in his long-term analysis of the industry, although he may be trying to move his company in the right direction at the wrong time. Data General is too small to become a generalist in this era of specialization.

DATAPOINT: HOW NOT TO PLAY THE SPECIALTY NICHE GAME

Sometimes it does not pay to be too early, too far out on the leading edge, pushing products that are ahead of their time in markets that are just not ready yet. You know what they say—pioneers have a lot of arrows in their backs. Datapoint hyped the office automation market before its time and came a cropper.

Datapoint was selling a product that sounded terrific: desk-top office processors designed for management (the term *executive work station* was not then in popular usage) that were linked together by a local area network. Datapoint called its local network, the ARC (attached resource computer) network. It was way ahead of its time, on the market well before Xerox had come out with its own network, Ethernet. Datapoint sold 5000 ARCNETS between 1973 and 1981 and saw its revenues climb 46% annually, reaching $400 million by 1981. Profits rose from $1 million to $49 million. Those were the glory days. Chairman Harold E. O'Kelley, who joined Datapoint in 1973 from Harris's Radiation subsidiary, won plaudits all around for his work in turning a once-ailing terminal company into a gleaming thoroughbred of the emerging office automation market.

And then—if you follow the industry, you know what comes next—Datapoint became front-page news, and the news wasn't good. It began in the spring of 1982, when the company reported a whopping quarterly loss. At midyear, the company reported that profits for the fiscal year just ended were $2 million, down from $49 million the prior year. Things continued to get worse: restated backlogs, management turnover, stockholder legal suits, divestitures, a major loss of credibility on Wall Street, and a free-fall stock price from $66 to $11.

Datapoint took a major-league tumble from which it is not likely to recover. It occurred just as the company was beginning to be mentioned in the same breath as IBM and Wang in reference to office automation. That probably was the source of the company's problems. Datapoint was beginning to believe its own press releases, but the customers weren't fooled. Although Datapoint's ARC network was systems oriented and technically well designed, it was difficult to sell. In order to utilize such an office automation system, customers had to fit their organizations completely to it, not the other way around.

In fact, despite all the publicity hype Datapoint generated over the ARC network, it later became evident that Datapoint was selling a large number of the ARC network processors as stand-alone items (without the network) to small businesses. Instead of being in the vanguard of office automation, Datapoint was drawing a substantial portion of its revenues as a traditional vendor of 8- and 16-bit minis. And it was being hurt by the same pressures affecting all the traditional minicomputer companies: the move to micros and super-minicomputers as the high-growth sectors. Meanwhile, Datapoint completely missed the market for stand-alone word processors, the springboard that launched Wang as an office automation leader. Playing the niche market is a tricky business. Datapoint played it wrong.

The immediate cause of the company's sudden reversals in 1982 stemmed from its effort to reduce its reliance on OEMs and enlarge its direct sales force. This is never an easy task. At Datapoint, it was a nightmare. The sales force was doubled in 1 year, a burdensome cost and a strain on existing sales personnel. Most of all, O'Kelley was tough—too tough. To make quotas, to keep earnings rolling along, and to keep the stock price up, his salespeople began to book bad business. Revenues were recorded before equipment was shipped, and for equipment the customer never really wanted, that was never intended for acceptance. Warehouses received products instead of customers. Earnings were duly recorded. Management was not aware of the extremes salespeople were going to in order to make plan. Financial controls were lacking. In Europe, Datapoint repurchased (for $100 million from TRW) the right to market its own products directly, requiring a costly buildup and reorganization over there.

At the same time, the company showed no intention of flagging in its efforts to become a premier office automation company. When things fell apart in 1982, Datapoint was in the midst of an ambitious plan to develop a large-scale PBX digital switchboard, an effort far too sweeping for a company of its size. Datapoint never shied away from things that were grand and sweeping. When announcing a new product or entertaining Wall Street security analysts, the company put on great Hollywood extravaganzas, at a tremendous cost. One year at its San Antonio security analysts meeting, Ray Malavasi, coach of the Los Angeles Rams, was luncheon speaker. Another year, Datapoint's vaunted R&D guru, Victor D. Poor, addressed the analysts remotely from his sailboat in the middle of the Pacific Ocean, adrift on a several-month leave of absence. He will now apparently take an even longer cruise, commencing a one-year leave of absence in April 1984.

There is little of the Hollywood aura at Datapoint today. Its products are mundane intelligent terminals and work stations that are being battered in the marketplace by the new wave of personal computers and work station offerings. Its traditional small business market is being jumped on by IBM, Wang, Hewlett-Packard, and a whole host of new-wave insurgents. Local area networks are now widely available and must of necessity be compatible with IBM. Datapoint's ARC network is not. A base of over $500 million in sales may insure its survival, and in fact profits did bounce back a bit to $8 million in 1983, but Datapoint will never be a leader or even a major factor in office automation. Datapoint's momentum and reputation have all but disappeared. Yet another turnaround is unlikely. There is precious little new in top management, products, or strategies. Datapoint will be a cyclical company. Customers have remained fairly loyal mainly because it's not easy to convert over to another vendor's software system, but growth prospects are subpar and the profit picture is equally dismal.

PRIME COMPUTER: SUPERMINIS AND SUPER-EGOS

Prime was a hot shot company during the late 1970s, surging ahead under the charismatic leadership of its former president, Kenneth G. Fisher. Suddenly in the summer of 1981, he departed over a disagreement with his board of directors. The fissure that ensued left the company a shadow of its former self. Maybe the company would have run out of gas anyway, caught in a changing minicomputer market and the need to become more than a one-product operation. What the future would have been under Fisher, we will never know. But the future without him is all too clear: Prime's chances of becoming a winner again have to be rated a long shot.

Beginning in 1975, Fisher took what then amounted to little more than an R&D lab with a breakthrough product, a powerful 32-bit superminicomputer, and transformed it into a computer company on the make. Sales surged 78% a year, from $11 million to $365 million over the ensuing 6-year stretch. Profits more than doubled each year. Prime's stock had the greatest price rise on the New York Stock Exchange in 1979.

Not only was Prime's 32-bit superminicomputer one of the first, it was a mini with a Honeywell mainframe software operating system, a powerful combination. (Prime's founders all came out of Honeywell.) Systems houses gobbled up the machine. It was a one-of-a-kind computer, vastly outperforming anything else around. It sold itself. Fisher's strength, however, was in marketing, and he leveraged the red-hot computer for all it was worth.

Prime was a fun place to work. Fisher was well liked, and he pushed responsibility down to lower management levels, running a decentralized operation. He kept out of nitty-gritty details and was a broad thinker, planner, marketer, and leader. The sales force produced, usually at the last minute of each quarter or year, but the orders did come through. The end-of-period surge became a norm. Fisher attracted good people and generally held on to them, except for the celebrated departure of one of his computer design geniuses, John W. Poduska, who subsequently started Apollo Computer.

Fisher was a Wall Street hero and a trusted, respected, well-liked leader to his employees. In other quarters, however, tension was building. On the board of directors the strings were pulled by David J. Dunn, a partner in Idanta Partners, 15% owner of Prime and the chairman of the company (though on an arm's length inactive basis; his offices were on the West Coast). Dunn's role at Prime was an adversarial one, constantly second-guessing Fisher despite the spectacular track record. Apparently, the split between the two men widened over Fisher's desire to keep pushing Prime's breakneck growth as a lean, mean specialty company. Dunn thought it was time to slow down, build backlog, and establish a more formal, broad-based organization. The fissure erupted. Dunn won. And Fisher's sudden departure set off a chain reaction at the company that saw most of the spirited producers, especially salespeople, jump ship. Momentum carried the company for a while. But it took

6 months to find a new chief executive officer, and the turmoil cost valuable time in product and market development. Competition in superminicomputers was heating up. Prime's products were aging. New markets were being held in abeyance. The momentum died, and so did the entrepreneurial, fast decision making, small-company atmosphere.

Joe M. Henson, the new chief executive officer, came from IBM after a 27-year stint there. Henson's career path at IBM had apparently topped out. His last two assignments were involved with the 3600 financial point-of-sale terminal and the new 3380 thin film disk drive products, both of which met with embarrassing delays and problems. Henson brought a number of fellow IBMers to Prime. Level after level of old-line Prime managers were let go. An atmosphere of tension and distrust developed in the company, as the guessing game of who was next intensified. Fisher's continued presence nearby did not help. He opened an office in Natick, Massachusetts, and kept in close touch with his old allies. One day Fisher had a Christmas luncheon with many existing and ex-Prime managers at a nearby restaurant. Henson happened to be lunching at the same place. Surprise all around. Tension worsened.

Henson set about organizing Prime into a small IBM, with centralized planning, support, and any number of other management functions. It is a structure more suited to a generalist company, like IBM, but Prime is too small to be a broad-based generalist. As a result, Prime has become overly structured. Creative freedom is stifled. The company is devoid of leadership technology and products. It has gone outside to Ford and Compeda for computer-aided design products and to Convergent Technologies for small computers. Prime's 32-bit computer is not particularly special anymore, so systems houses are looking elsewhere, such as to Convergent Technologies, for hot machines. The market for Prime's 32-bit supermini is now replacement and upgrade. Growth is slow, and plans to enter the office automation market have been delayed. Super 32-bit minicomputers are a commodity today, and Prime is losing market share. IBM and Digital Equipment are pouring hundreds of millions into R&D to put such machines on a single circuit board. Prime can't keep up in such a battle. Under Henson, its character has changed from a specialty niche company, yet it is too small to be a full-line computer industry generalist.

Profits in 1983 were only half the previous year's level. A classic product cycle transition took place while the company shifted to its new 9950 computer models, reducing orders for the older products. That condition may improve temporarily in 1984, but longer range, this company is not likely to flourish again. It may be profitable and expand in fits and starts, depending on the product cycle and economy, but the fun and excitement are gone. A band of former IBM managers, heavily dependent on staff work, cannot hope to stay up in such a fast-paced business—not by running the company in such a methodical, structured manner. Prime's traditional minicomputer markets are maturing. The efforts to move into new areas are minimal. The company is a captive of its old customer base. Its time seems to have passed. Prime is a likely candidate for merger with a larger computer company before long. The chairman, David J. Dunn, may already be preparing it for sale.

THE UPS AND DOWNS OF MOHAWK
DATA SCIENCES

Mohawk Data Sciences started in 1964 in the Mohawk Valley, the upstate New York home of the ancient Iroquois tribe. Mohawk was one of the wunderkinder of the IBM plug-compatible peripherals boom. It grew by leaps and bounds, turning a tidy profit of $6 million in 1959 and ranking as one of the industry's top companies.

Mohawk's only problem was that it leased its products to customers and the company could not afford to finance the lease base. Nor could it afford all its new manufacturing plants, as success led the company into many different product areas. Cash flow turned negative. The balance sheet was leveraged to the hilt. By the peak profit year of 1969, debt well outstripped stockholder equity. The stock, which had hit $111 the year before, started plummeting. (By 1983, it was in single figures.) On top of all that, IBM began to get tough on the peripheral companies that had been riding its coattails.

Mohawk operated at a loss for 5 years in a row. By 1975 the balance sheet showed $156 million in debt and only $13 million in net worth. That's about as close to bankruptcy as you can get without filing for Chapter 11 protection.

In 1975 new management took over and proceeded to take the company on a roller coaster ride of rising and falling profits. The previous president, Richard P. Rifenburgh, was replaced by Ralph H. O'Brien, who came over from Litton. O'Brien was enticed aboard with sizable stock options. And he did what every new management does to turn a company around: take a massive write-off and show a big earnings gain the following year. The stock options rose in value.

Profits hit $13 million that first year under the new management, double the former 1969 peak level. Then the company's profits ran out of gas, plummeting back to the 1969 level for the next 2 years. Then they went back up. Mohawk Data and O'Brien hit stride and in 1979–1981 managed to lift earnings to the $14 to $18 million range, decent progress but still only about a 5% after-tax profit margin, despite a low tax rate. It did not take long to hit the skids again. Mohawk's profitability in 1983 was well below the 1976 level.

Is there a lesson to be learned in this stop, start, rise, and fall pattern? The lesson is that a company such as Mohawk should do a better job of learning from its mistakes.

Mohawk's balance sheet is still too leveraged. Debt (almost all at floating interest rates) is over 40% of capitalization. Leasing still represents a heavy portion of revenues, causing a negative cash flow. As IBM and others have learned, leasing is a major disadvantage in this era of fast technological change, shortened product cycles, and competitive leapfrogging. Interest payments to support borrowings for lease financing almost equaled the company's profits in 1983. And Mohawk is gravitating right back to where it was 5 or 10 years ago, spreading itself too thin, making acquisitions into different markets, with a hodgepodge of different product lines. It is difficult to classify the company in any one sector; it dabbles in too many niches. The Trivex line of IBM-compatible, on-line terminals is under seige by IBM's new aggressive product and pricing strategies. The Qantel small business computers are in a market being swept away by the microcomputer companies. Mohawk's distributed data processing and key to disk data entry products are mundane, plain-vanilla entries.

Mohawk will not go out of business; it is still a viable company. Recent successes include signing of a $100 million Nationwide Mutual Insurance order and a fat New York State Department of Motor Vehicles contract. Mohawk has a respectable sales and service organization. The problem is that Mohawk is a $400 million revenue also-ran; a cyclical company with subpar profit margins. I do not expect this condition to change in the future.

11

The Risks of Playing
Tagalong: PCMs

The idea of creating computer products that plug right into IBM's computer system (plug-compatible) has been a tempting one for over 15 years. In the late 1960s, companies such as Mohawk Data Sciences and Telex pioneered the idea with such peripherals as keypunch data entry equipment and tape drives. They offered a product that was cheaper, more easily available, and in many cases more powerful than the equivalent product sold by IBM. And all you had to do was plug it into your existing IBM system.

In the mid-1970s the idea was extended to mainframes. Gene H. Amdahl, who was director of IBM's Advanced Computing Systems Laboratory in Menlo Park, California, left IBM and after some difficulty was able to raise the financing needed to create the first IBM plug-compatible mainframes. It was such a success that a whole new wave of entrepreneurs entered the market: Magnuson (which hired Amdahl's son, Carlton), IPL, Itel—now National Advanced Systems (a division of National Semiconductor), Two Pi, Storage Technology, the Japanese, and others.

The benefits of being a PCM (as the plug-compatible manufacturers are known) are obvious, and often quite substantial. Copying what another company does in its product saves a lot of time and money in product development. In the malaise that enveloped IBM in the 1970s, there was room for PCMs to get a foothold. IBM's prices were high, its product cycles were long, and it freely licensed its software operating systems, the basic program instructions to run the machine. A PCM could reverse engineer an IBM product—enhance it, refine it, and price it cheaply because it had little of IBM's software, R&D, and marketing costs.

The PCM mainframe market got a boost in 1975, when IBM canceled the development of its Future Systems line of mainframes, which was designed to be incompatible with its earlier 370 line. If IBM had gone through with the Future Systems mainframes, the PCM mainframe companies probably would have never been able to get off the ground. Today, the PCMs can only wish that they once again could compete against IBM the way they did in the 1970s. IBM is now unrelenting in exercising its competitive advantage over the rest of the industry. In 1979, IBM introduced its 4300, cutting the price by 60 to 80% for equivalent computer power. That led to Itel's bankruptcy and shortly thereafter to the demise of Magnuson Computer Systems. Amdahl's profits for 5 years now have never been close to the level of 1978.

IBM has also forestalled easy inroads by the PCMs by designing its systems in a more complex manner. Its semiconductor chips are now packaged in a multilayered ceramic substrate, the Thermal Conduction Module, that only IBM has been able to perfect. IBM has also changed the location of the mundane internal software instructions used to operate its computers. Instead of making them freely available in the software operating system, they are now "hardwired" into the hardware itself (that is, the circuits themselves are designed to carry out certain instructions, reducing the need for a separate program), creating "firmware." This makes it considerably more costly and time consuming for the PCMs to duplicate IBM's computers.

IBM has also cut its product cycles and accelerated its pace of technological development. Although IBM was never really considered a technological leader in the pure sense of that term (i.e., as it applies to Cray Research, Bell Labs, or even such companies as Tandem or Wang), the fact of the matter is that when IBM wants to get aggressive about technology and use that as a weapon in the marketplace, others have to stand up and take notice. In the peripherals market, where such companies as Storage Technology and Memorex were once in the technological forefront, IBM pushed ahead development of thin film head disk drive technology and jumped out in front of its PCM competitors by at least 2 years. IBM has also poured billions into automating production and is now able to lower its prices and retain its profit margins, while the PCMs get squeezed. In peripherals, IBM has instituted volume purchase agreements that tie in customer commitments for 2 years at a time. As for mainframes, they are no longer such a predominant revenue contributor at IBM. The company is more balanced. Before, when IBM used pricing and product actions in mainframes to combat the PCM competition, it had a major self-impact on its own revenues. Today, that is no longer the problem. IBM now charges fees for its software and is beginning to take some of the operating systems software out of the public domain (i.e., it is no longer freely available to all comers).

The PCM business will never be the same again. The PCMs lived by the sword, taking their flesh out of IBM's hide. Now they are dying or at least stagnating by the same sword, as IBM strikes back. Gone from the plug-compatible mainframe scene are Itel, Control Data, Two Pi, Magnuson, and TRW-Fujitsu. Amdahl has twice seriously negotiated the prospect of merging, once with Memorex and once with Storage Technology. As a group, the mainframe PCM vendors lost money in 1982. Amdahl's new 5860 computer model was delayed with technological bugs. National Advanced Systems (NAS) has become totally dependent on Hitachi for its mainframe product, for both development and manufacturing. NAS is only a marketer (for that reason we do not discuss it here) and has been in the red in recent years. Amdahl obtains the guts of its machines (the subassemblies) from Fujitsu.

The real competition for the plug-compatible companies is not IBM anymore; that war is lost. The competition is now among the PCM vendors themselves, with a real shoot-out coming soon between Amdahl and Trilogy Systems, the start-up by the former founder of Amdahl, Gene M. Amdahl. Although this match-up is as exciting as any in the computer industry, the spoils that will go to the eventual victor are limited. Since 1978, total PCM mainframe revenues have been at a $600 million plateau—only one-fifth the size of the PCM peripherals market. Although in the glory years, when Amdahl and Itel were riding high, the PCMs took 10% of the mainframe market, now they take half that. The PCMs have gone about as far as they can go.

The PCM peripherals market is much bigger, but the story is much the same. As a group, they have taken as much of the market as they are going to get: 10 to 15%, or about $3 billion in revenues. It is a mature business now, mainly an existing customer replacement and upgrade game and, more likely, a losing market share game. Many of the early success stories went into eclipse: Potter Instruments, Data 100, Mohawk Data Sciences, Memorex, and Telex. Memorex was awash in red ink in the 1970s and was acquired by Burroughs in 1981.

Like Memorex, Storage Technology reached the exalted $1 billion level and even made a cameo appearance in the lineup of Top 10 computer companies in 1981. Since then, however, it has stalled and is in a decline, depending on the eventual outcome of its own PCM mainframe and optical disk development to reverse the slide. Dataproducts is a printer manufacturer with potential that it does not seem to want to utilize. Telex is notable because it is one of the few PCMs to resurrect after being all but demolished by IBM.

If prospects for the PCMs are lackluster, the outlook is at least more positive than for the non-IBM-compatible mainframe manufacturers, the BUNCH. The whole world is evolving toward IBM de facto standards in communications protocol and hardware compatibility. Customers want computer equipment that will talk to each other and be able to tie together into a network. If a computer is not compatible or communicable, it will be left out in the cold. The IBM market and customer base offers enormous potential to the PCM that can play its cards right. Unfortunately, doing so requires taking on IBM head to head. That was never an easy task. Today, it is next to impossible.

AMDAHL: A SURVIVOR WITH NO PLACE TO GO

Amdahl was the real pioneer in creating the market for IBM-plug-compatible mainframes. In 1970, Gene Amdahl left IBM and, against all odds (RCA had apparently proved what a disaster an IBM-compatible strategy could be), secured the financing he needed to get his company off the ground. Today, as befits a true pioneer, the company Amdahl founded is a survivor (even though he is no longer involved in it, having departed in 1979 to found Trilogy Systems). Where others feared to tread, Amdahl made it through.

Appropriately enough, the company describes itself in a press release as a "phenomenon" whose story not only is unusual but is untold until now. Perhaps there is a reason for that. The story was left untold because most people saw it as a fairy tale, and one that did not necessarily have a happy ending.

Back in 1978 (only 3 years after shipping its first computer), Amdahl topped $300 million in sales, earning $45 million in profits. During the ensuing 4 years, however, profits plummeted, hitting bottom at $7 million in 1982. Sales expanded in 1983 to $778 million on the strength of the company's new 5860 mainframe line and profits finally, after five years, got back to the old levels. The pressure exerted by IBM is intense. Twice the company has sought a merger. Twice its deals were dashed, in part due to its Fujitsu relationship, the not-so-silent partner that owns 49% of Amdahl.

The immediate cause of Amdahl's problems in the early 1980s was the delay in the 5860 mainframe line. To compete in the plug-compatible market, you have to get your product out the door fast. Amdahl's 5860 line, destined to compete with IBM's 308X computers, fell behind IBM by 2 years. Amdahl had never found itself in such a position. Moreover, development costs went through the roof. R&D expenses for the 5860 line rose to almost 18% of revenues, way above the normal 8 to 10% industry range. The model 5870 is more than a year late.

Meanwhile, IBM's renewed aggressiveness has taken its toll. IBM is already cutting prices on hardware and software by 10 to 15% a year, and its next computer line is expected to be a blockbuster in terms of price and performance. It has already introduced its MVS XA extended architecture operating system, which could force Amdahl to add more instructions to its computer to remain compatible. As IBM continues to embed its operating system software into hardware, the costly technological game of remaining compatible will become ever more difficult. In fact, it may no longer be financially possible for a company with Amdahl's resources to develop a mainframe generation in time to be competitive with IBM. And even if it is financially possible, who will design it? The 580 line was designed by Gene Amdahl. Who will design Amdahl's next generation?

And what about Gene Amdahl? If the large-scale integrated semi-conductor wafer technology that he is betting on pans out, then Trilogy could replace Amdahl in the market. What irony!

Except for a temporary curtain call for the company in 1983, Amdahl's days in the limelight are over. Although there is still room left in the PCM market, Amdahl will have to be nimble if it wants to keep its place. The way I see it, for every good profit year, Amdahl will have to suffer through several poor ones. Because of IBM's aggressiveness, the window for shipments has been cut from 3 to 4 years down to only 1.5 years. And to even reach that point, Amdahl must go through 2 to 3 years of expensive engineering and product development catch-up effort. Amdahl is on a treadmill that will only worsen as time goes by. As its president, Gene White, admits, "We had a better price structure five years ago."

Moreover, the company faces some thorny technological problems. There is a ticking time bomb with respect to remaining compatible with IBM. The only solution is for Amdahl to have its own software operating system. The company is apparently pursuing this alternative (Aspen), but it may not have the resources to develop and maintain such software. Software has never been its strength compared to hardware engineering, and even in hardware, it is facing problems. Amdahl is wedded to air-cooled systems that may not be feasible once the incredible circuit densities emerge later this decade in machines capable of executing 40 to 50 MIPS compared to 14 MIPS in the current 5860 model.

Finally, there is the Fujitsu factor. This is a love–hate relationship. Amdahl will be dependent on Fujitsu's semiconductor and subassembly capability for a number of years to come. While this source of technology keeps Amdahl in the game—"the savings from this technology is a hard, cold business advantage," says White—it also stifles Amdahl and aggravates morale. Amdahl's place in the future is highly uncertain and most likely will diminish, though it may be of a size now that no one step by IBM could thwart it totally. The company has gone about as far as it can. It is a survivor with no place to go.

TRILOGY SYSTEMS: WHAT MAKES GENE RUN?

There is nothing humble or unassuming about Trilogy Systems. The wildly fantastic goal of this California-based start-up can be stated simply: Trilogy wants to become the most successful manufacturer of IBM-compatible mainframes at a time when the mainframe market is all but standing still, the plug-compatible landscape is littered with bankruptcies, and IBM is tightening its grip over what little potential for growth is still left. And that's not all. Trilogy plans to achieve its ends by perfecting a new semiconductor technology that, if successful, could rank as one of the most significant advances in the history of computing.

Can Trilogy be taken seriously? With anyone other than Gene Amdahl at the helm, Trilogy might have been laughed out of the industry. Instead, it has attracted $200 million in private capital and another $100 million through a public stock offering in the fall of 1983. (It still needs another $100 million.) Some major heavyweights in the industry, including Digital Equipment, Sperry, and Cii Honeywell Bull, have purchased rights to the semiconductor technology. These backers are betting on the track record of the Amdahls. (Gene Amdahl designed IBM's third-generation 360 computers in the 1960s and then founded and designed the computers for the company that bears his name. Carlton, his son, was the designer of Magnuson's computers.) If the Amdahls are successful—and it's a big if—they will have created a computer far superior to any that IBM is expected to come out with in the next few years, and Trilogy Systems will completely displace Amdahl for the lead in the plug-compatible market. In the process, they will have put together the greatest father–son act the industry has seen since the 1950s, when Thomas Watson, Sr., handed over the reins of IBM to Tom, Jr.

The stakes are high in this game, and Trilogy is betting everything on its gamble in semiconductors. The circuitry in Trilogy mainframes will be integrated on 4-inch square wafers, instead of the tiny thumbnail-size silicon wafers—the computer chips—that now predominate. Each wafer will have 20,000 to 40,000 circuit gates capable of operating at a much higher speed than any available today. Placing them on such a large wafer cuts down the number of wiring interconnections. There will be over 100 layers of wafers in each module the size of a fist. The close proximity of the circuits enhances speed and also allows space for extra circuits. These extra circuits will be used for diagnosing malfunctions and rerouting signals, thus producing a nonstop, fail-safe, fault-tolerant mainframe. The wafer will continue to perform even with as many as 300 faults among its nearly 40,000 gates—a reliability quotient that is as much as 10 times better than current IBM technology permits.

The Trilogy machine will have nine power supplies (two for backup), with output comparable to most computer power supplies used today (1750 watts) but taking up only one-tenth of the floor space of IBM's current largest dual processor, the 3084 mainframe. The main selling point of the Trilogy mainframe will be the advantages it offers in speed and power over the new line of Sierra mainframes that IBM plans to begin shipping in 1985.

But time delays and technology problems are reducing those advantages. Due to a major redesign, the Trilogy mainframe will not be out until 1986, 2 year behind schedule. The design was also reconfigured to make the computer a dual processor system, that slows its performance and reduces its advantage over IBM—even though it is still expected to be faster and more powerful than the Sierra. Nonetheless, Trilogy can't afford any more slip-ups if it still wants to make a big splash in the market.

Gene Amdahl has high hopes for his newest company. He claims the profit margins will be unheard of and that in the first full year of shipments "we will earn back our entire investment." Although one is hesitant to deride Amdahl for thinking big, there do seem to be very definite limits as to how far Trilogy can go. Trilogy has the potential to replace Amdahl in the plug-compatible mainframe market, but it is unlikely that it will go any higher than the 5% market share that Amdahl now has. In other words, it is unlikely that Trilogy will take much business away from IBM. Its main impact will be on the existing plug-compatible mainframe companies, namely Amdahl.

And even if it assumes plug-compatible leadership, Trilogy will still face the same problems that Amdahl does now. It will need to develop its own operating software that is compatible with IBM's. And it will have to keep raising the capital needed to continually push the technology forward for future generations of products. The computer industry is insatiable.

It is possible Gene Amdahl will never realize his ambitions to make Trilogy a mainframe company. With all the barriers to the mainframe business, Trilogy could instead become one of the growing number of semiconductor foundries that design custom circuits for computer manufacturers. Before it can do even that, however, it must make sure its semiconductor technology will work. That is no mean trick. The computer-aided design system needed to develop the 120-layered wafer module requires six mainframes. The schematics for the wafer module, if reproduced in humanly readable form, would require the space of 40 football fields. Now that's complexity. Costs are running $50 to $100 million over the original plan. The schedule is 6 months behind. In late 1983, after adding another layer of metal to provide interconnections between all the circuits and then turning on the electrical power, it didn't work. Initial delivery was pushed back to fourth quarter 1985. Expect more delays because this is unprecedented and new technological territory. Once the technology is perfected, manufacturing poses a whole other set of problems.

A forecast at this point is impossible; there are too many unknowns. The Amdahls have a proven track record. The technology they are promising is potentially revolutionary. Some heavyweight people in the industry have looked at it and found it to their liking. Anything can happen. We will just have to wait and see. What raises some more immediate questions is the rather grand style of living that prevails at Trilogy. It may be a start-up, but it sure does not act like one. Its facilities resemble a modern-day Taj Mahal, filled with mahogany, brass, pile carpets, expensive glass, and marble. (A fleet of BMW 633i's was apparently purchased well before the huge computer-aided design system was installed. There was probably an interior designer on the staff before any programmers were hired.)

This sumptuous living can be chalked up to Gene Amdahl's remarkable reputation in the industry. Does it also hint at something else? Does Amdahl still feel the need to prove himself, to show something to IBM and now also to his old company, Amdahl? On the walls of his office, he still proudly displays his many framed degrees, certificates of achievement, and awards. Does he still feel the need to convince others of his record? What is really behind Trilogy Systems? What makes Gene Amdahl run?

STORAGE TECHNOLOGY: CHANCES FOR A SECOND ACT ARE FADING

Storage Technology is the latest and greatest of the companies to score big in the market for IBM-compatible peripherals. But, like Amdahl, Storage Technology's best days seem to be in the past. The company has eaten about as far as it can into IBM's customer base, and in fact is now losing it back to IBM. The company embarked on an ambitious plan to become a full IBM-compatible computer systems supplier, including computer mainframes, but it bit off more than it could chew. The company is unlikely to ever regain the momentum it enjoyed during the 1970s.

Storage Technology Corporation was on a Rocky Mountain high for 10 years. Based in Boulder (one of the first companies to stake out Colorado as a high-tech area), Storage Technology surged from $4 million to $922 million in sales between 1971 and 1981. At its pinnacle, it became the ninth largest company in the computer industry. It garnered a whopping 55% of the market for IBM-compatible, high-performance tape drives. And, while IBM suffered in 1981 with delays in its new 3380 thin film disk drive, Storage Technology grabbed a 35% share of the disk drive market with its line of high-performance older generation magnetic head disk drives.

Then in 1982 things began to go sour. Sales growth slowed and then petered out completely by year end. Profits declined sharply for the first time in the company's history. In 1983, things worsened. Sales collapsed, plummeting 18% below the high-water $1 billion mark. Profits evaporated and the ink turned red. Storage Technology operated at a loss that continued into 1984. Finances became strained. The plug-compatible mainframe computer project became a cropper. It was too expensive and too late. Following a major build-up and promise by the company for 2 years it was terminated and written off at the end of 1983 at a cost of $28 million. The culprit was a wrenching product cycle transition in disk drives. While the company was developing a new thin film disk drive of its own (the 8380), orders for its old magnetic head drives came to a halt. In the meantime, IBM overcame its production problems and shipped some 20,000 units of its new thin film drive in 1983, a number that is expected to double in 1984. In 1984, Storage Technology will be up and running with its own drive and be able to ship perhaps 4000 of them, a far cry from the 7,000 or 8,000 it once hoped for, and even 4,000 may be optimistic. That would give it less than a 10% market share, a far cry from the one-third share of the past.

Storage Technology has lost its technological lead. The product cycle window has closed to a year or so at most, during which the company has a reasonable opportunity to compete for IBM business with a comparable product. And there are other factors behind the sudden loss of momentum.

The company incurred a massive reliability problem in late 1982. Thousands of older model 8650 disk drives were installed with poor quality, unreliable disk platter media obtained from another supplier. Retrofitting and replacing all those disks, a sizable and costly undertaking that is still not completed, has hurt the company's reputation for quality engineering. A manufacturing mistake of this magnitude can have unforeseen ramifications for years to come. This reliability problem, combined with the company's technological slip, creates a substantial hurdle that Storage Technology must overcome.

(It is 2 years behind IBM in thin film disk drive production and has lost several management and engineering personnel connected with this program. The company's new thin film 8380 disk drive appears to be technologically sound and may even be more compatible with IBM computers, requiring less conversion hassle, than IBM's own 3380. It is smaller in physical size, uses less power, and is easier and less costly to manufacture. It has more built-in redundancy, and its architecture allows greater performance and faster response time. Still, it is 2 years behind IBM, and IBM is not standing still in R&D on future such products, particularly a double density version of the product due out by 1985. It seems too late now for Storage Technlogy to obtain a decent return on its 8380 investment.

The dramatic surge in growth in the late 1970s, followed by the sudden drop-off, the reliability problems, and the red ink, has put an incredible strain on the company. The sales force lost heart during the late 1982–1983 transition period, and turnover ensued. There has also been a shake-up in top management. Erik T. Ringjob, executive vice-president of engineering and manufacturing, was the most notable departure. In 1983, Storage Technology's founder and chairman, Jesse I. Aweida, having previously given over the positions of chief operating officer and president to his brother Naim, took them back again. Many of the individuals connected with the thin film disk drive and reliability problems were dismissed. Aweida instituted a major structural reorganization, eliminating a 5-month-old experiment, a functional management structure (which cut across product lines and was organized around product, component, and engineering lines), and returned to the old manufacturing divisional structure.

Several new products that were under development were terminated, including a virtual storage system, a 3705 front-end communications controller, and a 3370 class thin film disk drive. The Communications Products Division was sold. This housecleaning by Aweida was essential to getting Storage Technology back on the right track. The company was becoming overextended with too many products and had taken its eye off its primary specialty sector, peripheral storage devices, where it once had market leadership and strong concentration.

Like Amdahl, Storage Technology is too big to be knocked off by IBM. It will survive and continue as a source for IBM peripherals. It has certain promising products, such as the Sybercache disk controller and the optical laser disk, now starting into production, that eventually could develop into a major market. From time to time, the company may experience healthy years of growth when the product cycle is on target, as it should be in 1985 with respect to thin film disk drive shipments. But facts are facts: IBM is no longer willing to give the independent plug-compatible companies much market share or breathing room. Storage Technology's heydays were in the 1970s. Its star shone bright in those years. It scored big while IBM slept. But to quote F. Scott Fitzgerald, "There are no second acts. . ."

The company's founder, Jesse Aweida—a Palestinian refugee, an expert in designing storage devices, and an accomplished downhill skier—apparently does not feel constrained by such a dictum. If not a second act, Aweida was at least hoping for an encore in which Storage Technology was to make its curtain call, no longer as just a peripherals company, but as a full-fledged compatible computer systems supplier. Storage Technology acquired Documation, a manufacturer of IBM-compatible high-speed printers. (It also made unsuccessful overtures to acquire Memorex, Amdahl, and Magnuson.) But the dream has ended. The computer project never saw the light of day.

Aweida definitely has a firm grasp on where the industry is going: "The future is in building devices that will run with IBM systems. Plug compatible companies cannot reverse engineer an IBM product anymore. There's not time. The IBM market will gain as the world goes compatible, so Storage Technology is in the right business." To have become a supplier of full-fledged systems would have required more money than Storage Technology had available. Joint financing could not be arranged. In looking to the future, Aweida was counting on all future growth to come from the computer and from the optical disk product. Now the computer is gone. The optical disk addresses a new market which is not yet developed and is still being pioneered. It may take a long time to become a big business. The tape drive market is not growing. Storage's new thin film disk drives, if ever successful, will only replace the older generation disk drive business it has lost to IBM. This company's future growth is now in question—considerable question. So is profitability. We would not rule out a takeover. Although Aweida is right in his assessment of the plug-compatible market, there is still the Catch-22 that has always prevailed in that market: The companies that ride on IBM's coattails are the ones that are most vulnerable when IBM suddenly decides to get competitive or to change its ways. Storage Technology got its start during a period of unusually favorable market circumstances that will not be repeated. Storage Technology will never be dull, but it will never again be the high-flier that it once was. There are no second acts.

DATAPRODUCTS: IT COULD'A BEEN A CONTENDER

Dataproducts is the largest, most successful printer company in the business. It makes high-speed line and band printers for use with minicomputers and mainframes. During the 1970s, when the first wave of "small" computers, the minicomputers, spread computing power to more and more users, Dataproducts surged in growth. Revenues rose from $55 million in 1973 to $270 million in 1981, a 22% annual growth rate.

The 1980s, however, is the decade of work stations and personal computers. On-line data networks provide information that appears on screens and most often does not have to be printed out. When a printout is needed, it is done through a low-speed, inexpensive dot matrix printer—the kind of printer Dataproducts did not make until recently. It looks like Dataproducts is not going to go anywhere big.

Actually, Dataproducts has always been a frustrating company to watch. The cyclicality of its profits has made accurate forecasting of its prospects impossible. Despite its strong growth in the 1970s, earnings fell in 6 out of the 13 years between 1970 and 1983 (peaking in 1978 and 1981). Sales expanded at a 17% rate during the past 5 years, but ranged wildly from year; to year, a 50% gain one year could be followed by an outright decline. Despite overall growth to $400 million in sales, the company remains one of almost a hundred different computer companies whose sales are $100 to $500 million.

Dataproducts is a nice sized company. It will remain a factor in the industry—it sells printers to some 90% of all computer companies—but it will not challenge for leadership. Its concentration on the traditional mainframe and minicomputer printer markets has precluded it from obtaining noticeable market share in the personal and small business computer sector, where cheap matrix printers are in burgeoning demand. Dataproducts entered the so-called dot matrix printer market late, acquiring Integral Data Systems in 1983. This led to a huge order by IBM for its PC that is fueling good growth temporarily at Dataproducts. But what IBM giveth it can also take away. This is no permanent panacea. Japanese firms are clamoring for this portion of the printer market, and smaller specialty companies, such as Printronix, that concentrate only in matrix printers are aggressive. While much of the company's printer market is maturing, this high-growth sector still eludes it, despite a contract from IBM.

Dataproducts' future prospects will most likely be similar to the past: cyclical and unpredictable. A big surge in 1984 will be followed by a sharp slowdown. It could have done a lot better. It could have been a billion-dollar leader in the industry. It was an early specialist addressing a niche. But the mainframe and minicomputer printer market matured and became cyclical and so did Dataproducts. The company never changed direction when the printer market shifted to an emphasis on microcomputers.

TELEX: A MIRACULOUS RECOVERY, BUT THEN WHAT?

Telex stared deep into the abyss in the 1970s. Could things get any worse for a company? After soaring growth in the late 1960s and early 1970s, the company fell into virtual bankruptcy almost overnight. It saw the market for IBM-compatible tape drives taken over by Storage Technology, and it ultimately lost the antitrust suit in which it charged that IBM's pricing policies were designed to drive Telex out of business. Debt soared. Its chairman passed from the scene suddenly in a violent death. In the end, the company was forced to withdraw from the market for plug-compatible peripherals. Everyone dismissed it as a past phenomenon from a turbulent, bygone era. It was said that Telex was just like all the rest of the PCM peripherals companies: They rose rapidly and folded just as fast, badly burned by leveraged balance sheets, me-too products, and overly liberal depreciation policies on leased equipment.

Not so fast. Telex is back. Although it is a minor player, in a narrower market niche—terminals—it is on more solid financial footing. The company is still involved in leasing, which may eventually come back to haunt it. It broke even in 1980 and topped $34 million in profits on $320 million in sales in 1983. Telex's business is predominantly IBM-compatible display terminals of the 3270 variety. Products are well designed with attractive differentiating features. Telex has 9% of this market, which is small compared to IBM's 55%, Raytheon's 15%, and ITT Courier's 12%. The market for IBM mainframe terminals is $800 million a year, growing 45% in terms of sales but less than 10% in profits. That's because prices are plummeting and IBM has become belligerent in its effort to retake some of its lost market share. IBM is able to cut prices because of the sharply lower costs gained by the automation at its Raleigh facility. And IBM is also introducing new products at a fast clip: the high- and low-end 3278 and 3178 terminals, which are successors to the old 3270 interactive terminal; the 3290 gas panel display terminal; and personal computing upgrade capability in many of its products, such as the 370 mainframe-compatible personal computer and the PC, which acts like a terminal.

The days may be numbered for the display terminal PCM market. The gains they made in the past several years are reversing in IBM's favor. And Telex knows this. It is slowly branching out beyond terminals, back into compatible printers, a controller, and tape drives. But a company this size, dabbling in several different computer peripheral market sectors, can become overextended quickly and lose the specialty concentration necessary for success.

Although Telex is currently on a roll, future opportunities in the IBM plug-compatible peripheral market are limited and coming under intense competition from IBM. Telex can harvest its lease base and introduce new products, but its comeback is now over. Where can it go from here? Unfortunately, not very far. But Telex has survived and has turned around and rehabilitated itself. It is a legitimate industry factor. And that is a credible accomplishment in the IBM PCM market.

Part 4

The New Insurgents

This is where the action is. Ten years ago, most of these companies barely existed, some not at all. Today they are remaking the computer industry. They are on their way to the top. . . . If only they can survive.

These are the new insurgents. In one way or another, they are all part of the fallout from the microprocessor boom. They successfully played the niche game—personal computers, floppy disk drives, word processors, superminicomputers—and then took off. Sales range from $50 million to $500 million. Less than $50 million, and a company is still a start-up in the computer industry. Over $500 million, and it becomes a different ball game. The company starts to get in the league where it is competing with IBM.

The $50 to $500 million range is the computer industry's equivalent of the Fertile Crescent. A company in that range is big enough to be recognized, to be taken for real, but still small enough to preserve the entrepreneurial creativity and freedom so necessary to be on the leading edge.

Opportunities abound. So do the hazards. The problems that confront the industry as a whole today are magnified many times over in the markets examined in this section: personal computers, software, new wave hardware, and office automation.

Most of today's insurgent companies will not survive. Some will never really make it big. Others will make a killing, and then exit quickly. Some will make it just by being in the right place at the right time. Others will scratch and claw their way to success. This is the fast lane of the computer industry. This is where the action is, the surging growth, the fun, the excitement, the breakthroughs. These are the companies that will own the computer industry of tomorrow. They are already well represented in the Top 100 rankings. Soon they will close in on the Top 10. Only IBM is safe. Not since the late 1960s has the industry seen such a wave of new competitors. And even then, it was nothing like it is today. Picking the winners from the losers was never tougher.

12

They're Everywhere:
The Personal Computer
Phenomenon

For those people (such as myself) whose job it is to track the comings and goings in the computer industry, a headline such as the one that appeared in the *San Francisco Examiner* on September 14, 1983, "Major Computer Firm Fails," can cause some momentary panic. Who are they talking about? What major firm? Did IBM suddenly go under? Did Burroughs or Sperry bail out of the business? Was Digital Equipment struck by some catastrophe? Reading the newspaper these days can give you gray hair. As it turned out, it was none of the above. The company referred to as "major" by the *Examiner* was none other than Osborne Computer. Considered something of a toy when it appeared on the scene in 1980 as the first portable microcomputer, the Osborne 1 proved a phenomenal success, becoming one of the early winners in the personal computer business. It is stretching things to call Osborne a "major firm," but its demise was of more than passing interest. In fact, its demise ultimately may be what is most memorable about the company.

Adam Osborne, an electrical engineer and the author of one of the first popular books about microcomputers, was also one of the first to grasp that personal computers are consumer appliances and should be sold as such. Osborne realized that price counted for a lot and that the best strategy was to aim low. The Osborne 1 was a no-frills, 8-bit microcomputer. It was CP/M compatible (CP/M is an operating system for personal computers) back when that was the industry standard. It was also designed to be carried around (from home to office, say, or on business trips—it fit under an airline seat). Making the Osborne "portable" was a marketing gimmick that caught the industry's attention, even though few people really used it that way (at 28 lbs., it was still too heavy and bulky).

With its tiny 5-inch screen (its major drawback), the Osborne 1 seemed more like a piece of Army field equipment than a computer. But with an $1800 price tag—considerably lower than anything comparable on the market—no one seemed to worry about appearances. The $1800 also included a package of free software, worth several hundred dollars if purchased separately.

For a while, the Osborne 1 was the best deal in personal computers. Adam Osborne beat the industry at its own game. *Fortune* magazine, after dismissing Osborne as a gadfly in 1981, devoted a whole article to him the following year. Then, things began to unravel. Other companies, such as Kaypro and Compaq, caught on and matched the Osborne with a better product (the Kaypro had a bigger screen). Osborne was late in coming up with a follow-up to the Osborne 1. Adam Osborne began to discover that managing a company was a lot less fun than starting one. Finally, IBM came along and turned the personal computer business all around. By September 1983, as the *Examiner* reported, Osborne was in court fighting off creditors. It was the first major bankruptcy of the personal computer business, but it won't be the last. Now that the precedent is set, the others will begin falling like dominoes.

Computer Devices, too late into the market, filed for Chapter 11 in November 1983. Victor Technologies, not IBM compatible, has suffered the same fate. Red ink has been evident at Vector Graphic, Fortune, Intertec Data Systems, and in the personal computer division of Xerox. Altos Computer Systems has experienced a severe sales slowdown during its transition from 8-bit to 16-bit products. Grid Systems, manufacturer of an innovative work station, has had marketing problems. In the home computer area, Atari (Warner Communications), Mattel, Coleco, and Timex have all had highly publicized downturns. Mattel lost almost $200 million in six months in 1983 and is now out of the business. So is Timex. Coleco's Adam computer had production problems, and despite Cabbage Patch dolls, red ink is gushing. Adam may not have long for this world. Kaypro planned an initial stock offering at $18 per share but settled for $10. (Don't worry. The founder's net worth became $25 million overnight anyway.) The same is true for Compaq, going public at an $11 per share price instead of a hoped-for $18.

So far, the record for dollar losses belongs to Texas Instruments (TI), the huge semiconductor manufacturer and one of the first companies to enter the personal computer business. In the first 9 months of 1983, prior to its grand exit from the business, TI lost $550 million on $400 million in sales. TI believed that low, low prices for its personal computer would give it market share and then economies of scale that would ultimately see it run in the black. The strategy worked for TI in semiconductors, but it failed in computers, just as it did in calculators and watches. Costs did not decline as fast as prices, although TI captured a good share of the market. Even after the bloodbath in calculators and watches, TI could still not get it right in microcomputers. Three strikes and you're out.

With this kind of fallout, what hope is there for the dozens of other companies that have entered the business, companies with names you probably never heard of before—Jonos, Access, Otrona, Spectra Video, Athena, Gavilan, Cromemco—and products with such names as Zorba, Chameleon, Escort, Courier, SV-318? The personal computer business has attracted between 100 and 150 companies (the number keeps changing).

The company that everyone is watching now with bated breath is the one that started it all: Apple. Having failed to come up with another blockbuster to follow the Apple IIe, Apple is experiencing serious problems. During the 1-year period ending in the summer of 1983, the company had seen virtually no profits. In fall 1983 I visited with John Sculley, who came from Pepsi-Cola to take over as president of Apple. I asked him what his greatest surprise was since joining Apple the previous spring. It didn't take him long to answer: "The shakeout happened 9 months earlier than I expected."

With IBM in the market, the shakeout was inevitable. How can as many as 150 companies hope to compete in a business where one company has over 45% .of the market? They can't. IBM has captured the office market (from Apple) and has now set its sights on the home market with the PCjr. The others can try to hang in by making their computers IBM compatible. Even Apple did this, belatedly, with its Lisa workstation. IBM compatibility is a strategy—in fact, it is the *only* strategy—but it is a strategy that will at best produce short-term results. IBM look-alikes offer only further inducement for the customer to go with IBM in the first place. Price may be an advantage at first, but not for very long. Which company can manufacture a computer less expensively: IBM, which will be selling over 2 million units in 1984, or a fringe company that may ship 25,000?

Even if IBM hadn't come along, there is no way so many companies could have survived in selling personal computers. If nothing else, they would have died while trying to get their products in front of potential customers. Retail stores and manufacturer-owned product centers numbered almost 4000 at the end of 1983. Even office buyers prefer to shop in stores rather than go directly to a manufacturer's salesperson. It's a tough sell. Computerland, the largest chain, with 650 stores, illustrates the problem facing companies trying to get their products on the market. At best, a Computerland store will push the products of five different vendors on its shelves. That's not very many. The only other alternative is to open your own stores. Here Radio Shack is the leader, selling only its own products out of some 450 computer centers and 8000 consumer electronics stores. With that kind of distribution, you can bet on Radio Shack surviving the shakeout. In an effort to make their products stand out, more manufacturers are turning to advertising. Apple now spends $75 to $100 million annually on advertising, while IBM's budget is over $100 million. Commodore, Hewlett-Packard, and Coleco are all in the $25 to $45 million range.

On top of all this, personal computer companies must contend with ruinous price wars (prices are now falling far faster than costs); abrupt product cycles (so short it is becoming impossible to recoup manufacturing investment); heavy R&D expenses (to stay up with the likes of Hewlett-Packard and IBM); and widespread customer confusion.

To cope with such a market, more and more personal computer companies are turning to executives from consumer products companies. Apple went to Pepsi-Cola; Atari's chairman is from Philip Morris; Texas Instruments went to Procter & Gamble; and Osborne went to Consolidated Foods. They may just as well have recruited in the Soviet Union or the People's Republic of China. In an industry that is consolidating and blowing apart at the same time, it is preposterous to think that even the greatest manager can lead a company unscathed through such a tumultuous market.

This is not to say that the business is devoid of opportunity. Far from it. The market for computers priced at under $10,000 was $8 billion in 1983 and growing at 50% a year. About one-fourth of this is the home market (computers priced at under $2200), which seems poised for explosive growth. Fewer than 5 million homes have a computer, out of a potential market of 84 million homes. Home computers may well follow the pattern set by televisions, which went from 1% to 70% household penetration in the 8 years between 1948 and 1956. In the office market, things are a bit more placid. At $6 billion, it is three times the size of the home market. Its future growth will be spread out over a longer period of time. Fewer than one out of five white-collar personnel now uses a computer (amounting to some 8 million machines). By 1990, the figure, according to Future Computing, Inc., will still be only about two out of five. Nonetheless, this market will undergo considerable change. In the beginning it was primarily small businesses. By 1985 it will be largely Fortune 1000 corporations.

Make no mistake about it, the personal computer business is in the prime of life. It is growing by leaps and bounds. There are phenomenal, explosive success stories such as Compaq Computer, which went from no sales in 1982 to $111 million in 1983, an all-time record in American business history. For all but a handful of companies, though, it will be a profitless boom. They may have the greatest computer known to man, but unless they can get it in front of potential customers, it won't do them much good. And unless it is IBM-compatible, it won't have much of a future—it is the IBM-type computers that all the software is being developed for. And even if it can clear both of these hurdles, will it have a price tag that will allow the company to make any money?

It is this jarring contrast of seemingly unlimited market potential pitted against the harsh all too limiting realities of the industry that gives the personal computer business its reckless character. Here (besides simple greed) is the reason why so many companies appear on the scene to go public and make millions for their founders, who then depart for greener pastures. They know the future leads only to bankruptcy or, if they're real lucky, possibly an acquisition by a larger firm. (The state of affairs in personal computers was aptly, albeit tragically, symbolized by the founder of Eagle Computer. On the day his company went public, making him a millionaire, he took his new Ferrari out for a spin. It went out of control, killing both himself and his sole passenger, his yacht designer.)

Even if a company can survive these turbulent market conditions, what will happen when the Japanese begin to make their presence felt? Once the rate of expansion eases, the product leapfrogging slows, and the turmoil settles, the Japanese will take a major market share, as they have in almost all other consumer electronics businesses. In 1984, Matsushita's Panasonic, Sanyo, N.E.C., and Toshiba will all be advertising IBM-compatible PCs in the U.S. market, priced in the $1500 to $5000 range and aimed at business. Panasonic's model is called Sr. Partner to compete against IBM's PC Jr. If IBM will be the General Motors and Japan the Ford, only the Chrysler slot is still up for grabs.

In time, another computer-related device will come along to replace the micro, as micros did to minis, and minis did to mainframes. Maybe a device the size of a thin cigarette pack, flexible and expandable during use to a 9- or 12-inch screen and keyboard, which can be plugged into any wall socket to communicate with anything, anywhere, with plain language programming and voice input, and which is more powerful than today's supercomputers, priced like today's throw-away calculators, and can be used for entertainment, business, education, shopping, banking, anything but sex. Another new wave of entrepreneurs will appear. And the cycle will start all over again.

IBM: THERE'S NO STOPPING IT NOW

It is telling that this review of the personal computer business begins not with an account of the pioneer, Apple Computer, but with an assessment of the Johnny-come-lately, IBM. It is telling because IBM's stunning performance in personal computers is only a prelude of things to come. Freed of antitrust concerns and seeking faster growth, IBM has become an even more overwhelming competitive force than it was back in the mainframe era.

IBM read the same market studies everyone else did in the late 1970s and learned that personal computers were becoming more than just toys for hobbyists and technical types. It learned that by the end of the 1980s some 30% of all data processing expenditures would be for personal computers. This may not have been convincing to everyone, but for a reasonably astute company like IBM it was enough. In fact, it was more than enough for a company that was coming off one of the most lackluster decades of its entire history. Even if the market studies were wrong, even if personal computers were not the be all and end all, IBM could not afford to sit them out. It couldn't allow another hot opportunity for growth to slip away, as it did in the minicomputer era 10 years earlier.

To latch on to the personal computer boom, IBM didn't do anything spectacular. It just did everything right. The company realized correctly that the market was not looking for a unique machine. The more humdrum, in fact, the better. Everything including its name—the IBM PC—is unspectacular and matter of fact. IBM barely even makes the machine. The operating software is from Microsoft, the processor is from Intel, and other parts are from Japan. Manufacturing is by SCI Systems of Huntsville, Alabama (and more recently, Teledyne, for the PCjr model).

IBM carried off a slight technological leapfrog when it used a 16-bit microprocessor, instead of the 8-bit processors that were standard at the time. A computer with a 16-bit microprocessor is capable not only of performing faster, but also of using more memory space. The move to 16-bit personal computers was almost inevitable, an event widely anticipated throughout the industry. IBM, in the right place at the right time, was more than happy to lead the way.

The only additional ingredient needed was marketing strength.

Here mighty IBM, with its vast, established marketing organization, proved its willingness to make the concessions demanded by this new specialty market. IBM spent over a year recruiting more than 700 dealers and sewing up the major retail chains, such as Sears. Even more significant to its marketing effort was IBM's decision to open up the market for add-on peripherals and applications software to third-party vendors. Instead of jealously guarding the software development for its computer (a strategy that would produce surefire disaster for most manufacturers, but one that IBM might have been able to carry off), IBM threw open the gates to anyone and everyone, gambling that it would recoup what it lost by gaining market share. IBM was right.

The numbers are staggering. Sales went from 25,000 units in 1981, to 190,000 in 1982, to over 700,000 in 1983, to an anticipated 3 million or so in 1984. IBM will sell more personal computers than any other kind of computer ever made. The $2\frac{1}{2}$–3 million personal computers sold will generate almost $4 billion in revenues, 45% of the total market and 7% of the company's business. By the end of the decade, personal computers will account for well over 10% of IBM's revenues.

IBM is giving further proof of how adept it can be by attacking the various specialty sectors within the personal computer market. In 1983 it introduced the XT, a high-performance version of the original PC. It also came out with another model, the PC XT/370, a personal computer that can accept and transmit data from IBM 370 and 4300 mainframes. It has also targeted the home market with PCjr. Although the PCjr is a bit stiff in price at $1300 it will still skim off a slice of the large and varied home market.

Suddenly, after playing no role whatsoever in its creation, IBM is at the center of the personal computer business. The question is no longer whether IBM will dominate. In October 1983, *Business Week* summed up the answer to that question with its cover that read: "And The Winner Is . . . . IBM." The new question is: How much room will be left for everyone else? Competitors (as well as manufacturers of IBM-compatible computers, such as Compaq) have benefited from the fact that the demand for IBM PCs has far outstripped the available supply. Because of shortages in parts, SCI has been unable to manufacture anywhere near the number of IBM

PCs that the market wants. This situation can't last forever. And when IBM gets up to speed, watch out.

APPLE COMPUTER: WHO KILLED CAMELOT?

Was IBM the undoing of Apple Computer? Was Apple the cause of its own demise? Can the company survive anyway, despite IBM and its own past mistakes? Must all good things necessarily come to an end? In Cupertino, California, the home of Apple Computer, these are the questions that try men's souls.

As nearly everyone knows, when Apple was good, it was very good: Sales of $1 billion after only 5 years; profit margins of 12.5% after tax; an initial stock offering that sold at 31 times forecasted earnings, twice what most technology companies expect when they go public. It was Camelot in Cupertino; Shangri La in Silicon Valley. Apple had the corporate atmosphere of a toy store at Christmas time. Some 300 Apple employees became millionaires.

Then disaster struck. Apple ran head-on into a brick wall: the IBM PC. At a minimum, Apple lost tens if not hundreds of thousands of sales. Far more important, however, it lost its respected (exalted?) position in the business. IBM now sets the industry standards, leaving Apple completely out in the cold. Software developers now concentrate on the IBM PC, not on Apple's products. Software development has become a chicken and egg situation. Potential customers wait to see what software is available before buying, while software developers wait for volume product shipments before writing programs. In the meantime, IBM is squeezing Apple out of the Fortune 1000 market. Sales to corporate offices, which represented 80% of Apple's sales in 1981, were down to 50% in 1983. And now IBM is targeting the home market. An elephant is stomping through the Apple orchard.

Nonetheless, aside from some tongue-in-cheek ads "welcoming" IBM to the personal computer business, Apple did little that was right to counteract the IBM threat. Perhaps it saw IBM as another Xerox. More likely, however, the company was blinded by its own success. Product development suffered. After the overwhelming success of the Apple II, the company stumbled badly with the Apple III, a slightly more powerful but incompatible version of the best-selling II. The Apple III was poorly priced and poorly supported. It was another 8-bit computer when the industry was already looking toward 16-bit machines. On top of that, it had operating problems. Production was suspended for a time while technical problems were corrected. It has never sold well. For all practical purposes, during the time that it laid claim to being the leading company of personal computers, Apple was a one-product company. The upgraded version of the Apple II, the Apple IIe, represented 97% of the company's sales in 1983. It has the cult status of a Volkswagen Beetle.

Apple was in the unique position of being a leading-edge innovator with a product designed for mass consumption. Unfortunately, Apple never decided whether it preferred its identity as an innovator or as the computer vendor to the masses. It quickly became a success at neither. And actually, the innovation was really patterned after many ideas originally out of Xerox's Palo Alto research facility that later made their way into Xerox's ill-fated Star computer. The Lisa, the most ballyhooed computer product of the decade—six pages in *Fortune*, four in *Business Week*, one in *Time*—is a painful example of a product development process that is out of touch with the marketplace and almost running amuck. Unlike the Apple III, the Lisa worked properly. It was no lemon. It was another Edsel. Limited software, a high price (despite an 18.5% price reduction), and initial non-IBM compatibility were all drawbacks. It also had the double whammy of being aimed at the corporate market. Had it been designed with total IBM compatibility in mind, the Lisa might have had a chance. Without IBM compatibility, it was a weak product in a market where Apple no longer calls the shots. Only 20,000 Lisas were sold in 1983, less than half the number originally anticipated.

Apple hopes to get moving again with its newest major product, the Macintosh. Although it was behind schedule and not available in 1983, Apple is predicting that the Macintosh will account for one-quarter of all sales in 1984, one-half in 1985, and will re-establish Apple as a serious presence in the personal computer market. I have serious doubts about that. The Macintosh is a neat computer. It is pretty to look at. It can produce graphics. It has a mouse—the handheld device that you can use instead of a keyboard to enter data. It's a *nice* computer, the kind you might like to give to your kids, or your mother. It's the perfect home computer, except that its $2,500 price tag is way too high for that market. But the Macintosh doesn't make it as a business computer either. It has limited capability to run business applications software, such as spread-sheet programs. It does not communicate with the the IBM PC (initially, at least); it does not run UNIX directly unless it is fitted with an expensive file server, and it has no hard disk option. Because of its proprietary design, new software must be developed just for the Macintosh. Over 100 software firms have signed up to write programs, yet most of the major developers are tied up writing programs for the IBM PC.

Lets face it, the Macintosh is a slick machine, attractive and easy-to-use. The early market response was strong. Dealer backlogs stretched four weeks. In part, this is attributable to the incredible hype the Macintosh received. The "1984" television ad cost $400,000 to develop. It cost twice that just to broadcast it during the 1984 Superbowl.

Macintosh's chance is to appeal to novice professional users, students, and early technological adapters. The company needs to sell 300,000 units in 1984 and over 500,000 in 1985. If it can't do that, Apple could be facing serious problems. After the Apple III and the Lisa, the Macintosh would become the third new product mishap in a row. Time will tell.

While Apple faces tumultuous industry conditions, it is also executing what appears to be a very wrenching internal transition. The regime consisting of cofounders Steve Jobs and Steve Wozniak and company president A. C. Mike Markkula, Jr., has given way to the new management team led by an outsider from Pepsi-Cola, John Sculley. Enticed aboard at age 44 for $3 million, Sculley is an old man at this adolescent company. His mission will be to establish a tough-minded, professional, highly organized, profit/loss atmosphere. In Sculley's view, Apple's greatest weakness has been its inability to bring products to market on an orderly basis, consistent with previous products. Sculley hopes to cut Apple's product development time from 3.5 years down to 1 year. Apple will also buy more peripherals on the outside rather than using internal production so as to get to market faster. Manufacturing will become more automated to be competitive with the Japanese (and IBM). Sculley is also redefining Apple's product development strategy. Product development groups will now try to coordinate their efforts more closely, instead of running off in different directions. The market focus remains fuzzy. Having struck out in its attempt to penetrate large corporations, it now seems to be interested in small businesses or the smaller offices of the large corporations. Yet the products seem more suited to the home or education sectors. And the avant garde television advertising hardly seems aimed at business.

Sculley says his goal is "to take high-cost technology and bring it down to low-cost products for the individual." This means personal computers for most of this decade but could eventually encompass other consumer technology products. Obviously, there is a danger in overmanaging Apple. Specialty companies thrive in a free-wheeling, undisciplined atmosphere. Already there have been a number of management departures from Apple, and massive personnel layoffs. Apple's 7000 employees at the peak were more than it needed, and even 4600 may still be too many. The Apple culture will dissipate. The fun will fade. More importantly, profits have already faded. Apple will not be able to achieve and sustain past profitability levels, although it may see a temporary revival in 1984 if the Macintosh takes hold. Price erosion in its heartland microcomputer market has just begun. The sudden lack of profits may derail Sculley's effort to turn the company around, making his job all but impossible. Sculley may live to regret his decision to leave Pepsi-Cola, where he had the potential to be chairman, for the wilds of Silicon Valley.

Although Apple has considerable assets—money, high-quality products, brand name recognition—it lacks a major ingredient for a specialty company: a market. When it was the only personal computer company, Apple had all markets by default. Now that it must compete for them, the company is at a loss. At first it corralled the office market. Now that IBM is there, it is selling to individuals. What happens when IBM and the Japanese, or such companies as Hewlett-Packard and Digital Equipment, start selling to individuals? The industry moved too quickly. Camelot is gone for good. And once it is gone, you can never go back again.

TANDY: THE MASTER MERCHANDISER

Wherever you look, coast to coast, from the main street of the smallest town to the downtowns of the largest cities, Radio Shack is there. It is the high-tech hardware store of modern times, the place where you go to purchase the nuts and bolts of the information age.

With over 1400 Radio Shack stores selling its computers, Tandy is the unabashed purveyor of computers to the masses. The company is not known for innovation, and its image is not one that attracts Fortune 1000 companies. Maintenance, service, and support could stand improvement. Yet all these things pale beside the fact that Tandy knows how to sell and has the resources to do it. Tandy is the leading merchandiser of the personal computer business, a role that will serve it well in the future.

Radio Shack was a bankrupt chain of consumer electronics stores when it was purchased in the early 1960s by Charles David Tandy, whose business at the time was selling leather goods. By 1975, the consumer electronics business was doing so well that Tandy (who died in 1978) sold off everything but Radio Shack. Personal computers now account for about a third of Tandy's $2.7 billion in sales.

When it comes to computers, Tandy sees itself as a distributor, although it also does some of its own manufacturing. It maintains one of the most extensive product lines in the business, ranging from a $10,000, 16-bit, multiuser small business computer to a $69 programmable calculator. In between there are home computers, portables, and a host of peripherals. Most recently, Tandy introduced an IBM-compatible computer. There are no holes in the Radio Shack product line. The company has 247 special service facilities and 31 factories. On top of everything else, it is also one of the biggest sellers of software.

Surprisingly, Tandy's major market is small businesses and not, as most people think, individual consumers (or corporations). Still, Tandy has been hurt by IBM's assault on the business. Tandy's share of total personal computer sales dropped from 20% to 10% between 1981 and 1983. Like Apple, Tandy is being hurt not only through lost sales but also by the maturation of the market, an inevitable process that has been vastly accelerated by the presence of IBM.

The institutionalized entrepreneurialism that characterizes the Tandy marketing effort has its limitations when it comes to computers. Each Radio Shack store is closely scrutinized on a profit-and-loss basis. Bonuses are based on store profit margins. Store managers are assessed carrying charges on excess inventory and bad checks. At a typical Radio Shack store customer service is viewed as secondary to the sale. This approach was fine when personal computers were still a curiosity item. Today, however, even small businesses want the backing of a "computer company," and consumers are gravitating to the more sophisticated home computers, away from the ones that are primarily game oriented.

Nonetheless, Tandy's overall record in retail sales is spectacular. Revenues have expanded 20% annually and earnings per share 38% each year during the past decade. Profits have climbed in each of the past 21 years. Return on equity ranged 29 to 46% in the past 8 years.

In the future, as the personal computer market is squashed through a compactor and only a dozen or fewer entrants survive, Tandy will be there as a master merchandiser and distributor. As to its profits, that's another matter. It will make no difference where it obtains its products, likely from the Japanese. Repair service, personnel expertise, quality, and innovativeness of products will improve. Tandy's TRS-80 and its successors will not be squeezed off any shelves in a shelf-space battle—it owns all its own shelves. Anyone can develop and manufacture a micro. In the future, the winners will be the low-cost producers—IBM, Commodore, and Japan—and the distributors like Tandy and Computerland. The company's retail store strength gives it stability. It will always make a retail markup on hardware, software, and services, although the markup may diminish.

COMMODORE: A STREET-FIGHTING COMPUTER COMPANY

Forget about being an innovator. Apple can try and fail at that game. Forget about the small-business market. Leave that to Radio Shack. Manufacture computers from the bottom up (including semiconductors and peripherals), and keep your prices low to gain market share. That's the Commodore strategy, and it works—at least it used to.

Commodore introduced a personal computer in 1977 priced at $595. Demand skyrocketed, so it raised the price to $795. Orders doubled, but relations with dealers became strained, and the company got a bad reputation for service. So Commodore took its act to Europe, where it priced its computer at $1295. It was a hit. Commodore took over 70% of the European market. Only in 1981 did the company turn its attention back to the United States, where before long it was repeating its winning ways.

During the Christmas 1982 selling season, Commodore stole the show with its VIC-20 home computer, which it sold for $200. It sold a million of them, taking fully half of all home computer sales. U.S. sales, which were $30 million in 1978, reached $305 million in 1982 and more than doubled to $681 million in 1983. Profits increased 85%. Between 1978 and 1983, Commodore's growth rate was double that of Apple and Tandy.

Commodore achieved its position by being a cutthroat street fighter, outfoxing classier personal computer companies. Being vertically integrated in semiconductors and peripherals, Commodore gets its products to market fast and cheap. It also closely coordinates product development and marketing. Commodore outmaneuvered Texas Instruments, a technically superior company, and Atari, a supreme marketer. The linchpin to its strategy is volume production of hardware. Commodore figures that a massive machine population will generate ample third-party software development. It is right. Over 1000 programs have been written for the VIC-20, and the largest selling how-to computer book is a VIC-20 operating guide. The VIC-20 is so popular it is advertised on cereal boxes in Canada and is termed a *Volks Computer* in Germany. By pushing computers in volume, Commodore creates a pull-through for peripherals (which it also makes) and clears the way for millions of upgrade sales in 1985. But the home market is a tough one and there are some dark clouds on the horizon. Although Commodore surpassed Texas Instruments and Atari, how will it do against IBM and, eventually, the Japanese?

These questions may be academic depending on how Commodore copes with an even bigger question: How will it continue its winning ways without Jack Tramiel at the helm? Tramiel shocked everyone by his resignation in January 1984. It was his management style that enabled Commodore to keep up the fast pace of the personal computer business. A World War II concentration camp survivor, Tramiel is a feisty, autocratic, freewheeling businessman. At Commodore he was tough on his management team and on costs. Decisions were fast and unequivocal. His style created turmoil in management ranks, but the job got done. There is no time for committees or staff meetings in this business. To stay on top, a company must keep breaking the sound barrier. Commodore was good at it with Tramiel running the show, but what about now?

Tramiel's abrupt departure is a signal that the company may be headed for problems, that it may have gone as far as it can go in home computers. After all, it was just a matter of time before Tramiel's strategy of low price, volume production, and vertical integration caught up with him. A company that lives by the sword dies by the sword. Invariably another competitor will take the same approach and be better at it than Commodore. Televideo Systems is doing it to the traditional terminal manufacturers and has an eye on personal computers. Low cost is always a tenuous advantage.

Even with Tramiel at the helm, there were problems. His management approach left little room for financial controls and organization—which can become a real liability when a company begins to shoot through the $1 billion mark. In 1983 there were widespread reports of production problems.

Commodore is solidly entrenched in the home computer market. If the new president, Marshall F. Smith, age 54, who came over from Thyssen-Bornemisza, one of Europe's largest industrial corporations, and is a friend of Commodore's chairman Irving Gould, continues to follow Tramiel's lead, Commodore may have a few good years left. But despite his faults, Commodore had better prospects with Tramiel than it does without him. One might have more confidence about Commodore's prospects if, following Tramiel's departure, several other members of management had not followed him out the door. And if Tramiel had not accompanied his resignation with the statement that he intended to sell off some of his 2 million shares of Commodore stock.

SCI SYSTEMS: HOW DO YOU KEEP 'EM DOWN ON THE FARM?

There is joy in Huntsville, Alabama, these days—thanks to mighty IBM. Huntsville is the home of SCI Systems, a company that most people never heard of before IBM selected it to make the circuit boards that form the innards of the IBM PC. As the fortunes of the PC keep rising, so do those of SCI. If only it can stay happy as a supplier to other people's computers, it will do quite well.

The company was started in 1961 as Space Crafter Inc. (on $21,000 in capital) to help build Army and NASA satellites. Along the way, it established a reputation as a builder of reliable, quality subassemblies for other computer companies. By 1979, however, it still did only $37 million a year in business. Five years later, all that has changed. SCI will probably do about $450 million in business in 1984, over 60% of which stems from one OEM customer: IBM. SCI got the IBM job by competing in a fly-off against the Japanese in an experimental 90-unit production run. SCI was declared superior in quality and price and is now the sole source supplier to IBM of all PC circuit board subassemblies and most of the boards for the model XT as well. SCI also produces the guts of the IBM Displaywriter word processor and its 3278 terminal.

How does SCI do it? In the tradition of the south, SCI is a lean, mean manufacturer. That translates into "no unions and no employee frills." At SCI's plant just outside Huntsville, in the town of Arab, total labor overhead costs run in the area of $12 an hour. Although IBM is also nonunion, it cannot begin to touch that kind of low-cost labor. The labor costs at a typical IBM plant are more than double what they are at SCI, given the company wage scales and fringe benefits. SCI produced 2.5 million boards for IBM in 1983. Because the average IBM PC requires 4.5 boards, this translates into more than 550,000 PCs. Almost three are assembled each minute. SCI sells the four or five boards to IBM for $400 a set, generating $220 million in revenues in 1983. IBM in return puts on the housing and retails the PC for over $2000. Because of the shortage in semiconductor components, SCI's Arab plant was at 50% capacity in 1983. In 1984, it will produce at least 5 million boards for over 1 million personal computers, generating $450 million in revenue. SCI's backlog is almost $1 billion. The bottleneck is components. Even though it is Intel's and Motorola's second largest customer, and IBM owns 18% of Intel, SCI cannot obtain anywhere near enough semiconductor components to meet demand. Thus, production is component limited.

SCI clearly has the potential to do more than just build what goes inside other people's computers. Its ability to produce quality products in volume is an important attribute. SCI is accustomed to intense testing and zero defects. It knows how to manufacture at low cost. Its volume production gives it a steady stream of earnings or what Olin King, the company's tough but laid-back president, likes to call "investable profits." The tremendous production volume also offers an opportunity for extensive vertical integration, into sheet metal and plastic molding. SCI's defense business provides it with engineering talent. Its substantial size and IBM customer relationship give it credibility. The company can eventually use these strengths to leverage it into its own end-user product markets . . . maybe.

Right now SCI is heavily dependent on IBM, clearly a good bet for the future. It also counts among its customers several other weaker computer companies, such as Monroe (which was acquired by Compucorp from Litton in 1983). As King puts it, "Three years ago 20% of business with IBM was O.K., today 60% is fine, but I don't want it to be 90% . . . there has to be a balance."

Any attempt to enter the direct end-user computer market will require more R&D product innovation, an end-user sales force that must be created from scratch, as well as maintenance and service capability. All that is a tall order. SCI is already spread pretty thin, involved in a diversity of products and markets, going hell-bent just to satisfy IBM, doubling in size each year. Managing this situation is a strain. You can see this just by looking at Olin King's office—stack after stack of yet to be read magazines and other reading material cover his desk and window ledge.

SCI's future is irrevocably tied to that of the IBM PC. That's not a bad linchpin to depend on, but it is beyond the direct control of SCI itself. As a manufacturer of other companies' products, SCI has found a niche. The company will undoubtedly grow much larger by staying with what it does best, without marketing, service, or noticeable internal product development. Eventually, however, it will attempt to spread its wings and broaden out. And therein is the catch. A company cannot stay one dimensional forever, but the longer it waits to expand its capabilities, the more difficult the adjustment and the higher the risk, despite the fact it can leverage off its large revenue base and manufacturing capability. SCI should stick with OEM manufacturing and become an alternative to the Japanese for the U.S. computer industry.

SCI's momentum is surging and will continue a few more years before it begins to moderate. It would take another customer like IBM to keep it growing at its current rate, and as everyone knows, there is only one IBM. There is a place in the business for this type of manufacturer. SCI is different. Look for it to prosper.

TANDON: PAR FOR THE COURSE IN FLOPPIES?

The personal computer business would not be the same today without the presence of Sirjang Lal Tandon, nicknamed Jugi, the man from the Punjab region of India, near Bombay, who gave us the floppy disk drive. Without this low-cost, compact disk storage device (which has completely eclipsed tape drives in the small computer market), the personal computer would never have become the success story that it is today. Though not as dramatic as the advances in integrated circuitry, the development of the $5\frac{1}{4}$ inch floppy disk drive must be ranked equal, if not greater, in importance.

Tandon was a manufacturer of disk drive components outside

of Los Angeles (where it began in 1975) when Jugi sensed an opportunity in the emerging personal computer market. By 1979 Tandon, no longer just a components supplier, was making the whole disk drive. Sales went from $3 million in 1977 to $300 million in 1983. Tandon seemed to have the market all to itself. At one point, it ran an advertisement saying it no longer competed in the disk drive business because "You Can't Compete When You've Got No Competitor."

This kind of cockiness relects the personality of Jugi Tandon himself, who became quite rich as his company prospered. He is worth $200 million in stock and is the owner of 11 luxury automobiles (including two Rolls, three Mercedes, and a Lambourghini) as well as a new 30-room, $15 million house. (Some 60 other Tandon employees have also become millionaires, including a former assembly-line worker whose stock is worth $6 million.) But Jugi better be careful. The market for floppy disk drives is headed down the back nine, and the course is loaded with traps. The market for rigid (Winchester) disk drives is picking up steam, and Tandon has yet to prove itself there. The company hopes to be first and foremost in the market for $3\frac{1}{2}$ inch microfloppies, but that market is just emerging. Meanwhile, the market for $5\frac{1}{4}$ inch floppies, which represents two-thirds of Tandon's revenues, will probably top out in 2 years' time, like tape drives did a few years ago. Tandon could begin to run out of steam before the eighteenth hole.

Tandon's ticket to stardom was simple: Emphasize manufacturing technology instead of product technology and become the first low-cost producer in the business. Tandon manufactures, it does not merely assemble. Disk drive parts (components, heads, stepper motors, etc.) are produced in India by a subsidiary headed by one of Jugi's brothers. Vertical integration extends all the way down to the actual disks. This allows Tandon price leadership across a broad product line: $5\frac{1}{4}$ inch floppy disk drives (a $400 million market of which Tandon has 65%); $5\frac{1}{2}$ inch rigid disk drives (already a $500 million market of which Tandon has 17%); 8 inch rigid disk drives; $3\frac{1}{2}$ inch floppies; and a $\frac{1}{2}$ inch cartridge tape drive. Most OEM customers purchase more than one product.

Tandon announces its products early with ultralow prices, confusing the market and forestalling computer manufacturers from committing to other vendors. Then Tandon delivers at the stated cost. Order backlog has skyrocketed, from $45 million in 1981 to $121 million in 1982, and over $250 million by 1983. One order by IBM alone in 1983 was for $310 million.

Jugi concentrates on customer relationships and marketing, traveling around the country signing contracts in the tens and even hundreds of millions of dollars. Because he is close to his customers, new product response is well aimed and timely. Tandon develops what the market wants, not what it thinks the market may need. The business is simple: little selling, no software, existing technology—nothing fancy. Manufacturing and engineering are everything. Low cost and low prices put the market in Tandon's lap. The customer list reads like a Who's Who of the microcomputer and word processing markets: IBM, Hewlett-Packard, Wang Laboratories, Tandy, Commodore International, Apple—more than 700 OEM customers in total.

Tandon's future seems assured. But actually, it is no more assured than any of the other young companies that have appeared in the personal computer market. Although Tandon derives 40 to 50% of its revenues from IBM (an aspect of the company that will be to its benefit for a while), it will be hurt by the wave of dropouts occurring among personal computer manufacturers. Tandon was burned by bad receivables from Victor Technologies in 1983. Tandon earned its position by having the lowest prices, but it can't stay that way forever. Japanese competition is an ever-present consideration. Moreover, Tandon has become a big company in a very short period. Jugi runs the show. It will be difficult to maintain control with the current narrow top-management structure.

The demand for micro peripherals will continue to surge in the years ahead, but the products and technologies will change. Tandon is king of the floppies but is second fiddle in the newest growth area—rigid Winchester $5^{1}/_{4}$ inch minidisk drives. Seagate Technology stole the march in rigid minidisk drives, and Tandon must play catch-up there. Tandon will not dominate the business in the future as it has in the past. Forecasts and plans do not count for much in such a volatile business. Predictability will be limited.

(Unlike our experience on the golf course with Jugi. On that occasion my associate, whose investment company owns a sizable number of Tandon shares, pulled out a computerized earnings forecast to get some quick, forthright guidance from Jugi as to its accuracy. Jugi's prediction proved correct. That's one way for an outsider to analyze a company.) Tandon's low-cost strategy and close reading of the market will serve it well, but in time, current advantages may diminish. Look for a few more great years ahead for Tandon, but don't count on sending your kids to college with the stock. Tandon will reign supreme in floppy disk drives but has yet to prove itself in the even bigger and faster growth market, mini-rigid disk drives.

SEAGATE TECHNOLOGY: RIGID DISK DRIVES AHEAD OF THEIR TIME

Around 1979, Alan Shugart had an idea that in retrospect seems quite logical, but at the time was considered highly risky and daring. Shugart saw the booming business in floppy disk drives and decided that there was a market among microcomputer users for hard disk drives. Known as Winchester drives, these are more expensive but capable of storing far more data than are floppy drives. Although rigid disk drives are fixtures at mainframe and minicomputer installations, no one had thought of ever using them with microcomputers. Shugart decided to be the first.

In 1981 the company Shugart founded, Seagate Technology, shipped $10 million worth of rigid disk drives. They were almost a novelty item then, but not for long. By 1982, 8% of all micros were equipped with a rigid disk drive. Seagate produced 50,000 and took half the market. In 1983 the company shipped 200,000 drives and recorded $110 million in revenues. Sales are expected to reach at least $300 million in 1984, when one out of every five microcomputers will use rigid disks. By 1986 the ratio will be one to three. That's a wave anyone would love to ride. Seagate's goal is to reach $1 billion in sales by the end of this decade. The only problem between here and there may be burnout. Too much, too fast can take a toll. And Seagate is heavily dependent on IBM as a customer, shipping almost half its production to IBM for use with the PC as of late 1983.

Already, Shugart's interest seems to be waning. Living on the picturesque Seventeen Mile Drive in Monterey, California would distract anyone. Shugart seems hurried, unsettled, and casual. His photo in the annual report reflects an open-shirt informality. The second in command and cofounder, Finis F. Conner, is likewise already phasing out of day-to-day operations. Shugart is now chairman, and Conner is vice-chairman.

Lack of attentiveness on the part of these two founders is partially to blame for the hoax that was pulled on Seagate in 1983. It seems a Dr. Sidney Friedman signed on with the company as a $95,000 research scientist with preeminent qualifications: holder of over 300 patents; science advisor to every president since Kennedy and to the governments of Great Britain and West Germany; consultant to over 150 large corporations, including IBM, Motorola, Texas Instruments, TRW, Xerox, Intel, GE, RCA, Memorex, and the Department of Defense; holder of two Ph.D. degrees cum laude in physics and in electrical engineering from Oxford University; and fluent in 13 languages. Not a bad resume. Ten days after joining Seagate, Friedman was unmasked as an exconvict on probation in Los Angeles for a similar hoax. He was arraigned on grand theft and held in Santa Cruz County Jail. Shugart and Conner must pay closer attention to the business or someone may walk off with the whole company.

Despite such mishaps, Seagate's position at present appears impregnable. Product capacity was 3000 units per day in mid-1983, and 1 million per year by year end. That is scheduled to double in 1984. The customer base is first class: IBM, Digital Equipment, Hewlett-Packard, Wang Laboratories, Apple Computer, and others. Seagate's product line is narrow, concentrated in the low-capacity 5- and 10-megabyte end of the market. It lacks vertical integration, although it will introduce its own disk drive controller product in 1984. The company does not manufacture its own disks, as does Tandon. Moreover, the disks that it uses are based on oxide media technology, even though plated media (as Tandon uses) permits a higher recording density. Nor does Seagate manufacture its own magnetic recording heads. Competition is intensifying with the onrush of Tandon into the rigid disk market. Prices are falling 25 to 30% annually, and Seagate may not be able to bring down costs as fast as Tandon because of the lack of vertical integration. There will certainly be a price war. Seagate expects a 10-megabyte rigid disk drive to sell for a little over $400 in 1984; Tandon anticipates a price possibly as much as $100 cheaper. The race is on. And Seagate will need substantial external capital financing in the future to meet its expansion requirements. The stream of profits and depreciation are outweighed by the capital expenditures for plant and equipment, so cash flow is negative, necessitating continuous borrowing or stock financing.

I expect Seagate to ride the microcomputer rigid disk drive tidal wave over the next few years and remain the market leader. Its position, however, is precarious. The market will be volatile and competition intense. Seagate's founders may be long gone in a couple of years, just when they may be needed most. This company has been launched in a whirlwind but does not have an anchor to windward. It could be a big winner or a big loser—it's hard to predict. The company is far too high a risk for my nerves, but it is in the right business and promises pure excitement for a time. Seagate will never be dull.

VERBATIM: HIGH-TECHNOLOGY RAZOR BLADES

Over the long haul, it's not who makes the razors that counts. It's who makes the blades. Verbatim is the world's leading supplier of high-technology razor blades—the floppy disks that have proliferated with small computers. The typical personal computer consumes 50 floppy disks in its time. By 1988, the market for these disks alone is expected to reach $1 billion, up from just under $200 million in 1983, as seen in Figure 12.1. Verbatim is the market leader, with 37%. If it stays on its toes, Verbatim has a good chance of keeping its premier position. But it won't be easy.

Competition in this market is intense. After Verbatim there is Dysan (15%), Maxell of Japan (14%), and 3M (13%). IBM and TDK are also important factors. And that's just the beginning. Everyone is getting into the act—Fuji Photo, Xydex, and many others. Al-

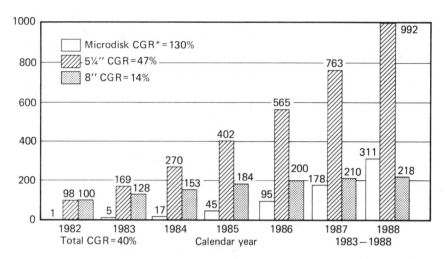

Figure 12.1. World flexible disk market (units in millions). *Source:* Verbatim Corporation.

together there are 28 competitors, but within 2 years, there will probably be some consolidation. Such companies as Nashua and Memorex (Burroughs) that do not keep up in R&D, marketing, and manufacturing may fall by the wayside. But as competition consolidates, prices are coming under pressure, making it tough even for the survivors. Traditionally prices have fallen 10 to 15% annually, and cost reductions have kept pace with them. Now that may no longer be the case. During the fall of 1983, prices in Europe eased by 15% in just 3 months, possibly an ominous trend. Prices in the United States are similarly beginning to erode more quickly.

The business of manufacturing floppy disks appears on the surface to have all the hallmarks of a low-technology, commodity-oriented operation. Just stamp'em out, pack'em up, and ship'em. Actually nothing could be further from the truth. Manufacturing disks involves more than 70 steps for the disks alone, not including the jacket and packaging. It is an area in which the technology is changing constantly, as these disks become capable of storing greater amounts of information. The early floppy disks in 1970 stored 26,400 bits per square inch. By 1983, the bit density was over 1.5 million per square inch. To accomplish this, the chemical process required for coating the disk has to be maintained at the highest levels of quality and reliability. Another technological trend is greater durability. The coating on the media is becoming thinner, yet durability is increasing because of longer lasting lubricants, higher cohesive strengths, and greater adhesiveness. The density of the individual tracks found on disks is also increasing. To ensure that the tracks on the disk remain stable, the basic film substance of the disk must be able to withstand expansion and contraction due to changes in temperature and humidity.

Verbatim is quite strong technologically. Although many of its competitors go outside for the coating processing, Verbatim keeps this in house and is better able to control costs and meet demand—a key consideration in such an explosive market. Verbatim also has as its senior vice-president of R&D, Geoffrey Bate, a Ph.D. and one of the world's foremost experts on magnetics.

Beyond its technological leadership, mass distribution is Verbatim's strongest suit. As in the record and publishing (not to mention the razor blade) businesses, rapid distribution is a key factor in success. Verbatim has 400 distributors that serve thousands of retail stores. The company also sells directly to the major microcomputer and word processing manufacturers, such as IBM, Apple, Tandy, Wang, Digital Equipment, Xerox, Burroughs, and Lanier.

The newest marketing effort is the building of a direct sales force of some 200 salespeople during 1983–1984 to cater to larger stores and Fortune 500 corporations. This cuts out at least one distribution middleman and allows closer scrutiny of store merchandising, ordering, and inventory levels. Consumer catalogs and the education market are other selling channels. Warehousing, dispersed manufacturing plants for quick delivery, advertising, and better positioning of products are other efforts Verbatim is pursuing.

Verbatim is a well-managed company that has all the advantages that accrue to a specialist company. It is in one business and one market, with full concentration and narrowness of focus. Verbatim has an entrepreneurial spirit and creativity. Personnel policies are enlightened: Each employee gets a 13-week paid sabbatical every 7 years. President Malcolm B. Northrup seems to understand the challenges that face his company. His goal is "to develop managers to operate consistently with high profitability, making the correct decisions with little facts. You can't wait more than a couple of days in this fast-moving business." Verbatim's objective is to reach $1 billion in sales by 1988, growing at least 40% annually. It seeks return on equity of 25%. In terms of market share, its goal is to maintain its one-third share of existing markets and achieve a 25% share in new product areas.

Verbatim has an awful lot going for it, but the future won't be a cakewalk. The technological hurdles that face this company cannot be underestimated. The technology in mass storage is steadily shifting in the direction of laser and vertical recording techniques and thin film head disk drives. Although these technologies are all aimed at the high end of the market, their impact on Verbatim's market is inevitable. Huge companies such as Eastman Kodak, 3M, and the Japanese companies have hefty R&D budgets and a strong interest in this business. The Japanese are already making a strong push. Maxell has increased its share of the U.S. market sharply, much of it coming out of Dysan's hide. The 3½ inch microfloppy market is about to take off. Growth in the traditional floppy market is already being affected by the popularity of hard disk drives. The basic floppy disk market is getting sloppy and may soon be out of control altogether. Disks are appearing on retail store racks, steeply discounted in price. Channels of distribution may soon be so abundant that they will be beyond the influence of the vendors. IBM, a large Verbatim customer, is pulling the manufacturing of some of its disk requirements in house. On top of everything else, technical personnel trained in magnetics and mass storage technology are hard to find. Verbatim began to experience some of these pressures in late 1983 as profits moderated.

Verbatim has the resources and the will to make it. But this market cannot go unscathed by the fallout in the personal computer business, so Verbatim's destiny may be out of its control. It is a company with its work cut out for it.

13

The Future of the Computer Industry: Software

It used to be that a neophyte, upon being introduced to the world of computers, was told first about the concepts of hardware and software. A great deal was said about the former, as little as possible about the latter.

For today's neophytes, the situation is becoming exactly the opposite. They may hear more about such programming languages as ANSI COBOL, FORTRAN, PL/1, and Assembler than they will ever want to. It's not that software wasn't important before. It's simply that it is more important today. This is due partly to basic demographics. There are a lot of computers out there. Consequently, there is greater incentive to write software. (Was there a recording industry before there were record players?) Part of it is also because of economics. There are more computers because they are cheaper. Because they are cheaper, they return less money to those who make them. So, those who fancy a lot of money turn their interests to software, where a good markup is still within the realm of the possible. Software's move to center stage is also part of the maturation of the industry. Customers are more sophisticated today. They are no longer dazzled by lots of blinking lights and split-second calculations. They may still be neophytes when it comes to the intricacies of computer technology, but they know the route to greater productivity lies as much with the software as it does with the hardware.

Ten years ago, fewer than one out of every five dollars that users spent on data processing went to software. Today the split is about 50–50. By 1990, the ratio will be 4 to 1 in favor of the programs. Now that's a revolution. The total market for software supplied by all U.S. companies (hardware manufacturers and independent software companies combined) was $14 billion in 1983. By 1988, software sales are expected to be $50 billion. More than 70% of this increase will be revenues from packaged applications software: $8 billion in 1983 and $35 billion in 1988. A little less than one-third of packaged software sales are programs written for personal computers. Expenditures by U.S. corporations on software packages expanded 50% in 1983. In terms of occupations for the future, according to *Forecasting International* and *U.S. News & World Report*, the second and third largest number of new jobs over the remainder of the century will be in CAD/CAM (computer-aided design and manufacturing), and software development. There will be over a million new jobs in each category.

The software market is booming. But unlike the personal computer boom, this one will not be profitless. Far from it. Software will be enormously profitable for those who play their cards right. And therein lies the problem. It is very difficult to play your cards right in software. There is no easy way of producing a program. It is more an art than a science. Everyone agrees on that. Everyone would like to do something about it, but no one seems to have any good notion of where to begin. The programmer's muse is an untamed one. Great software, like great writing, adheres to no known schedule of production. Moreover, the level of perfection demanded in programming is far higher than it is in almost any kind of writing or, for that matter, in most human endeavors. As Frederick Brooks wrote in his book, *The Mythical Man Month*, "If one character, one pause . . . is not strictly in proper form, the magic doesn't work. Human beings are not accustomed to being perfect, and few areas of human activity demand it. Adjusting to the requirements for perfection is, I think, the most difficult part of learning to program." *

* Frederick P. Brooks, Jr., *The Mythical Man Month: Essays on Software Engineering* (New York: Addison-Wesley, 1982), p. 8.

It is also important to remember that there really has been nothing like software before. The idea of the computer, or some sort of "mechanical brain," was kicked around since at least the nineteenth century. But for software, what real precedents are there—player piano rolls? To get an idea of the challenge facing the software industry, imagine the following: The automobile has just been invented, a wondrous development hailed by all as a boon to humanity. There is one problem, however: No roads. There are no roads because never before has there been a wheeled vehicle of any kind. Hundreds of cities and towns dot the landscape, isolated outposts, surrounded by dense thicket and forest. (Don't ask me how they got there—remember I'm asking you to *imagine*.) To make use of this new invention, roads must be created. Nothing like that has ever been attempted before. There is a great deal of confusion and disagreement. In what direction should the roads be built? Which cities and towns should be connected? Who will build the roads? How will they be paid for? How much time will it take?

You get the idea. The software market is a wilderness, one that is as lush with opportunity as it is fraught with unknown peril. Those who set off in the right direction, with the right resources, will find their efforts rewarded many times over. Others may find themselves at a dead end, lost in the middle of nowhere.

Nonetheless, as a practical matter, software can be an awfully nice business to be in: no manufacturing, little fixed asset requirements, little investment, and costs are comparatively easy to control.

On the other hand, its reliance on skilled personnel makes it risky. People are the key to any software company's success. And they can walk out and never return.

The type of software most people are familiar with is *applications software*. These are the programs that enable computers to do such things as word processing, payroll, accounting, and even play games. If you have ever bought a computer, chances are you had something specific in mind that you wanted it to do. The applications software can be written to appeal to a broad group of users (such as general-purpose word processing programs), or they can be prepared for a highly specialized market (word processing for lawyers, say, or for journalists).

Then there is *operating software*. As its name implies, operating software directs the operation of the computer. Unlike a musical instrument, which can be made to produce random sounds in the absence of a score, a computer cannot do anything without an operating program. There are several kinds of operating programs.

1. **Operating Systems.** Direct the internal operation of the computer and manage the flow of data between the computer and its peripherals (e.g., IBM's MVS and DOS).

2. **Systems Software.** Assists the operator of the computer in controlling, monitoring, and measuring the computer's internal operation to help it perform more efficiently (e.g., Computer Associates' Optimizer).

3. **Systems Implementation Software.** Used by programmers to help in the writing of other programs (e.g., Applied Data Research's AutoFlow). It includes such things as assemblers and high-level programmer languages. These are the only devices available to date to make software development a more productive activity.

4. **Database Management Systems.** Stores, indexes, and organizes for easy retrieval of vast amounts of data (e.g., Cullinet's Integrated Database Management System).

If it were left up to the manufacturers of musical instruments, how much creative variety might there be in our music today? Most likely not very much. Thousands of individuals, working alone for the most part, have composed the music of our culture. So it is too in software. Ten years ago, almost all computer programs were supplied by the computer manufacturers themselves. There was no software industry to speak of. Now the hardware manufacturers' share of the software business is dropping. Some 4000 independent software firms, the largest being such firms as Cullinet and Management Sciences of America (MSA), account for about a third of today's $14 billion market. By 1988, their share will be 50%. Moreover, by the end of the decade, the software market will be so huge it will no longer be a specialty niche the way it is today. It will fragment into hundreds of niches and slices. Leaders, such as Cullinet and MSA, will rank among the industry heavyweights, on the Top 25 list and maybe even close to the Top 10. They will be displacing the hardware companies.

In some ways, software is far more market driven and prone to specialization than hardware could ever be. The trick for companies in the software business is to choose a market that is large enough to be profitable, yet uniform enough so that packaged software can be sold without having to do a lot of customizing. The retailing market, for example, is far too broad. But retail auto parts stores, because there are thousands of them with similar needs, offer a great software market opportunity. (And as we will see, one of the turnkey companies—firms that buy computers from someone else, add their own software, and resell the entire system—have enjoyed great success selling to the retail auto parts market.)

Accounting is another peril of the software business. The expense of writing a program must be treated as a cost of goods sold. It is an operating cost rather than an R&D cost that generates tax credits. Although software is obviously valuable, in an acquisition it carries little or no book value. The company making the acquisition risks having its profits seriously diluted because of the accounting.

And then there is the looming presence of IBM. There is little likelihood that IBM can dominate software the way it has mainframes or personal computers. The software market is too wide and too varied. Moreover, because there are few economies of scale in software development, IBM's only major advantage is in marketing. Still, because of its enormous installed base of equipment, the company must be reckoned with. Any move it makes is likely to send ripples through the industry. Lately, IBM has been microcoding or hardwiring more of its systems control programs into its mainframes (building certain software program instructions into the semiconductor circuitry), making it more difficult for third-party vendors. IBM is also on a campaign to help users of its computers reduce the software maintenance costs they incur whenever IBM changes its operating software. It is doing this by offering users access to unattended remote computers at its IBM Data Services Center in Tampa. Users can call up and receive the updated programs from these computers over the phone. In the past, an IBM mainframe user received frequent updates, or "patches" that were inserted in the program by programmers—a time consuming activity. Freed from the job of making constant, mundane modifications,users have more time to develop their own software, reducing their reliance on third-party suppliers.

The bottom line is that software is an uncharted wilderness. Almost anything can happen, and it probably will. The only certainty of the software market is its inevitability. All the computers at work today are worthless without software. The more a user wants to do with a computer, the more software is required. Software is the king of the insurgent specialty markets. It is the grand musical score to the proliferating computer equipment. It is the No. 1 computer business of the future. No wonder some 4000 companies are already in it, 800 in microcomputer applications software alone. For those firms, it is music to their ears.

CULLINET: A COMPANY THAT KNOWS HOW TO SELL

Cullinet is not quite the largest software company in the business, but it is one of the best (you will find many users of its software agree on this point). And in more ways than one, Cullinet has emerged as a leader in the young, explosive software market—a position it should be able to keep.

When it was founded in 1968, Cullinet was one of the first companies to sell only software. Then years later it became the first company to go public and issue its stock to outsiders. And in 1982, it became the first software company to have its stock listed on the New York Stock Exchange.

To get that far, Cullinet had to have something extra going for it, that certain verve and pizzazz that enable a company to stake out a market before its time and then keep its act together until that time finally arrives. For Cullinet, that extra something boils down to marketing. It's important to keep in mind that Cullinet's founder, John Cullinane, is not a programmer at all. He's a master marketer. Cullinane knew that before one line of code was put up for sale by Cullinet, potential customers would have to be educated, not only about the idea of software, but about the idea of buying it from an independent company.

It is obvious that Cullinane has done his job well. Cullinet's sales, which were only $2 million in 1975, swelled to $110 million in 1983 and are expanding at 50% a year. Revenues per employee are over $120,000, compared to $62,000 in 1978. Profit margins are 23%, and return on equity is 20%. As the business has grown, so has the product line. The total price value for Cullinet's line of software products (one of each) was $1.6 million in 1983, five times what it was in 1980. Nearly two-thirds of its product line is new. Can anything stop Cullinet? We don't believe so. In this, the golden age of software, Cullinet will be the first billion-dollar software company.

Software at Cullinet means database management programs for IBM mainframes. Database management is one of the most important concepts in software, and programs that perform that function represent a large chunk of the overall software business. Most computer applications, from accounting to word processing, involve the storage and retrieval of data. Database management programs allow a large grouping of data (information about company orders, sales, costs, personnel, pricing, etc.) to be stored together and then retrieved in a number of different formats, by a variety of users. It eliminates the need for duplicate files and makes business information more accessible and therefore more valuable.

Cullinet began its major assault on the database software market in 1973 when it introduced its Integrated Database Management System (IDMS), acquired from B.F. Goodrich and adapted for the mass software market. IDMS, which competed with a similar product offered by IBM, was aimed at IBM computer sites where the information in the database was constantly changing and therefore had to be updated all the time. Over the years, Cullinet has added to this product a data dictionary (a kind of index that makes it easier to locate data), a teleprocessing monitor, a back-end database management processor, and other enhancements. In 1984, Cullinet will begin offering a "relational" database system, a relatively new concept in database management in which the software determines the relationships, among data during the actual processing, rather than having those relationships determined by the structure of the database. (Think of a database system as being like a family tree. A relational system can tell who is a cousin and who is a grandfather just by reading the names. A nonrelational system must follow all the individual branches of the tree to determine who is related to whom.)

Database management is a complicated business, so we won't go into the technicalities. It is enough to say that computer users who buy Cullinet's software are very pleased with it, as indicated by the 25% preference rating it received in a survey by the Hayden Publishing Co.* Only IBM was higher with a 31% rating, while Cincom and AG Systems were preferred in 11 and 10% of the responses. The year before Cullinet topped even IBM. Not only is the software rated highly, another survey found that Cullinet was considered No. 1 in customer support and satisfaction, too.

Had Cullinet waited for the market to come and say its products are great, it might still be waiting—in bankruptcy court. That's where John Cullinane's marketing expertise came in. Selling Cullinet's software would not be easy under any circumstances. To begin with, the software is a big-ticket item, over $350,000 in price. That means a customer's top management must be persuaded, not just the data processing people. Who could do that selling job? Smooth-talking salespeople? They wouldn't understand the product. Technical people? They don't know how to sell. After years of tinkering, a solution was arrived at: seminars.

If you can't bring Mohammed (Cullinet) to the mountain (the customers), then bring the mountain to Mohammed. Cullinet used to give seminars and presentations by the hundreds. Now it gives thousands of them. A typical IBM computer systems customer once sent technical and software-oriented personnel to attend. Now, since the average sale amounts to several hundred thousand dollars, the customers are sending along senior management, even presidents and chairmen. The presidents come and hear what IDMS can do

---

* 14th Annual Audit of Brand Recognition of the Computer Market 1983, Hayden, Inc., Hasbrouck Heights, N.J., 1983.

for them. They ask their data processing technical personnel sitting beside them if all the benefits of such complicated software are really true. The answer is yes. The sale is closed. Cullinet wins 80% of the business it bids on; it once lost 80%. There were over 100 salespeople and over 9000 cumulative software product installations in 1983, compared to under 2000 in 1978. Those seminars really sell.

Cullinet is not resting on its laurels. It began to move into applications software in 1982 with financial and manufacturing programs, accounting for 4% of revenues in 1983. It also acquired Computer Pictures in 1982 for graphics software to supplement its IDMS. A data center and training site for its customers are additional new avenues of growth. In the future, the company's strategy is to use its basic database software and broad range of customers to launch a major thrust, not only into financial and manufacturing applications software packages, but also into information databases themselves and data processing services. Having taken 15 years to expand from nothing to $100 million in sales, Cullinane believes it will be "much easier to move from $100 million to $500 million," now that the company is an established leader and is accepted by large customers.

Although Cullinet is still behind IBM and Cincom Systems in cumulative installations, the market for database software is big, almost $250 million in 1984 and expected to top $1 billion by 1987. Only one-third of all IBM computer installations now have this type of software. IBM has about half the market, while Cullinet is responsible for 10 to 15%. New customers for Cullinet in 1983 totaled over 300, and the customer list is impressive: Chase Manhattan, GE, General Foods, and Coca-Cola. At Cullinet's current rate of expansion, it should reach a half billion in revenues by 1987.

Despite such accomplishments, no company is perfect. Cullinet does operate in the IBM-compatible arena, and IBM's database software is improving, especially with its recent introduction of a relational database system. Cullinet's IDMS is over 10 years old now and growing more vulnerable by the year. Competition by such independents as Cincom Systems and Software AG still lurks. IBM is playing around with the microcode in its mainframes, but there is no way IBM could ever render all non-IBM-developed software incompatible. If it did, it would make some $200 billion of its customers' own software development investments worthless, and these customers would rather switch to Amdahl than lose that investment. But Cullinet may find that staying compatible will be more expensive than it used to be.

The database software market will eventually slow in growth. Cullinet will need to get into other software markets in a big way to continue its growth. Financial and management controls become strained when a company expands by over 50%. In Cullinet's business, there is little ongoing stream of repeat revenues (perhaps 25% of the total) and no backlog. The company must close business and ship reels of tape each quarter to achieve its profit objectives. There is no coasting. Retaining the high profit margins as the company broadens out will be a challenge.

Management is young. The senior people just below Cullinane average 34 years of age. The president, Robert Goldman, is a software genius, but running a corporation is a different matter. And this company is highly stock conscious, fixated on stock price to the point of showing slides at investor meetings that chart the stock price performance, and even taking a Wall Street security analyst (not me) who was critical of the company and tossing him out of a new-product press conference—us Wall Street folks are not used to such physical treatment.

Believe me, that's not why I view this company positively. In this business, when you come across a company like Cullinet that can create good products and also knows how to sell, there is a good chance that you have come across a winner.

MSA: THE IMPRINT OF IMLAY AND IBM

Management Sciences of America (MSA) was founded in 1963 to develop custom software and do management consulting. It barely survived. By 1971, the company had programmed and consulted its way into bankruptcy court. The next year, John Imlay, a colorful, high-profile innovator took over as president. He dropped the consulting and, instead of custom software, pushed the company into packaged applications software. It was an idea whose time had come. MSA took off like a shot.

Unlike Cullinet, which has concentrated in one very specialized software area (database management systems), Imlay's strategy at MSA was to build (both through internal development and external acquisition) a wide range of integrated software packages that could be marketed across a variety of industries. The mainstay of MSA's product line is a series of financial management programs for mainframes that do such things as general ledger, financial forecasting and modeling, accounts receivable and payable, purchasing, inventory, fixed-asset accounting, payroll, and taxes. Manufacturing software was acquired from Xerox's Arista Manufacturing Division in 1982 and is aimed at manufacturing control. In total, MSA has some 5000 mainframe customers, to which it has sold 9000 packages.

And then there is the exploding personal computer market. MSA is one of the leaders there through its acquisition of Peachtree Software in 1981. Already, Peachtree has grown from sales of $3 million in 1981 to $20 million in 1983. Over 100,000 personal computer programs have been sold.

MSA owes a lot to Imlay. It owes even more to IBM. A few years ago, when IBM began endorsing independent applications software packages, MSA was one of the manufacturers so anointed. IBM tells its customers in need of financial software packages to go to MSA. The same thing happened with the IBM PC—IBM commissioned Peachtree to develop the software. By riding IBM's coattails in both micros and mainframes, MSA is the leading supplier of applications software packages, with 5% of that highly fragmented market. Revenues in 1983 were $145 million, with profits of $13 million. Sales over the next few years should expand by at least 40% annually, and profits by 35%.

Marketing is paramount. MSA has over 150 salespeople and 100 product and industry specialists as backup support. Several non-IBM mainframe computer companies also sell MSA's software to their customers. In microcomputers, Peachtree sells through 2000 retail stores. Retailing skill, involving such techniques as video demonstrations and on-site displays, is critical to success in that market.

Although it is larger than Cullinet, MSA's profits are less, its growth rate is slower, and its revenues per employee are not as good ($75,000 compared to Cullinet's $120,000). This is partly because MSA covers a much wider product spectrum, which could be a problem in the future if the company is not careful to avoid spreading itself too thin. In the meantime, MSA suffers from a more immediate problem. Despite its varied product mix, MSA has a selling cycle syndrome that is terribly frustrating and risky.

It seems that corporations are so tied up during the first 4 months of the year in closing their books and dealing with their auditors and the Internal Revenue Service that any thought of improving the financial control system by buying new computer software is put off until late spring. Then it takes 6 months for the customer to evaluate alternatives and maybe even to see if the budget will allow for the purchase of such software. As a result, MSA closes much of its business, typically 40% of the total year's revenues, in the last quarter. But costs stretch throughout the year, and most new marketing support personnel are hired and trained early in the year.

Since MSA earns virtually nothing in the first three quarters of the year and then rakes it all in during the last 3 months, if any slight slippage ever occurs in closing business late in the year, the shortfall will be sudden and unrecoverable in that year's profits. Moreover, another accounting controversy exists. Revenues from customer support agreements (covering software package enhancements and improvements, which represent almost one-quarter of total company sales) are recorded in a lump sum when received, usually in the fourth quarter. The cost of providing this service is spread throughout the year, however, so revenues and earnings are artificially inflated temporarily, further exacerbating the seasonal pattern. In 1983 this seasonal dependence hurt profits. International revenues fell a little short of expectation but costs were fixed. Profits came in flat, quite a surprise after everything had pointed to another good gain all year, until the last minute.

Although MSA seems to be spreading itself a bit thin in numerous different applications software markets, there are big prospects if the software continues to be first rate and the company can keep control of itself. The IBM relationship and the personal computer software market will be driving forces. In the future, expect more acquisitions of software products and more concentration on the international market. Management owns half the stock in this company, so they'll run it their way. And that's been the right way so far. MSA calls itself The Software Company. It has the magic formula—an IBM connection. This business has an outstanding future. MSA is one of the best in the business. And John Imlay will insure it stays that way.

INFORMATICS GENERAL: DOING TOO MANY THINGS, NONE OF THEM WELL

Why is Informatics General such a frustrating company? Let me tell you. It is one of those companies that is permanently in transition, going from nowhere to nowhere, with elusive profits. It seems to be embarked on a perennial revitalization program. It appears to have difficulty focusing on a single market or business, preferring to dabble here, there, and everywhere. It does not seem to possess the characteristics needed for success in the software business: dynamics, innovation, creativity, single-mindedness of purpose. It is a company of large revenues ($198 million in sales) and little profit (5% pretax margins). It appears content to muddle along with annual sales growth of 10 to 20% in a business that is growing at more than twice that rate. It is similar to Computer Sciences, another company with potential but apparently going nowhere.

In all fairness, it should be pointed out that Informatics General is at least now making money. Through most of the 1970s, it ran in the red. Back then it was a subsidiary of Equitable Life, serving in part as a technical staff to support the health insurance claims processing business. In its outside activities (systems software and commercial data processing), it stressed market share over profits and lost over $5 million from 1974 to 1979. Since it was sold to outside investors by Equitable, profits have climbed steadily at more than 20% a year, though they are still at low levels. Sales, however, have been lackluster, expanding only 14% a year.

Informatics's revenues consist of 40% software, 35% data services, and 25% professional technical services. Part of its lackluster revenue performance stems from the slowdown in the data services market. Like all companies that offer remote time-sharing services, Informatics has suffered from the changes in that market (see Chapter 9). It also lost business in 1983 when Equitable took more data processing in house.

To get out of the doldrums, Informatics's key strategy for the future calls for a renewed concentration on software. Growth in that part of the company's business topped 20% annually from 1978 to 1983, but profit margins have been low, 5% before tax. It's the same old story: too many widely scattered products addressing too many markets. Informatics offers applications development software and inquiry/report writing software for cross-industry markets, as well as applications software packages for life insurance administration, law office management, and accounting firm management, among others. It would be difficult for any company to market effectively such an array of software. And Informatics is not especially accomplished in the art of selling to begin with.

Another strategy is to focus just on those vertical markets where the company has proprietary niches: law firms, insurance companies, the distribution and apparel industries, accounting firms, and government data libraries. Informatics can provide these customers with a specialized combination of services, including software, data processing, professional facilities management, and systems engineering. Revenue growth from these niche markets has been good: 24% annually. And profits have grown over 40% since 1979 but from a small base; so unfortunately, the profits from these vertical markets are still only half of what they are in cross-industry markets. Even though vertical-market profits are expanding twice as fast as those from the rest of the firm, it will be a while before they are a meaningful stimulation to overall corporate profits.

Informatics has potential: a broad base of customers, some good software and services, and it's in all the right markets. It suffers because it is in the backwater of these markets. It has to play catch-up in most areas except a handful of specialized vertical niche markets. The company is big but sluggish. Walter F. Bauer, the longtime chairman, is 60 years of age and has managed the firm too autocratically and too monotonously for too long. The president, Bruce T. Coleman, is younger. His background is in software, where Informatics is strongest. But as long as Bauer remains in charge, don't look for big dynamics here. If Coleman ever gets the reins, this company might change its stripes, shake off its lethargy, and realize its potential more fully. But don't hold your breath. Informatics has been a frustrating company for two decades. It has not done all that bad, but it could do worlds better. By the time it decides to go for it, it may be too late. This company would make an excellent acquisition for a number of other data services or software companies.

APPLIED DATA RESEARCH: IT TAKES MORE THAN A GOOD PRODUCT

Not too long ago (in 1979 to be exact), Applied Data Research was twice the size of its archrival, Cullinet. By 1982, however, Cullinet was bigger. It's not that Applied Data stopped growing. In fact, it maintained a solid 30% a year growth rate between 1976 and 1983. Cullinet simply grew faster, at 50% a year. So did the entire packaged software business, at 40% a year. It's not hard to fall behind in this business. You can't do *almost* everything right; you have to do *everything* right.

At Applied Data, the weakness is marketing. If for some reason you were not impressed by the fact that Cullinet came up with seminars to sell its database software, then consider the experience of Applied Data. This company didn't come up with seminars or anything like it to market its products, and today it is paying the price. Despite a 120-person sales force and excellent products, this company is bucking for the status of an also-ran when it should be leading the way. The problem begins with management. Applied Data is run by software development people who have the unfortunate notion that good products sell themselves. In a perfect world they would be right. Unfortunately, this is not a perfect world. A company that lacks effective marketing can find itself losing ground quickly.

In 1979–1980 a number of different problems converged at once: Large sums of money were needed to finish work on a newly acquired database management system, while at the same time, a number of other new products were seriously delayed. Customers who were awaiting the new products decided to license existing products on a short-term basis and defer their payments. On top of everything else, a long overdue marketing buildup was commenced, including the signing on of some European representatives. The company went into heavy debt—over half of its total capitalization, compared to virtually no debt at most software companies. Debt is always burdensome given the high cost of interest, as Applied Data soon discovered. Earnings dropped to around 6% after tax, and interest payments began to grow. That's what can happen when a company neglects marketing and product line development and then must play catch-up on a crash basis.

Today, Applied Data has its act back together—sort of. Its marketing, products, and balance sheet were all much healthier by 1981. Profits bounced back, though the margins have never returned to the levels of the mid-1970s. In 1983, however, the company suffered from a product cycle transition. A new product, IDEAL, was late, and competitive software product announcements interrupted business, leading to temporary red ink despite strong orders. So the company continues to show flashes of brilliance, punctuated by unexpected disappointments.

Perhaps the most confusing or controversial aspect of Applied Data is its accounting. Virtually all revenues are recorded up front, upon installing the software at the customer site. Yet the terms of 3- to 5-year leases or permanent license agreements often permit deferred payments spread over a period of years. Maintenance contracts, to upgrade the software, range 1 to 4 years in length (and the cost is obviously spread over this period), but again revenues are all recognized immediately upon the signing of the contract. Revenues and costs are not evenly matched. Current revenues are inflated. And there is virtually no way of predicting future sales or profits because there is little in the way of recurring revenues. The business depends on what the salespeople do in any particular quarter. And since clients spread their paychecks out over a long period, cash flow is usually negative.

Applied Data Research is in the right business, with generally good software products. Its potential is excellent, but its performance has been short of optimal: not bad, but not brilliant. It's a story of good but not outstanding growth, of respectable but not big profits, of fits and starts, and of spurts and fallbacks. The company's objective is 30% growth by 1988. That's good, but it's not quite up to the industry rate. It all traces back to financial management, accounting, marketing, and various product acquisitions (such as cable TV software) that misfired. The company has succeeded despite all this, and that's saying quite a bit. Applied Data Research is in the heavyweight class in the software arena all right, but it could have been a contender for the title.

COMPUTERVISION: CREATING THE FACTORY OF THE FUTURE

In 1969, the year Computervision was formed, the idea of an automated factory was just a gleam in the eye of far-thinking technology gurus and futurists. It was more hype than substance, the kind of idea the computer industry likes to come out with to shake people up a bit. It is controversial (because of the inevitable unemployment it will cause) as well as being sort of eerie. The idea of a big factory, humming along with no one inside—just robots and other computer-controlled mechanical devices—seems right out of the Twilight Zone. Today, 15 years later, it is still more dream than reality. Fewer than one out of five manufacturers have installed even a rudimentary form of factory automation. Yet the notion that industrial automation is the wave of the future no longer seems a pipedream. For American manufacturers, looking worriedly over their shoulders at the Japanese, it is considered a necessity for survival.

Actually, industrial automation doesn't start on the factory floor. It starts in the drawing room when the design and development of new products is carried out. This is where Computervision got its start, selling systems for computer-aided design (CAD). When a new product is being designed, the whole job becomes much simpler if it is done at a computer terminal. Drawing and drafting are eliminated (for the most part). Inspection and modification are easier. A design can be tested and retested dozens of times. Stress and structural analysis can be performed. Documentation for the design can be produced automatically. Productivity gains of as much as 5 to 1 are possible, depending on the application.

There are numerous markets for CAD systems—electronics, ar-

chitecture, automotive, aerospace, and a variety of equipment manufacturing industries—as well as a myriad of specific applications:
structural, mechanical, electrical, and civil engineering. Each one
requires special software. (Aha! Now you see the market potential.)

Computervision's strategy right from the start was to provide each
customer with a complete turnkey system, consisting of Computervision's own specially developed computer processor, as well as
all the software, peripherals, and support that the customer needs.
This total system approach was vital in the early days when Computervision was almost the only source for CAD/CAM. (CAM stands
for computer-aided manufacturing.) A heavy emphasis on developing complete customer trust and satisfaction has been another
key part of this strategy. Years ago when customers were unsure
whether CAD/CAM would work for them, they took a big risk in
committing to such expensive systems. Computervision guaranteed
satisfaction or would take the system back and refund the money.
GE, an early customer, took them up on their policy, and when GE
was ready to try CAD/CAM again later, it went right back to Computervision and subsequently became a major customer.

The strategy has paid off. Computervision's sales climbed from
$8 million in 1972 to over $400 million in 1983, a 43% annual
growth rate for more than a decade. With 25% of the market, Computervision is the leading CAD vendor, followed by IBM (20%),
and then Intergraph, Calma (Schlumberger), and Applicon (GE).
Turnkey systems are about two-thirds of the market, with the rest
being mainframe-based systems. The market is expected to grow
30 to 35% annually between 1983 and 1988, from under $2 billion
to $7 billion.

By relying totally on its own proprietary system, however, Computervision runs the risk of being surpassed by competitors. This
already happened once. The computer processor in Computervision's original system was a 16-bit minicomputer that eventually
was surpassed by superminicomputers, such as Digital Equipment's
32-bit VAX computers that are used by other CAD companies. Computervision was late in developing its own supermini and refused
to buy it on the outside the way Intergraph did.

Lately, however, the company has relaxed its all-or-nothing approach to product development. It is now acquiring software from

outsiders, such as the Medusa three-dimensional mechanical design and drafting package from Cambridge Interactive Systems. It also has a relationship with Sun Microsystems for intelligent work station terminals. In 1983, Computervision took things a step further, teaming up with IBM in secret nondisclosure joint R&D to offer a turnkey CAD system that could be tied into an IBM 4300 mainframe computer, permitting large-scale database management, which was not possible using Computervision's computer processor. This arrangement also qualifies the company as a value-added remarketer of IBM 4300 computers, to which it can add its CAD applications software and provide complete systems integration.

Like many others in this wild and woolly industry, Computervision has established an IBM connection. Why not? Computervision has firmly established itself as a leader in the market. The major restraint on its growth was customer attachment to IBM hardware. Now any IBM user can get a complete CAD system from Computervision and still be compatible.

Over the long term, Computervision will move more deeply into CAM (factory floor systems that take the data out of CAD and put them to work) as well as computer-aided engineering (CAE). The company will follow a strategy of being a total system supplier with a broad array of software for many CAD, CAM, and CAE functions. However, as the market fragments into specialty niches, this approach may be difficult to maintain. Customers have become sophisticated about factory automation and are mixing their systems with different vendors' products and software. The pioneering stage is over. New CAD/CAM start-up companies are flooding into the business, 100 in 1982 alone. Competition will undoubtedly intensify as more computer hardware and software companies get into this market and cut prices to obtain initial penetration. The Japanese know how to manufacture better than anyone and will surely begin to provide CAD/CAM systems based on their expertise in this discipline. And as Computervision reaches the $1 to $2 billion sales mark, it will find it more difficult to be creative, to get new leading-edge products to the market fast, and to stay flexible.

On top of everything else, the CAD/CAM/CAE market is one that is extremely sensitive to the ups and downs of the economy. Some of the markets Computervision serves, such as mechanical product manufacturing, are cyclical. Civil engineering projects are dependent on government spending. Automation of these industries is a deferrable expense during periods when business is bad, as Computervision discovered when its orders softened and profits temporarily tailed off in both the 1974–1975 and 1982 recessions. A resurgence commenced in 1983, spiked by a $100 million order from the U.S. Navy.

Computervision has a lot going for it. It is the leader in CAD, with over 5000 customers and an installed base of over $1 billion in equipment. It spends a hefty 11% of revenues on R&D. A "greenhouse" venture has been set up as an autonomous operation, with separate funding to nurture and sponsor new ideas and creativity. Talented engineers who yearn to spin off and start up a new venture do not have to leave the company to pursue their dreams. Computervision has big objectives: 35 to 40% annual growth; $1 billion in sales by 1986; $2 billion by 1989, and a return on equity of 25%. According to its chairman, Martin Allen, it also wants "to improve the industrial system" and overall "quality of life." These ambitious goals seem more than mere dreams. Allen and his team are dedicated and hard working, instilled with a Yankee work ethic. They are low key, with a certain straight-laced moral fiber. They take a no-frills, spartan approach to things. The day I interviewed Allen, we sat in his office munching tuna fish sandwiches and drinking soda over the noon hour, between his appointments. No airs here. This company has been through tough times and has been tested. It has a concern for its customers and employees. In my opinion, Computervision will go a long way. The market will be enormous, and this company will remain the leader. Success has not gone to its head. It is hungrier today than in the past. And Allen, the founder and pioneer, will remain in charge for some time to come.

INTERGRAPH: THE RIGHT WAY TO BE A SPECIALIST COMPANY

Intergraph started out in 1969 in Huntsville, Alabama, doing consulting studies for NASA and the Department of Defense. In one study, the company (known back then as M&S Computing) analyzed the CAD systems that were available for creating large-scale integrated circuits. It did not take very long for Jim Meadlock, the company's founder, to realize that this was a market with potential. But instead of going head to head against Computervision and other early entrants addressing the electronic and mechanical design markets, Meadlock decided to go after the mapping market. M&S (the name was changed to Intergraph in 1980) was off to the races in 1973 with its first CAD system for mapping and civil engineering. It pioneered the database management software that links data inside the computer to the picture on a graphics terminal. This remains its biggest technological strength. Later, other software programs were added to serve such markets as general cartography (energy exploration), utility facility management, plant design (chemical, petroleum, and power generation industries), architecture, mechanical and electronic design, and construction markets.

Still, the overall business thrust remains the same: computer-aided design. By keeping its focus narrow, by being a specialist in CAD alone, Intergraph has made it big. The company never tried to do everything.

It buys its large computer processors from Digital Equipment (VAX 32-bit superminicomputers, over 500 of them by mid-1983, making it Digital's largest VAX customer) and from Motorola (the 68000 microprocessors). Intergraph supplies its own proprietary software: Integrated Graphics Design Software and database management software.

By 1978 the company reached $20 million in sales and just over $1 million in profits. Five years later, the CAD business pushed revenues to $252 million and profits to $29 million, a 66% annual rate of growth in sales and 90% in profits over the span. Intergraph ranks a clear third in the market, behind only Computervision and IBM, and it is closing ground. It experienced no slowdown during the 1982 recession. Profitability is high, 20% margins; R&D is 13% of revenue, a hefty level. As the company markets its existing software and systems to an increasingly larger number of customers, there exists tremendous operating leverage.

Intergraph has a number of winning strategies. It intends to maintain its concentration in CAD, avoiding the temptation to overreach into CAM and other related sectors. It combines its software and hardware into a completely integrated, fully functional turnkey system. It does not sell just CAD software for other vendors' mainframe computers or for low-end microcomputers or graphics terminals. Customers can carry out an entire design project on its CAD system. An architect can do site planning and then design the building's foundation, structure, interior, air conditioning, electrical system, and plumbing—in short, create the whole building on the computer. The company follows a cross-engineering discipline strategy with its software packages, so that different data in a large project such as the one just mentioned can be integrated by the customer. Intergraph thinks like a computer systems company, not just a graphics terminal company. The graphics are really only a by-product of all the data anyway. It's the ability to manipulate and describe the data that is key.

Over the remainder of the decade, Intergraph must contend with competitive thrusts from two directions. At the high end, IBM and other mainframe and minicomputer companies are buying CAD software and adding it to their computers. From the other side, the intelligent work station and personal computer manufacturers are also coming into the market. The fully dedicated systems suppliers, which do not specialize in the hardware aspect of the computer industry, may get squashed in the middle. Price competition is rising. As the number of entrants proliferates, pricing becomes more important. When that happens, it is harder to make a good return on investment. Customers become confused, and that tends to make them gravitate to IBM despite its rather mediocre CAD software.

Over time, computing in general will become predominantly interactive. By concentrating in interactive graphics, Intergraph is a specialist company that figures to flourish for a long time. It is loaded with technical talent, over 500 engineers and technical people. Marketing has been built up to where salespeople number almost 100. The founder still runs the show and keeps the company on the straight and narrow, with the discipline, creativity, and humbleness that will insure future success. Meadlock's wife is also a long-time member of top management and a large stockholder. And Intergraph was disciplined with hard times early on. A number of employees who were paid in stock in lieu of cash hit pay dirt in later years when the shares surged and the company went public.

The facilities are modest, resembling old World War II Army barracks, outside Huntsville. This is high-tech among the cotton fields. No glitter. No fancy headquarters as a monument to management. Just work and a single-mindedness of purpose. Intergraph is an insurgent winner, the perfect example of a specialist strategy in the era of specialization.

TRIAD SYSTEMS: COMPUTERIZING MAIN STREET

Triad is the largest and most lucrative turnkey company in the business. It got that way by staking out a large and lucrative market: the thousands of auto parts dealers across the United States. Here Triad found a market narrow enough so that one system would fit all users but large enough to allow Triad to become a substantial company.

The system Triad sells is complete, from soup to nuts: hardware, software, service, training, and future software enhancements. The entry-level price for a Triad system is $50,000. By reducing receivables and inventory levels, and accelerating inventory turnover, the typical retail auto parts store recoups its investment in 9 to 18 months. The Triad system is well suited to its market. It better be. When a small retail business puts all its financial, accounting, inventory, and order entry procedures on one system, that system better work right. Nearly one-third of Triad's sales are follow-up business from existing customers. Sales were up 75% a year in the 3 years between 1978 and 1981, surging from $15 million to $78 million. By the end of 1983, Triad had sold 56,000 of its systems, garnering 75% of the auto spare parts computer market.

In the meantime, however, Triad has encountered one of the inevitable disadvantages of competing in a vertical market. In 1982, when the auto market hit the skids, so did Triad. Sales went flat that year, and in 1983 they were still up only 10%. Profit margins went from over 20% down to single figures. Triad's solution to this problem is to branch out into other vertical markets. It is never easy to develop another hot leading-edge product, to repeat the success of the first one. In its efforts, Triad has experienced mixed results. Because of its success with auto parts dealers, Triad reasoned it could do the same with a system for tire dealers, using the same software. Unfortunately, that turned out not to be the case. The same software could not be used. Triad had to start over again from scratch.

So the company decided to put its energies into another effort: retail hardware stores. This market seems to have even greater potential than auto parts. Although both markets have the same number of stores—about 38,000—only 10,000 to 12,000 auto parts stores are large enough to warrant a computer system. Already, the hardware market is off to a better start than the auto parts market, $20 million in annual sales after 3 years, gaining fast on Triad's $70 million auto parts business. The first move outside the original market is the toughest. Once the learning curve takes hold (i.e., after enough experience is gained), software and marketing for other vertical markets can be developed faster, with fewer mistakes. But it still takes time to get a reputation. After being in the hardware market 3 years, Triad has won endorsements from a number of national chains, five of which represent one-third of the market, including True-Value (7000 stores), American Hardware (3800 stores), and Ace Hardware (more than a thousand stores). Triad has 212 national accounts endorsing its auto parts system to over 10,000 independent stores, giving it 98% of the turnkey computer business that has become available so far by these outlets. Some 50% of Triad's total business derives from national accounts. That kind of sponsorship cannot be won overnight. It takes years of proven performance. The turnkey market is tough.

Looking to the future, Triad will adopt various strategies to meet some serious challenges. To open up more market opportunity, it is unbundling its prices, selling just a portion of the software or a scaled down system. That way an entry-level system can be bought for as little as $20,000, instead of $50,000. This may also forestall any challenges from personal computers that might make an inroad by being programmed for one job, say inventory.

The extent of Triad's vertical integration is unusual for a company its size: computer hardware assembly, operating and applications software, and direct sales and service. This level of overhead may not be advisable. The company may be trying to do too much, when it should be concentrating on software development and marketing. Such vertical integration could become an Achilles' heel, rendering the company inflexible and overwrought with hardware investment requirements.

The grand strategy, and the most ambitious objective, is to develop a total of six separate vertical markets by the end of this decade and 10 in 10 years, each having a sales potential for Triad of $100 million. Triad wants to "automate Main Street U.S.A.," according to its annual report. That's probably overreaching a bit. This company can do well just by pushing ahead in the hardware market and reaping the benefits of a cyclical recovery in the auto parts market. Software is critical. Any turnkey company that gets too big, too fast, by entering too many vertical markets, will become overextended. Triad is the class of the turnkey companies. Its future is solid because it is a specialist, offering a distinctive, heavily software-based system to a niche market.

REYNOLDS & REYNOLDS: TEACHING AN OLD DOG NEW TRICKS

Reynolds & Reynolds was started in 1866. Not many businesses, much less software companies, can lay claim to being over a century old. For most of its history, Reynolds has been a supplier of business forms. Ever since the automobile was invented, Reynolds has sold its forms to auto dealers. Reynolds virtually had that market all to itself, but it was not one to sit around and let the world pass it by. When the computer era came along, Reynolds met the challenge. First it started doing batch data processing for its auto dealer customers. Then when it became fashionable, it moved into on-line, time-shared data processing. Finally, it began selling entire turnkey computer systems. Reynolds buys its computers from IBM and NCR, develops its own software, and sells a system that does everything an auto dealer could possibly want in the way of data processing.

It has been a good business. Reynolds has made steady progress, becoming one of the 100 largest computer companies. The problem is that, since the late 1970s, Reynolds has been unable to go any further. The automobile market is becoming saturated, and it has become cyclical. Moreover, Reynolds has been getting some stiff competition from Automatic Data Processing in recent years. Reynolds showed no revenue growth in 1981 and 1982. Profits plummeted, and its computer business actually fell into the red. Overall, Reynolds's sales have expanded 15% annually over the past decade, to $252 million in 1983, but its profits have climbed only 7% a year. In late 1983 and during 1984, Reynolds is enjoying a resurgence in the auto dealer computer systems business based on the healthier state of the automobile sales. Profits began to bounce back but still not back to the record reached back in 1979. The question is sustainability. Sales of business forms, growing about 10% a year, still account for just under half of the company's total business.

So Reynolds is trying to crack other markets, but it can't seem to get it right. It is not without opportunities. It sells business forms to 8000 contractors (plumbing, heating, and electrical) as well as to 3000 physicians' offices. Unfortunately, Reynolds discovered that those markets require a lot of customization, were uneconomical to reach with direct sales representatives, and were resistant to the idea of laying out $35,000 for a computer system. The contractor turnkey effort was terminated in 1983. An effort to perform data processing for accountants has also been terminated, and tax preparation processing was scaled down to become a regional rather than national effort. Overall, Reynolds has been far too hesitant in its diversification efforts, waiting too long to make a decision and then making only a halfhearted effort. The investment of money and personnel into such efforts has been too limited. Too much talk and no action. The company's worst move was its effort to produce computers and terminals in house. This attempt at vertical integration was terminated in 1983, 3 years after it started. Reynolds now relies on the IBM PC and NCR's UNIX-based computers for its turnkey systems.

Reynolds's turnkey and data processing forte has always been software. It should stick to that. Recently, the company added a new wrinkle to its auto dealer systems, a word processing feature designed to help the dealers generate new business through mailings, instead of just using their computers for bookkeeping and accounting. Reynolds will also continue its effort to go after the market for doctors' offices. And lately it has been giving renewed attention to its forms business, adding thousands of retail stationery store distributors to go after that market.

Still, the big challenge will be to diversify away from auto dealers. After 5 years of trying, the results are dismal. Reynolds management would do well to step back and take stock of itself. Management at Reynolds is patriarchal, all managers having spent their entire careers at this Dayton, Ohio, company. The Grant family has owned a controlling interest since the 1930s. The folks at Reynolds have the highest of values and ethics. Perhaps they have been a little too courteous for too long. Reynolds needs to get tough, to bet big, to shake things up. After all, nice guys finish last.

A PIECE OF THE ACTION: FAST-EMERGING SMALLER SOFTWARE COMPANIES

There are numerous software firms with annual sales of under $100 million. And many of these have already made an important mark in the business. Niches vary from applications software for manufacturing and banking to mainframe systems software. They are too small at this stage to warrant a detailed discussion, but short summaries of some of these promising entrants follow.

Computer Associates International

Computer Associates will soon be joining the ranks of Cullinet and MSA. Started in 1976, in just 7 years it had sales of $90 million. The company swelled considerably in size following its 1982 acquisition of Capex. A leader, like Computer Associates, in the IBM systems software market, Capex accounted for one-third of the combined entity when acquired. More acquisitions appear to be on the agenda.

Computer Associates was an early leader in providing systems software for IBM installations that use the DOS operating system— mostly medium sized computer installations, about two-thirds of all IBM customer sites. Capex's product offerings included systems software products for IBM installations that use the OS operating systems, generally larger computers and more extensive configurations. Because DOS and OS are the two principal operating systems used with IBM and IBM-compatible hardware, Computer Associates now covers the waterfront.

Computer Associates is also making moves in applications software. It now offers Capex's line of financial modeling, forecasting, and budgeting software for IBM-compatible mainframes and certain Hewlett-Packard minicomputers. In 1982 the company also added an applications program for manufacturing and wholesale distribution. It is also taking on Cullinet with a new relational database management software. Computer Associates is scoring in a number of software markets and moving into new ones fast. It is going to be a heavyweight very quickly.

Pansophic

Pansophic specializes in systems implementation and applications development software used by the computer personnel involved in design and programming of new computer applications, as well as the control and security of existing programs. This is an over $1 billion market expanding at an almost 50% rate. Pansophic is also in database management systems. Its revenues have grown close to 30% annually since 1978, to $50 million in 1983. It competes with several of the established leaders—Cullinet, Informatics, and Applied Data Research—and is strongly positioned in its sector.

Two software products have been instrumental in putting the company in the forefront of the industry. One is EASYTRIEVE, a database management system that provides for the efficient retrieval and reporting of data from computer files without costly and time-consuming development of computer programs. EASYTRIEVE stands as No. 4 on the list of the most popular computer programs to date. The other is PANVALET, an operating system program that acts as a librarian to store and maintain source programs and protect them from inadvertent or unauthorized destruction or modification. PANVALET is No. 3 on the list of software products installed to date, with a total of over 4600 installations in 1983. Pansophic has a broad, direct sales force, recently supplemented by an OEM program to have applications software firms, such as Policy Management Systems, market Pansophic products to their own customers.

Pansophic has 7000 customers itself. Its software products have a long life cycle, making for a predictable stream of ongoing business. Continuous support fees comprise one-third of revenues. The company's objective is to expand 30% annually. Some of its software products are mature now, and it has made several marketing and new product development mistakes. Growth is coming from newer, less established products.

ASK Computer Systems

ASK has the distinction of being the most successful high-technology company ever founded and run by a woman. Sandra L. Kurtzig started ASK in 1978, when she was 26. It became a $50 million company in just 5 years. The objective is to top $100 million by 1985, to expand at a 40 to 50% rate. ASK staked out the manufacturing sector and has developed a wide array of applications software, all on a turnkey system, for such manufacturing management jobs as inventory, materials and engineering design, control of work in process, purchasing, and cost accounting. More recently software for such financial tasks as accounts receivable and payable, general ledger, order entry, scheduling, and planning has been added. The software runs on Digital VAX and Hewlett-Packard System 3000 computers. Competition stems mainly from IBM, COMSERV, Hewlett-Packard, and Martin Marietta, but ASK is the largest independent supplier of software for manufacturing.

The challenge is to retain a narrow, specialized focus. ASK has flourished by concentrating on manufacturing software, yet it has subsequently branched into financial, microcomputer, and database management software. This is still a small company. Perhaps it is trying to do too much, to be in too many different aspects of applications software. The manufacturing discipline itself is broad, offering a huge market opportunity. Yet the company's attitude is that, having mastered one market, it is time to move on to other areas. It could become overextended fast. Meanwhile, ASK steamrolls along, headed for a 50% growth year in 1984. And Kurtzig is in the record books as the first woman in Silicon Valley to achieve $50 million in net worth as the creator of a high-tech company, and she is barely over 30 years of age.

AGS Computers

AGS Computers is a $140 million company that has expanded at upwards of 50% annually during the 5 years ending 1983. Much of the growth has been via acquisition. Software, however, comprises only one-third of sales, or $50 million. AGS got its start doing custom programming and systems development projects for AT&T, Citibank, and other large, New York area corporations. From working with Bell Laboratories, it has considerable skills in UNIX operating system software. Then, through two acquisitions, the company got into the packaged software products business, concentrating on project and resource management and systems development related programs. Finally, the third leg of the stool is distribution of microcomputer products (such as Altos, Nippon Electric Company, and Televideo Systems) to computer and software systems integrators and retail stores. This high-volume, low-profit business is surging. Overall, AGS's mix of services and software is low in profit and not well focused. This company has technical skills and is fishing for avenues of high growth. Too many acquisitions have diluted its single-mindedness of purpose. More than half of sales in 1983 were from operations acquired over the previous 3 years. The record is good, but this hodgepodge of businesses will be difficult to manage. This company is confused.

Hogan Systems

Hogan is small, at $30 million in sales in 1983, but it has exploded from just $3 million in 1980 and appears to be a real comer. Hogan specializes in applications software for banks, offering all kinds of programs: a deposit system, loan processing, profit analysis, payment collection, terminal transaction processing, a card system, and financial information. It provides one-stop shopping for bank applications software, all under one umbrella. That is, these programs all work together, allowing a large integrated system to perform a number of tasks. The market is large: 400 banks and thrift institutions in the United States, of which Hogan already has 100 as customers, and another 400 abroad. These are large customers who buy large ticket items. Each of Hogan's software sales averages $900,000. Not many more than a dozen salespeople call on these prospects. There are fewer than 300 employees. This is leverage. And it's profitable: 25% margins. There is also volatility. One sale makes or breaks a quarter's profits, as the company discovered abruptly in late 1983. The focus is narrow. Hogan does one thing, banking applications software, and it does it well. Prospects for continued high growth appear favorable.

Policy Management Systems

Policy Management Systems provides applications software for the property and liability insurance industry and also offers certain data processing services for this vertical market out of four data centers. It essentially automates all insurance processing functions. As of mid-1983, 318 out of the total 1675 U.S. property and liability insurance companies, including the Kemper Group, were customers. Revenues went from $13 million in 1978 to over $60 million in 1983. Profitability was over 22% before tax in 1983. Contracts are 6- to 8-year license agreements, up to 40% paid up front (some ranging as high as $1 million or more) and at least 60% paid monthly (some as much as $38,000 a month) over the 6- to 8-year license period. This provides a highly predictable future flow of revenues. Policy Management Systems was spun out of Siebels Bruce & Company in South Carolina in 1981 and is still 50% owned by that insurance holding company. It is an extremely successful vertical-market applications software company, similar to Hogan in the banking market. It is a gold mine that should continue to flourish.

Wyly

Wyly's history is replete with harrowing financial horror stories, turnaround attempts, and a frustratingly dismal profit record over the past several years. Though revenues are $153 million, profits have not been higher than 5 million in any year for more than a decade, and were still almost nil in 1983, following a whopping loss in 1982. The business is a hodgepodge of software (37%), data services (49%), and turnkey systems (14%), following the termination of the used computer remarketing business. Half the software business is systems software, mostly mainframe performance monitoring and job scheduling programs, growing at a good clip. Applications software is largely for banks and financial institutions and accounting software for cross-industry customers. Wyly was still making numerous small acquisitions and going in multiple directions in 1983, and it was losing money again. The company has some significant revenue but does not appear to be going anywhere.

Microcomputer Software

The market for microcomputer software came into its own in 1983, with total revenues surging to $1.3 billion, a 75% increase over the prior year. By 1988, revenues are expected to be over $7 billion— about 14% of the total software market.

These figures only tell part of the story. Because of the retail mark-up, total sales of microcomputer software were $2.2 billion in 1983 and will be over $13 billion in 1988. Those kinds of numbers demand respect.

On the surface, it seems as if nothing could be easier than to write a personal computer program, form a company, and sell it. One hot software program and sales skyrocket into the millions, much of the revenue dropping right to the profit line. Overhead is minimal. And there certainly do not seem to be any major barriers to entry in the business. In 1983 there were 5000 companies selling personal computer programs. By the end of 1984, there will be 11,000 software programs available for the IBM PC alone.

So where's the rub? Well, like so many other aspects of the computer business, and in particular anything at all related to personal computers, things are not always what they seem. For starters, companies that come up with one great software program seem to have difficulty coming out with a second one. VisiCorp and MicroPro International have both produced major bestselling programs— VisiCalc and Wordstar. But both companies have found themselves in virtual eclipse only 12 months after seeing sales reach all-time heights.

Coming out with a follow-up bestseller is not the only problem. It seems that any best-selling program is immediately swamped by dozens of imitators. Some compete on the basis of price while others add extra features to leapfrog the original.

VisiCorp rode the fortunes of VisiCalc for some four and a half years until sales began to disintegrate in 1983 under pressure from

Lotus's 1-2-3 integrated spreadsheet program. Product leapfrogging is now so intense that the commercial viability of a typical personal computer software program is down to about a year.

Development, marketing, and advertising costs are skyrocketing. VisiCorp started selling VisiCalc on a $500 budget in 1978. It spent $10 million on its follow-on product, VisiOn, only to find itself forced to cut the selling price from $495 to $95 almost before it hit the market. Lotus raised $5 million to launch its 1-2-3 and spent $1 million of that in a few months just to advertise its introduction. And don't forget the big expense of training the retailer to sell the program effectively, and even training the consumer how to put it to use. Lotus trained over 1000 sales personnel in some 500 stores on its 1-2-3 product, and is advertising and holding training seminars for users all over the country.

As if these conditions were not enough, the retail distribution channel is getting clogged up. A store can only be proficient in selling so many programs. And there are even signs that some of the once abundant venture capital for personal computer software start-ups is beginning to get more scarce. Certain stocks, such as MSA and Lotus, slid sharply in the first half of 1984 and profit problems, such as the ones that have occurred at VisiCorp and MicroPro International, seem to be occurring more frequently.

Altogether, there are about a half dozen independent personal computer software firms that are clearing at least $40 million in revenues. Then there are the leading personal computer hardware manufacturers, of which the top six are each doing $60 to $110 million in software sales. Finally, publishers and other media purveyors are getting into the act, including CBS and Reader's Digest, to name just two. Here we take a look at four of the better known independents:

Microsoft

Microsoft is the leader in microcomputer software, topping $68 million in sales in 1983. Microsoft was founded in 1975 by 19-year-old William H. Gates III. As a Harvard dropout pursuing the software business, Gates developed numerous microcomputer software language products. The big breakthrough for Microsoft was its IBM connection that began in 1980 when IBM contracted for it to develop an operating system for the PC. Microsoft developed MS-DOS and it became an industry standard (the way CP/M once was) in only a couple of years, based on IBM's stunning PC success. Microsoft gets royalties on every PC sold, some $10 million in such royalties to date. It will also supply software for IBM's PCjr. Its Microsoft BASIC language had 1.5 million installations by 1983. The next big thrust will be into applications software programs for micros. This firm has an IBM connection that will take it to still greater heights in the future.

Lotus Development

Lotus shot from nothing in 1982 to $53 million in business in 1983 and probably will be well over to $100 million in 1984. Lotus is also riding the microcomputer boom with its 1-2-3 spreadsheet software package. It is surging so fast it is likely to be the microcomputer software leader in 1984, displacing Microsoft. Its new software, Symphony, adds word processing, communications, and more record keeping functions to 1-2-3. Lotus is one of the few micro software companies that has gone public. There will be many others to come. Its founder, Mitchell Kapor, netted $5 million in the initial public offering in late 1983, not bad for 2 years' work.

Digital Research

Started in 1976, Digital Research was one of the early micro software companies, having developed the CP/M operating system that was the industry standard for the 8-bit generation of micros. Its revenues were $48 million in 1983, but it faces a transition away from just operating systems and into applications software.

MicroPro International

The WordStar word processing software package for micros launched MicroPro International to $45 million in sales in 1983. But there have been problems along the way, including a question of survival in 1982, management changes, and personnel layoffs. Now it is launching other packages in hopes of doubling in 1984. This company has had a roller coaster existence and the future appears to be similarly boom–bust.

14

A New Wave: The Next Generation of Minicomputer and Mainframe Companies

Hardware has definitely lost its uncontested dominion over the realm of computers, but it is not about to be banished from the kingdom altogether—not yet anyway. In computers, as in mousetraps, there is always room for a better way. For those companies that can master the industry's new competitive conditions (fragmented specialty niches, standardized technology, overly brief product cycles, etc.), there is still lots of opportunity out there.

Already a new wave of companies is finding this out with products aimed at the traditional mainframe and minicomputer markets. Instead of simply pumping out computers that are distinguished by being cheaper or more powerful than the competition, these companies are making computers that have something else going for them: a radically new architecture.

The trend toward multiprocessor fail-safe computers is at the forefront of the new wave. Up until now, most computers have been designed with one central processing unit. This single-processor architecture—referred to generally as the Von Neumann architecture, after John Von Neumann, the Hungarian-émigré mathematician who played a prominent role in the early development of computer technology—is a simple, efficient design, but one that poses a great risk to the user. What happens when the processor (or any other part of the system) breaks down? Unless you happen to have another computer on standby—an expensive and unwieldy safety precaution—you are out of luck. In the early days of batch processing, when computers were given work one batch at a time to complete before the next batch, such breakdowns, albeit annoying, were not as pressing a concern as they are in today's environment of continuous interactive, on-line processing. A computer system with a multiprocessor or parallel processing architecture is becoming essential in many organizations (such as banks, airlines, and stock exchanges) that depend on computers to perform customer transactions around-the-clock. Multiprocessor architecture also opens the way toward major improvements in computer performance that can be likened to the greater power of an automobile engine with dual carburetors.

Tandem was the first of the new-wave hardware companies with its line of dual-processor, nonstop computers. At a time when most computer hardware was being reduced to a commodity-like existence, Tandem outfoxed the market with a radically new hardware design that users desperately wanted (although, as we shall see, software plays a great role in it). Tandem revenues went from virtually zero in 1976 to $450 million in 1983. It is so far ahead of the market that, after 8 years, it is still without significant competition, although that situation is now changing. Tandem will not be alone for long.

Another key aspect of the new computer architecture is flexible modular design. In the past, a computer system was judged on the number of terminals it could support at any one time—1, 2, 4, 16, 32, and so on. The new wave of hardware will be judged on how many actual computers (not terminals) can be linked in networks, sharing processor power, software programs, data, and images with one another, and on the ease with which this sharing can take place. In Tandem's current system, thousands of Tandem computers can be connected in a network covering as many as 255 geographic locations. This networking capability is the main selling point of the most successful of the new office computer and work station

companies, Convergent Technologies and Apollo. They have networking as a standard feature. In the coming era of systems integration, this capability will be a feature without which no computer
company can hope to survive.

Of course, these advances in computer architecture would have
been impossible without the major increases in microprocessor
performance—advances that show no sign of abating. Microprocessor chips are available from Intel (the 86 series) and Motorola
(the 68000 series) that can be configured so as to equal in power,
at under one-tenth the cost, the Digital Equipment VAX-11/780
superminicomputer that was introduced in 1978. New microprocessor chips, created through a process known as complimentary
metal oxide semiconductor (CMOS, for short), will have 30,000 to
50,000 gates. Older chips, based on emitter-coupled logic (ECL) or
transistor-to-transistor logic (TTL), are capable of only 2000 gates
per chip. Vast improvements in performance are also possible because of a microprocessor operating system, UNIX, which is rapidly
becoming an industry standard (even IBM may soon announce UNIX
availability across all product lines). UNIX will be the standard
and will take a major role in this new-wave supermicro phenomenon.

For the old-line minicomputer companies already battered by
personal computers, these new-wave start-ups are another unwel-
come development. There is no way such companies as Digital
Equipment, Data General, or Hewlett-Packard can ever hope to compete with these upstarts. They are too committed to past computer
hardware design architectures, and the myriad software programs
developed for the existing products. To change now to a whole
new line of incompatible equipment would be devastating to their
customers who use current products and software. They could not
upgrade to the new products. In short, these companies cannot
participate fully in the microprocessor era. To remain compatible
with their old product lines and at the same time try to come up
with new performance standards they would have to create expensive, custom-made chips, and even then the performance of their
computers will be no match for the new-wave architectures. It's a
double-bind: new chips and new architectures.

The old-school companies are constrained not only technologically but also by way of habit and practice. Engineers do things the traditional way. Thinking is narrow and unoriginal. Bureaucracy, hardening of the arteries, bloated organizational structure, decision by committees, loss of the creative entrepreneurial spirit—all this makes it more difficult and time consuming to get new products out of R&D.

With no obligation to the past, no inhibiting commitments, only the new wave has the freedom to take the industry in new directions. Small and entrepreneurial, they also have the energy it takes. This is the beginning of the new industry order. And already there are close to 100 such supermicro companies in the business. The list of start-ups is bulging: Sun Microsystems, Synapse, Stratus, and others. Who cares about the potentially troublesome hurdles still ahead—marketing difficulties, widespread customer confusion, the looming presence of IBM? That's all the more reason for the captains of this new industry order to take their companies public, make their millions, and then keep all options open for a possible quick exit. After all, that's part of the new order too, isn't it?

TANDEM COMPUTERS: THE NONSTOP WORLD OF JIM TREYBIG

Tandem can be summarized in one word: Treybig. Tandem's founder, James G. Treybig, is a colorful iconoclast, a guru, a radical thinker about computers and management who has created a company as unusual as his style. Tandem had over $400 million in sales in 1983, up from nothing in 1976. From six customers in 1977, the list has expanded to 758, with a total installed base of some 6,397 processors. Tandem's computers are no backwater, secondary product. They are critical to the on-line transaction processing of major banks, airlines, and telephone companies. And the customers know it. Customer loyalty is the highest in the industry, above even IBM.

What makes Tandem run? For openers, the product—the NonStop computer. It never stops. That is the very basis of its design and function. In a Tandem system, two or more processors operate in parallel as an interactive network. If one processor fails, the rest of the system keeps running. This multiple computer architecture not only minimizes the risk of system failure but also protects the data from being damaged or destroyed. Because of its unique design, it is easy to add more computer processors to the network. Originally, a single Tandem system could operate with 16 processors. By 1979, with the introduction of EXPAND software, up to 4080 computers could be attached in as many as 255 different locations.

The key to Tandem NonStop computers is software—extensive, complicated, sophisticated software that allows the computers to work together, yet also work around any unit that may have failed. The software includes an operating system, database manipulation programs, database inquiry and report writing programs, program development aids, communications software, and the like. Established mainframe and minicomputer manufacturers cannot duplicate Tandem's fault-tolerant computer systems. It involves more than just hooking a few extra processors together. It requires all new architecture and software.

Almost as important as the product strategy at Tandem is the management style and leadership of Jim Treybig. Treybig's Texas drawl and self-assuredness, combined with his sincere care for and trust in his employees, is renowned in Silicon Valley. This is where people-oriented, California-style, high-tech management culture all started. Treybig is both the gospel and the keeper of the creed. Everything, from product shipment schedules to employee lifestyles, figures into his management philosophy. Tandem may be the closest company yet to creating a truly democratic atmosphere. Everyone benefits from the company's success more or less equally. Treybig's office is no different from that of the lowest-paid programmer—small and unassuming. There is an atmosphere of trust at Tandem. Everyone is in it together. All understand the essence of the business. Friday afternoon beer busts include everyone from the president to the plant janitor. Everyone communicates, from the highest to the lowest level, allowing cross-pollination. Every employee gets a 6-week sabbatical after 4 years of employment. Recreation facilities include a pool as well as volleyball and basketball courts. Single parents, prevalent in the high-tech country of California, bring their kids over on the weekends and grab a few hours in the office while their offspring splash around. Treybig pays attention to his people and reaps the benefits: Productivity rises. And Treybig fights for creativity, to preserve the small-company atmosphere. Tandem has the most sophisticated company-wide electronic mail system of any of the 40 computer companies I visited for this book. And it is used. Some 4000 employees can query the boss from as far away as Kowloon, Hong Kong, by merely hitting a few keys. Tandem is different. It is almost a cult.

Looking to the future, Tandem faces a number of challenges. Despite the happy atmosphere, there has been management turnover at the top. Three of the four founders (all but Treybig) have departed. Many early members of management, after they cleaned up financially with the stock they held, lost the will to work at the torrid pace and left. As Tandem gets larger, heading toward the $1 billion level, it will be difficult to retain the small-company creative atmosphere. Growth slowed to 35% in 1983 after almost doubling in every prior year. The company pushed growth too hard during the recession, at an unsustainable rate, and incurred accounting restatement problems once it discovered some business was booked prematurely. After that, it had to tighten up its financial controls and procedures, sacrificing some freedom and decentralized authority. Some competitive newcomers on the horizon will use inexpensive microprocessors to provide computer redundancy, instead of the highly sophisticated hardware-software solution developed by Tandem. And Tandem, like other more traditional computer vendors, is now committed to its architecture and software, rendering it less flexible in this era of microprocessor technology. Its 16-bit design cannot easily be upgraded to 32-bit capability.

Tandem wants to eventually be one of the two or three surviving mainframe companies, reaching $1 billion in sales within a few years. Treybig believes a high-tech company must grow or it will be destroyed. Tandem is likely to flourish for a number of years. It will continue to make sizable inroads into the mainframe market, and competition will be minimal. Tandem's products are so necessary for computer users that demand for them will continue to be strong. And as long as Jim Treybig is still around, this company will hold together.

CONVERGENT TECHNOLOGIES: MAKING COMPUTERS FOR OTHER COMPUTER COMPANIES

Convergent was formed in 1979 by a couple of ex-Intel managers who conceived of a product that would integrate the "converging technologies" of 16-bit micros, storage devices, and local communications networks, all in one system. All these technologies were widely available and certain products on the market utilized one or the other, but no product combined them all so effectively and innovatively as Convergent's. Convergent's product was a full-fledged work station—actually a system of work stations, all tied together, sharing data, storage, and peripherals—and it was a 16-bit architecture. A 16-bit microprocessor, as compared to an 8-bit machine, provides faster operations, greater accuracy, and sharply expanded main storage capacity. The newer 32-bit chips will vastly obsolete the 16-bit chips, as power and capability will be enhanced geometrically. Higher level program languages can be used, making the machine easier to operate. More than one application program can be used at the same time. High-resolution graphics are possible. Machine performance can equal that of minicomputers and even certain mainframes.

With a price tag of $8,000, Convergent's integrated work station was a breakthrough in performance, flexibility, size, and price. It had 1 million bytes of memory, was multifunctional, and, most importantly, could be clustered into local networks. Later, a $4,000 individual, stand-alone work station was also introduced. Convergent set a new standard, a new performance curve. It leapfrogged into the minicomputer and terminals markets with a new approach that was more flexible and affordable and could be expanded piece by piece. The minicomputer companies quaked. So did the makers of small business computers and the old-line distributed data processing companies. Convergent availed its products to other computer manufacturers in need of such systems. The response was overwhelming, leading to the second strategy.

This second tack called for Convergent to concentrate on the OEM market exclusively. Convergent would do no direct selling. It would be the innovator and manufacturer. No sales organization, no service, and no maintenance. Keep it simple. A small company should specialize in what it knows best. Burroughs signed up, then NCR, then a long list of prominent computer companies: Four-Phase Systems (Motorola), Prime Computer, Gould's Systems Engineering Laboratories, Thompson-CSF, Raytheon, ROLM, C-3, M/A Com, Datapoint, and AT&T. Burroughs bought 48% of the company's output in 1982; NCR bought 16%. Burroughs was over 50% of the business in 1983. Although it was still a start-up, Convergent had instant credibility. To entice and seal customer relationships with such blue-chip computer vendors, Convergent sells them stock purchase warrants and gives certain important ones manufacturing rights. Manufacturing rights could be a vulnerability if those rights are ever exercised. The company could lose a huge portion of its business. Convergent's international marketing is done by TRW. That's all right when you are a start-up but risky once a company is established. Just ask the folks at Datapoint, who paid $100 million to reacquire their international marketing rights from TRW. In just 3 years, Convergent has signed an extensive lineup of OEM customers, but overdependence on the OEM channel may become a disadvantage eventually. It's an easy trap to fall into, an easy way to obtain size fast. But control over the end market is lacking.

Right now, Convergent Technologies is laughing all the way to the bank. The company shot from $13 million in sales in 1981, to $96 million in 1982, to over $164 million in 1983. Sales could top $300 million by 1985. The company has also added two new product lines: the 32-bit MegaFrame superminicomputer and the NGen line of work stations. The 32-bit MegaFrame is a multiprocessor system using the Intel 80186 and the Motorola 68010 microprocessors. Those components can be bought these days for $25 to $30 each. The MegaFrame was developed on a crash basis in 1 year. It is a parallel processor, so several can be hooked together and expansion of the system is easy. It has a tailored UNIX operating system and sells for $17,000 to $110,000, depending on the size of the configuration, anywhere from 8 to 128 work stations.

NGen is the new family of work station products, using the Intel 80186 micro. WorkSlate, the microportable product in this line, was featured on the cover of American Express's 1983 Christmas catalog, selling for $900. This product will use Intel's new 386 32-bit micro, once available. Convergent's strategy is to leverage the hell out of commercially available microprocessors in any number of innovative, price-competitive (based on volume) products from personal computers to superminis to intelligent work station terminals. It started a wave. Now there are waves of others coming right behind, all using the same microprocessor components, the same UNIX operating system software, and employing innovative design architectures. Convergent is not alone anymore. And the endless line of new microprocessors is swamping the traditional minicomputer and even mainframe computer companies.

Convergent was early, but its path will not be smooth. Already there has been great self-impact and disruption caused by the new generation of NGen work stations. Orders for the old integrated work station line fell off in 1983, as customers awaited the new NGen in 1984. Sales flattened out for three or four quarters in a row and profits plummeted. There were simply too many new products all at once, impacted by a shortage in the new 32-bit microprocessor chips. Because the company must now manage three distinct product pursuits, its ability to focus is being weakened. This splitting of the company into three pieces could be risky where it's growing at such a torrid pace. There are too many products, with too short a life cycle. Keeping effective managerial control will be a challenge. There is little quarter-to-quarter predictability or backlog to fall back on. The handful of large OEM customers have wide flexibility in ordering. Convergent has insufficient control over the inventory pipeline or the ultimate sell-through by the OEM computer vendor customer. Dependence on Burroughs as a customer for over half the business is a terrible risk.

The biggest uncertainty of all is the founder and president, Allen H. Michels. He is a hard-driving, glib, wisecracking power wielder. Michels calls all the shots but seems overly haughty. His management team is intense, with a lot of vitality and energy. But one gets the impression that this culture exists because Convergent has been a money train. Growth has been exceptional, and risk has been rewarded. Michels' unique fire and brimstone approach to management has worked like a charm so far. But is that style a foundation upon which a long-term enterprise can be built? One wonders.

APOLLO COMPUTER: A NEW-WAVE COMPANY SHOOTING FOR THE MOON

Apollo Computer is the best and brightest of the new wave. It has done all the right things. Apollo has taken advantage of a customized 32-bit VLSI microprocessor (Advanced Micro Devices); low-cost random access memory chips; high-resolution graphics display technology; rigid disk drives; the UNIX operating system; Pascal high-level language; and networking architecture to link its computers together. Its product is a powerful, flexible work station that sells for as little as $10,000. It is equivalent in power to a Digital VAX or an IBM 370/158, but it is the size of a desk-top terminal. Speed is almost 1 MIPS. Internal memory ranges from 1.5 to 3.5 megabytes, depending on the model. The product line is called DOMAIN, for Distributed Operating Multi-Access Interactive Network. These are 32-bit superminicomputers of a new order, a new class—superminis packaged almost as microcomputers. Theoretically, other established computer companies (IBM, Digital Equipment, Prime Computer) could have done the same thing, but reality prevented it. Only new companies like Apollo can start with all new architectures, ride the new technology curve, and leapfrog the old-line companies.

The market Apollo is addressing is the technical and professional one of scientists, designers, modelers, and software programmers. Computer-aided design is particularly well suited to Apollo's products and is more than half the company's market at present. Digital Equipment once dominated the technical computer market with minis and later superminis that sold for $25,000 to $500,000. That sector is now being captured by desk-top computers that range from $13,000 to $30,000 in price and superminicomputers that go for $27,000 to $80,000, all built with 32-bit VLSI microprocessors and new networking architecture. Apollo computers can be linked together in a network, sharing data, software, and images. At the same time, each computer or work station is a powerful processor in its own right, capable of performing 15 separate processes concurrently.

Apollo has done more than just design a fast machine with communications software. It has allocated the resources to back its products up. It has built a sales force as well as a maintenance and service organization. It also has an ongoing stream of new products, such as the new supermini-class work station announced in 1983, offering a nearly threefold price/performance improvement over the existing 2-year-old product. All the while, the company is retaining its concentrated focus on one market—powerful, compact, high-performance 32-bit interactive computers for technical, scientific, and engineering customers. The strategy has worked beautifully. Having started up operations in 1980, Apollo generated its first sales, $3 million in 1981. It turned a tiny profit on $18 million in sales in 1982 and recorded over $80 million in sales and a $13 million profit in 1983. It will likely reach sales of over $150 million in 1984. The company shipped its first thousand computers by mid-1983.

Apollo is the undisputed leader of the 32-bit microprocessor technology product parade. It also carries with it a couple of disadvantages. Three of the founders and top management, including John W. Poduska, Sr., the chief executive officer, are technical types that we surmise are more enamoured with breakthrough products and technological advances than with the inevitable tedium in managing a large company. They were all instrumental in developing the Prime Computer product line. We suspect they are in it for the thrill of technology rather than to build a $1 billion company. Once things get a little boring or unchallenging, they may set their sights on other ventures. Poduska was vice-president of R&D at Prime Computer and is no doubt a technological genius, but these are hardly the qualifications for a chief executive officer of what is likely to be a sizable company in a very short period.

Another risk is Apollo's heavy dependence on two computer-aided design customers, Auto-Trol Technology and Calma (GE), and one computer-aided engineering firm, Mentor Graphics. These three companies combined account for over 50% of total sales. Until the customer base broadens, any setback by one of these customers would have a quick negative impact on Apollo's sales.

Apollo is in the right place with the right stuff. Its innovative products will sustain its burgeoning growth for quite some time.

EMULEX: A NEW-WAVE PCM

Consider the following: As of the end of 1983, 31,000 VAX super-minicomputers, 300,000 LSI-11 computers, and 323,000 PDP-11 minicomputers had been installed by Digital Equipment. A company could do quite nicely selling plug-compatible products aimed at this market. And Emulex has done exactly that. From $5 million in 1980, sales ballooned to $45 million in 1983 and are likely to reach $85 million in 1984. Profits are exceedingly high: 26% margins. Originally, Emulex's product was tape drive controllers. Later it added disk drive controllers. Over 20,000 such disk drive controllers have been sold in the form of plug-in boards that can be inserted into Digital Equipment computers at customer sites. Next came a line of communications controllers for Digital computers. All these greatly enhance the capability and flexibility of Digital machines at low cost. Emulex sells board by board. Digital will sell only the entire computer. Finally, full tape and disk drive peripheral subsystems were added to the product line. At this stage, there is a good balance among disk controllers (44%), communications controllers (26%), and full disk and tape drives (17%).

Emulex's strategy is to address the Digital Equipment market with niche products superior to those offered by Digital itself. Digital has sold more computer units (not including personal computers) to more individual sites than any other manufacturer. Emulex has sold more controller boards for Digital machines than any other third-party supplier. It's a tremendous target market. Emulex reaches its customers through dealer remarketers that act as middlemen in reaching end users. It also uses OEM systems houses that soup up Digital computers and add other hardware or software for specific applications. Direct sales are small but expanding as the company grows. Being a relatively small company attempting to reach a broad, fragmented customer market, the indirect sales route was the only way possible. In doing this, though, Emulex faces an inevitable and wrenching transition to direct end-user sales, a costly buildup, and a sensitive issue once the dealers see the company competing against them.

In the future, the company will begin to branch out from the Digital-compatible market. Though it has penetrated only 5% of the Digital controller market, that was the easy portion. It is planning to introduce an IBM-compatible personal computer disk drive controller board. It will also expand its own Digital-compatible 5 1/4 inch rigid disk drive business. Emulex's advantage is its niche approach to large installed computer bases where a single product can sell readily to thousands and thousands of customers. The market already exists. The products are low-ticket items that can be stamped out like cookie cutters. Marketing costs are minimal for now.

However, as Emulex achieves size, this approach may not be as easy anymore. Emulex is not exactly creating an original product, nor is it going after an original market. It is in the plug-compatible add-on business, in this case with Digital instead of IBM. Digital may be an easier target than IBM, especially in 1983–1984, when it is in such organizational and product disarray. Still, the PCM business is risky. Digital can make moves to thwart Emulex as it becomes a greater threat. Emulex can still alter course quickly at this stage. Its business is largely at the board level, supplying components rather than full-fledged computers or peripherals. But sooner or later it will want to move into end-user products, such as the disk drives it is already involved in. This is another transformation fraught with complications and problems. Most companies that begin as component suppliers cannot make the changeover to end-product emphasis.

Emulex is on a tear. It is exploiting niches by supplying innovative, advanced products based on VLSI technology. Technology has made it possible for Emulex to outdo Digital in certain narrow product areas, and Emulex has made a thriving business out of it. It's a new-wave company in an old plug-compatible market. It will surge for a few more years before it hits the inevitable transitions that companies like it must go through.

ENCORE COMPUTER: WHAT'S LEFT AFTER YOU PASS YOUR PRIME?

Encore Computer had yet to sell a single product at the time this book was published, but it is already a company to be reckoned with. Like Trilogy Systems (Gene Amdahl's new start-up), Encore has credibility because of the people who are leading it—a team of heavyweights headed by Kenneth G. Fisher, the ex-president of Prime Computer.

Fisher made Prime the wonder company of the 1970s and is sure he can outdo that performance in the 1980s. Encore (like Convergent and Apollo) is going after the work station market and a lot more, with a 32-bit multiprocessor-based product that uses the UNIX operating system. The key will be a unique architecture based on development work done by Hydra Systems (acquired by Encore), C. Gordon Bell, and a team of Carnegie-Mellon experts. A massive networking system will be available in which up to 256 Hydra processors and over 100 work stations can be linked in a local area network, parallel processing if you will. Like many of the other new-wave hardware companies, Encore is betting that major market opportunities will emerge as the traditional minicomputer and mainframe companies find themselves unable to adapt to the new architectures of the microprocessor era. Specific market niches that Encore plans to go after include computer-aided design, transaction processing, federal government systems, graphics, and business data processing. Initial capitalization for Encore will be some $20 million. A direct sales force is being built. Vertical integration will be limited to final assembly and testing (and to the R&D laboratories) so as to maintain flexibility and a low-cost structure. Too much integration into components and peripherals leaves a company highly vulnerable to built-in overhead costs, an overstretched R&D budget, and inability to focus on the mainstream business.

With this approach, Fisher has established the prerequisites that he believes will allow Encore to avoid the hazards facing other new-wave companies: weak marketing; lack of a strong follow-up after the initial product breakthrough; problems in managing rapid growth; and customer confusion over the proliferation of networking alternatives in the coming era of integration. Fisher is structuring Encore to take advantage of these conditions.

If nothing else, Encore has a lineup of management talent that is all-pro all the way. In a mere 6 years, Fisher led Prime from a $7 million floundering start-up to a $350 million operation, an 88% compounded rate of growth. Henry Burkhardt III was a cofounder of Data General in 1968 and a key member of the management team there until leaving in 1976, when the company was running $200 million in sales. Burkhardt is steeped in computer design, manufacturing, software programming, and finance. C. Gordon Bell was with Digital Equipment from 1960 to 1983, most recently as vice-president of engineering and chief technical officer. At Digital, Bell was responsible for research, design, and development of all computer hardware, software, and systems, particularly the VAX 32-bit superminicomputer product line. Robert G. Claussen was vice-president of domestic sales at Prime for 7 years. Julius L. Marcus was group manager–engineering at Digital. And the list goes on. This is an impressive group.

Fisher's goals for his new company are big. He wants to earn a 60% return on investment. The sales objective is nothing less than $1 billion by 1990 and 10% net profit margins. His products will offer a 5 to 1 price/performance advantage over existing mini and supermini competition. Some products will be developed in house; some technology will be acquired. Most of the product line sectors will function as independent business units (IBUs). Marketing will be done centrally, as will finance and manufacturing. Development will be done at the more remote, small, creative IBUs.

That's the plan. It is a plan with chutzpah. It has to be. Surviving in today's industry requires no small amount of chutzpah. Anyway, Apollo and Convergent Technologies have already staked out the work station market. To survive, Encore has to offer something better. If anyone can pull this off, Fisher, Burkhardt, and Bell are the ones. Even if it is only one-quarter as successful as planned, this company will triumph. Stick around for Fisher's, Burkhardt's, and Bell's Encore. It will be quite a show.

CRAY RESEARCH: ALONE AT THE TOP, BUT NOT FOR LONG

In the rarified and highly select world of supercomputing, the market belongs not to one company, but to one man: Seymour Cray. In the northern reaches of Wisconsin, far away from Silicon Valley or any other high-tech center, Cray labors away at the craft for which his name has become synonymous: the design of the world's most powerful computers.

Cray, you must understand, is a bit of a hermit. He's a genius who is only comfortable wearing lumberjack flannel shirts and going to the laboratory near his home in Chippewa Falls. At Control Data in the early 1960s, he invented that company's line of 6600 and 7600 mainframes. He also created the architecture and design of the 205 supercomputer that Control Data still sells today.

Although Control Data, at Cray's wish, built him his laboratory in Chippewa Falls, after a while Cray tired of the structured environment of the large company and bailed out. This was quite a surprise at the time and caused Control Data to leave the supercomputer market for most of the 1970s. Cray, meanwhile, started his own supercomputer company in 1972. It became the dominant force in supercomputers by the late 1970s. Nonetheless, Cray found that his position as chairman and chief executive officer kept him out of the laboratory too much. So in 1981, he relinquished all his titles (including his board seat) and returned to his lab, becoming the exclusive R&D contractor to his firm, doing the things he does best: designing the most powerful computers in the world.

As you may have surmised by now, such an activity is one not best suited to committee work, the Japanese approach. Even mighty IBM admitted defeat in the 1960s and never tried again. Only Seymour Cray has a track record here.

A supercomputer is a high-speed, very powerful mainframe computer. To be technical, it is a *vector processor* with a complete set of instructions that make it uniquely capable of operating on arrays of numerical data. A supercomputer is many times more powerful than even the most expensive commercial mainframe. While an IBM 3084 mainframe is capable of processing at 27 MIPS, the Cray X-MP supercomputer can perform at 630 million floating point operations per second (MFLOPS).* That makes the Cray machine 23 times more powerful than the IBM 3084. The X-MP is also quite expensive, costing over $12 million, compared to $8 million for the IBM 3084. (By 1990, Cray intends to have a supercomputer that will operate at 10,000 MFLOPS, similar to the goal of the Japanese in their supercomputer project.)

---

* In large numerical calculations, the decimal point "floats" over many positions to yield much greater accuracy. FLOPS is the common measurement used to compare supercomputers.

Supercomputers are used for a variety of scientific jobs: weather forecasting, petroleum exploration, nuclear research, fluid dynamics, aerospace design, structural analysis, stress testing, and biomedical research. Some 60% of all machines are bought by the government. The Atomic Energy Commission, the U.S. Weather Bureau, the Department of Defense, scientific research laboratories (e.g., Jet Propulsion Laboratory, Cal Tech) and universities (e.g., M.I.T.) are typical customers.

The market is small, but Cray Research has found it to be lucrative. In 1972, when the company started out, it had a staff consisting of a handful of the world's best large-scale computer designers, in addition to Cray himself. In 1977, after installing three machines, the company was profitable. Profits have climbed each year since. Cray sold 9 machines in 1980, 13 in 1981, and 15 in 1982. Things slowed a bit in 1983 (16 were sold) but are picking up again in 1984, with 22 expected to be shipped. It cost only $8.5 million to design the Cray 1, and it sold for $9 million. Profits have expanded 35% annually in recent years, and revenues topped $169 million in 1983.

Competition has not been much of a factor to date. There was none until Control Data reawakened with its model 205 in 1982, leapfrogging the original Cray 1 and causing Cray to adjust prices and bring out the X-MP to put it back in the vanguard. On the horizon, there are stirrings from the Japanese: Fujitsu, Hitachi, and Nippon Electric Company (NEC). The first two already have products for the Japanese market, but they have not yet been seen in the United States and software is lacking. It is expected that Amdahl eventually may sell the Fujitsu machine in the United States.

Regardless of some potential competition, there is no doubt about Cray's continuing leadership in this market, as long as Seymour Cray is the brains behind the development effort. However, it is likely that the business will become more price competitive and that retaining 75% market share will be a challenge. While innumerable pretenders have tried and failed in supercomputers (Texas Instruments, IBM, Burroughs, and Control Data), there will be further attempts by others—the Japanese, perhaps IBM again, a little company called Denelcor; and a new Control Data spin-off, ETA Systems, headed by the other Control Data master computer de-

Supercomputer Model	Performance M FLOPS[a]	
Cray 1/M	250	
Cray X–MP	630	
Cray 2	1000	(available 1985)
Control Data 205	400	
Fujitsu VP–200	500	
Hitachi S–810/20	630	
NEC SX–2	1300	(available 1985)

[a]Millions of floating point operations per second.
Source: International Data Corporation, National Bureau of Standards.

signer, Lloyd Thorndyke. Control Data's intentional spin-off of its supercomputer operations signals its desire to avoid the heavy investment requirements there and possibly its eventual retreat from that business altogether.

The ultimate question is the long-term market potential of supercomputers: How many users are out there who could possibly want one? It may be only a $200 to $300 million a year market, with 100 to 200 potential users. Cray already has three-quarters of the business. This market is economically very sensitive. When the government budget came under scrutiny in 1982 and the oil exploration business tailed off, Cray suffered an order slowdown. Cray adjusted by cutting the price of the 1/M supercomputer in half (to $4 million) and priced its 1/S similarly, to open up a whole new world of commercial supercomputer users. The strategy seems to be working. General Motors, Grumman, and Nippon Telephone signed orders in 1983.

Other challenges loom. With the introduction of the Cray 2, the architecture of the Cray line will be changed dramatically. The Cray 2 will be completely immersed in cooling liquid, with three-dimensional circuit density. And what about Seymour Cray himself? He is only one man and can't go on forever. But for as long as he does, Cray Research will remain the leader in supercomputers.

Cray Research has a certain style, patterned after Cray himself. It is small, cohesive, focused, informal, personable, approachable, and above all, humble. The annual report states: "We take what we do seriously, but don't take ourselves very seriously. . . . There is laughing in the halls . . . . people are professional without being stuffy." The attitude and behavior of this company based in northern Wisconsin and Minnesota are certainly different from those of Silicon Valley Companies. Supercomputers are a nice niche, but small. Such machines may be of strategic importance, but the Japanese may be wasting a lot of development dollars trying to build a business in such a specialty niche. Bet on Cray's individual innovativeness over Japan's committee approach.

FLOATING POINT SYSTEMS: THE SUPERCOMPUTER AS A MINICOMPUTER

Way back in 1970, Floating Point Systems realized there was a market for a high-speed scientific computer packaged as a minicomputer and sold at a minicomputer price. The company's first product was a 38-bit word length machine capable of mathematical calculations of up to eight decimal digits of accuracy. (Commercial computers give only two decimal points of accuracy.) Later, its product line came to include a 64-bit machine with accuracy out to 15 decimal points. This computer cost in the area of $300,000, but it offered scientific users a cost per calculation far lower than if they used a traditional minicomputer.

Floating Point has a strong position in a niche market. Its computers are ideal for such things as processing signals from X-ray scanning and analyzing seismic oil exploration data. But this market is only so big. To break out of it, the company has entered the simulation market with hardware and software aimed at that faster growing area. Revenues and profits began to surge in 1979, then collapsed in 1982 when the oil exploration market sagged and the recession stalled the overall minicomputer market. By late 1983, however, business had picked up once again.

Floating Point has a unique relationship with other vendors. IBM, Digital Equipment, Sperry, and Apollo all have endorsed Floating

Point's products and will market them in conjunction with their own equipment in situations where a customer needs such a scientific computer.

The problem is that the company is still too narrowly confined. Its market is still too small to allow much growth. The softness in the oil exploration field has also been a bad influence. In addition, Floating Point is dependent for 40% of its business on GE, which uses Floating Point computers in its X-ray scanner machines, and therein lies the Achilles heel. GE's Medical Systems announced it will switch sources for its array processors used in its next generation of X-ray body scanners in 1985 to a Floating Point spinout, startup company, Star Technologies. The loss of this business is a major setback and will have an impact by 1985. Star is not the only challenge, there have been several employee spin-offs attempting to mount competitive alternatives. In the meantime, the shift toward the simulation market brings overtones of a mainframe-style marketing requirement, which is a whole different ball game from what this minicomputer company has heretofore been accustomed to.

We expect Floating Point Systems will achieve a respectable record in the future having topped $100 million in sales in 1983. But a 25 to 35% rate of expansion may be difficult to reach, and from such a small base does not get this company very far, very fast anyway. It will retain its solid position in its narrow market and will grow, but it will be overshadowed by the wave of 32-bit micro companies, as each thrusts for a billion dollars in sales.

STRATUS: MAKING WAVES IN FAULT-TOLERANT COMPUTERS

Tandem was the successful pioneer of the market for nonstop computers, but in the hot specialty niches—and nonstop computing is one of the hottest—pioneers don't stay alone very long. The first company to set foot in Tandem's domain is Stratus, started by former employees of Data General.

Stratus decided in early 1980 that by using microprocessor chips it could put two identical sets of logic circuitry on a circuit board quite cheaply and achieve nonstop, fail-safe computing. Duplicate disk drives and power supplies ensure that every aspect of the computer runs in parallel. This way Stratus comes up with the poor man's fault-tolerant computer for $140,000, half the Tandem Computer price. Stratus took the hardware approach (cheap) rather than Tandem's software approach (expensive) to achieve parallel processing capability. The advantage is more than price, it is also ease of programming. The limitation is that only 32 computer processors can be attached together, compared to thousands at Tandem.

In only 3 years, Stratus has made some notable strides. Various blue-chip customers, such as Ford, 3M, and Merrill Lynch, use the Stratus/32. The company has its own direct sales force in the United States, while Olivetti distributes the product abroad. It took just over 2 years to go from inception to the first sale and less than 3 years to turn a profit, by the end of 1982. This illustrates the trend with new-wave companies of coming out of the blocks at lightning speed. The technology won't wait. Micro-based products age fast. A company must go from idea to shipment in 2 years or less, or it will be leapfrogged and become obsolete. Sales in 1983 were over $20 million and could be close to $50 million in 1984.

This is the era of micro-based, 16- and 32-bit, new-wave computer architecture and design. It is not going to stop anytime soon—there will be more convulsions, quakes, upheaval of the old order, blitzkrieg inroads by 2-year-old companies into established markets, and geometric leaps in computer power, performance, and price. Stratus is attempting to do to Tandem Computer what Tandem did to the traditional micros and mainframe companies. And Stratus is one of many. It's a wave. Stratus is riding the wave. Look for this company and others of its ilk to make a big splash.

15

The Promised Land of Computers: The New World of Office Automation

Although we are fast becoming a nation of twenty-first-century information workers, you would never know it from the looks of the typical office today. Filing is still done by hand: paper files in manila folders in big, metal, filing cabinets. Written material is drafted by voice or by hand, then transferred to typewriters, although there may be a few word processors here and there. Duplicate copies are created by hand, one sheet at a time, at a copying machine that sits all by itself. In short, most offices are still a backwater of technology, barely beyond the pen-and-ink stage. It is as if farmers were still using first-generation tractors and milking their cows by hand.

It won't stay this way for long. It can't. The imperatives of the information age won't allow it. Companies are learning the hard way that they are at a competitive disadvantage unless they can control their information. *Information float*—when key information is completely inaccessible or takes too long to obtain—is becoming as much of a problem as interest rate float. The quality and timeliness of a company's response to customer inquiries have big effect on business. The response "I'll call you back after I check the records" translates into lost revenues.

The office itself is becoming transformed from an overhead cost into a business profit center. Computers (in addition to improving efficiency and therefore lowering costs) actually generate increased revenue by enabling management to exert better control over such things as receivables, inventory, debt, cash, and capital expenditures.

If that's not enough to get people thinking about office automation, then the sheer size of the emerging information bureaucracies (both public and private) will do the trick. In ways that cannot be underestimated, the office is replacing the factory (which replaced the farm) as the center of commerce. Already 35 million people— 40% of the entire labor force—work in administrative positions. The total white-collar payroll, from clerks to chief executive officers, is already over three-quarters of a trillion dollars. The typical company spends one out of every four dollars on office expenses, and yet the office invariably is the last place where anyone thinks of making an investment to improve productivity. The typical office worker is backed by a capital investment of $5000, compared to $30,000 for blue-collar workers (although they may not always be working, but then neither are office workers) and $55,000 for agricultural workers (although the government may pay them not to use any of it). No wonder office productivity rose an inconsequential 4% in the 1970s, compared to a 90% rise in factory productivity.

What alternatives are available to improve office productivity? More copiers? More dictation equipment? More word processors? That would be fine if copying, dictating, and typing were separate and discrete activities, and the only goal was to see that each one was performed more quickly. But that is not the case. The information that begins with a handwritten memo on the desk of an executive could easily find itself traveling through a typewriter, a word processor, into a desk-top computer (as electronic mail), face-down on a copying machine, transmitted through a PBX over telephone lines by a facsimile machine, and so on. The drag on office productivity is not the speed with which each of these individual activities is performed. Productivity is being held back because of the barriers that prevent these activities from being part of one continuous information network. That's the promise of the Office of the Future: the creation of office information systems in which everything from dictating machines to copiers to desk-top computers to mainframes are all hooked together so that the information contained inside any one of them can be retrieved at the touch of a button from anywhere in the network.

So what's holding it up? Why isn't this electronic Xanadu here yet? Obviously, technology has held it back to a certain extent. Word processors and personal computers—two key elements of the electronic office—only became economical within the past few years. Then there is the old trap of what sounds good in theory versus what actually works in reality. In theory, a Fortune 500 company could save millions through office automation. As a practical matter, many companies are reluctant to invest thousands of dollars in electronic equipment to be used by secretarial employees. Such benefits as convenience, the quality of the work environment, and speedier access to information are not easily quantified in dollars.

Above the clerical level, the job of selling office automation is even tougher, even though the cost justification is easier to come by. Managers and executives like to associate personally with one another, to sell themselves and ideas. Computers aren't their style. There is a gut-level fear in large corporations that the Office of the Future will be one in which personal exchange is reduced to a minimum, in which all communication is done via messages left on a computer terminal, and that the only real warmth will be from the glow of the computer display. At the managerial level, where people don't even type, there is a real animus toward any keyboard technology. And despite all the proselytizing for executive automation, only 5 of the 40 chief executives interviewed for this book had any kind of computer device in their offices. The solution to managerial fear of technology probably will not come until there is a generation of office workers accustomed to computers since childhood.

Finally, the whole concept of office automation is still overly broad and nebulous. There are as yet no standards or uniformity in such things as information exchange and communications protocols. Moreover, there is little homogeneity in the market itself. Offices are as different as they are alike. And the technology is constantly changing. Companies, such as Lanier, that staked out an early lead in the word processing market, soon found themselves outflanked by the vendors of shared word processing systems and by the personal computer companies. Traditional companies, such

as IBM, are coming at the market from the traditional data processing point of view. Others, such as ROLM (and eventually AT&T)
are coming at it from the communications side. It is hard for vendors
to stake out a niche or an identity from scratch.

Nonetheless, office automation is happening—right now. Companies are taking it seriously and looking around for the right vendors. Computer companies that have not yet formulated a strategy
may find that it is already too late. At the very minumum, they
will miss the enormous market development that is occurring right
now.

Desk-top computers alone are penetrating the office market at a
rate of over 1 million units annually. Computer keyboards in the
office are approaching a cumulative total of 10 million. The office
personal computer work station revolution has begun, the secretarial word processing transformation having preceded it. By 1985
one-quarter of all white-collar personnel will have access to a desk-
top computer, by the end of the decade perhaps it will be half. The
total market for what is generally known as office automation equipment is already $13 billion a year and growing at nearly 40%:

Device	1983 Shipments ($ billions)	1983 Growth Rate (%)
Desk-top Computers	5.0	50
Word Processors	2.5	22
PBXs	1.3	12
Electronic Typewriters	0.5	15
Intelligent Copiers	0.5	30
Nonimpact Printers	0.4	35
Facsimile	0.3	13
Terminals	1.0	10
Communications	0.5	50
Software	1.5	85
Total Market	13.5	37.5

Sources: International Data Corporation; Salomon Brothers Inc.

IBM is certain to be the major office automation company. It is the only one with such broad-based marketing and support already in place. It knows how to sell to the Fortune 500. Although IBM was late getting started with personal computers and word processors, it lost no real ground. In only 3 years of serious effort, IBM has sent the competition scattering. It is approaching the office market the way it staked out the computer room back in the 1950s and 1960s—with an eye toward capturing two-thirds or more of the market. It is also showing considerable flexibility in this effort, establishing joint ventures and cooperative relationships with the likes of Microsoft, SCI, Computervision, Comsat, ROLM, MSA, and Intel, to name a few.

IBM is leveraging its position as the dominant supplier of computer equipment and then adding on the essential communications services: Satellite Business Systems for long-distance data, a ring-net local area network for intrabuilding communications, and the equity ownership in ROLM for the PBX link. Because of its established size and installed customer base, IBM's products become standards around which other manufacturers have to align themselves. The PC, the as yet unannounced local area network, and IBM's Systems Network Architecture (SNA) are all standards around which the industry is beginning to conform. Wang, the only computer firm with a real track record in office automation, announced in late 1983 that its office products would be communications compatible with IBM.

Still, no company is perfect. Not even IBM. It has had problems establishing compatibility throughout its own product line. A System 38 computer cannot be connected to a 308X mainframe, or even to an IBM PC. In fact, IBM's line of office automation products is not as integrated as Wang's. Communications capability is still behind, even though whatever IBM comes out with in this area (unless it is an incredible disaster) is likely to set a standard. Overall, IBM's products are not as easy to use as those offered by Wang, Lanier, Apple, and others. If products that are user friendly are what it takes to win in office automation, though, you can bet that IBM will be designing its products toward that end. Office automation is not just another niche to IBM. It's the future of the computer industry.

AT&T has to be counted as a definite factor in office automation. Though it is new to the computer industry (and competition in general), AT&T comes with a number of unique and significant assets. First of all, it is completely unencumbered by past commitments to older architectures, designs, software systems, or a customer-rental equipment base. It has the potential to leapfrog existing systems by designing products based on Western Electric's extremely powerful 256K memory chip component. AT&T has the resources of Bell Labs and Western Electric. Above all, AT&T has money—lots of it. The new AT&T has some $35 billion in assets, $15 billion in book value, and $56 billion in annual sales. That puts AT&T at No. 4 on the Fortune 500 list, ahead of IBM. If AT&T cannot mount a serious, credible effort in office automation with these advantages, it will come as a surprise to the whole world.

AT&T is making the System 85 PBX the spearhead of its office automation effort. Although it is off to a slow start, AT&T has taken a page out of the ROLM/IBM book by agreeing with Wang Laboratories and Hewlett-Packard to jointly develop the software capabilities that will allow easier tie-in of those companies' products to the System 85. Convergent Technologies will supply work station and other computer products. Olivetti will do some international marketing and provide some office products. Expect more intelligent telephone terminals and local area network announcements soon. AT&T is also preparing its line of 3B 20S 32-bit superminicomputers for the office market. These computers were designed by Western Electric and have been used internally at AT&T since 1980. Priced at $245,000, with a UNIX operating system, the 3B 20S is being equipped with software for filing, word processing, and electronic mail. It was the centerpiece of AT&T's unsuccessful bid for the U.S. Forest Service computer contract, which it lost to Data General.

The market is moving fast, and AT&T needs to get its act together. Time is critical, and that's the one thing money cannot buy. Only time will tell whether this communications giant can cut it in the outside world. (For a more detailed discussion of AT&T, see Chapter 8.)

After IBM and AT&T, there will be a second tier of companies, such as Wang and ROLM, which started out as niche companies

(Wang in word processing, ROLM in PBXs) and then expanded successfully from there. Of course, there will be droves of small specialists in word processing, PBXs, work stations, facsimile, graphics, and so on. The office market is big. In the years to come, it will dominate the industry. In the coming era of systems integration, the technologies that are created to make the Office of the Future a reality will become the pièce de résistance of the industry, the same way that the microprocessor was the crowning achievement of the hardware era.

WANG LABORATORIES: THE ORIENT EXPRESS OF OFFICE AUTOMATION

If any company is capable of riding the surge in office automation to challenge Digital Equipment for the No. 2 spot in computers, it is Wang Laboratories. Although its first successful commercial product was an electronic calculator and it was an early leader as a niche company in word processing and small computers, Wang is now the company most clearly identified as a pure office automation systems company. With that kind of reputation, it can go a long way. Wang has both management and marketing to go the distance. The only question is whether any one company has enough resources to tough out the fight against IBM.

Wang Laboratories was founded in 1951 by An Wang, a native of Shanghai who came to the United States in 1945 and studied at Harvard's Computation Laboratory. There he invented and patented components of the magnetic core computer memory that were later sold to IBM. In the mid-1960s, An Wang inaugurated a strategy to sell proprietary products directly to the end-user market. The first such product, an electronic calculator, was a huge success, pushing the company's revenues to over $25 million a year by 1970.

Soon thereafter Wang began to pursue two other emerging markets: small computers and word processing. The early days were slow because these markets were still embryonic (the microprocessor had just been developed), yet the company kept busy laying the necessary groundwork for the success that would soon come its way. It built an effective, large marketing force. Manufacturing was integrated vertically all the way down to the component stage. Most importantly, Wang developed an innovative computer product line both for small business users and large customers wishing to carry out distributed data processing. Easy systems integration and networking have been a hallmark of Wang's product line right from the start.

Wang Laboratories is in every way An Wang's company, with his stamp of discipline, conservatism, low profile, and humbleness evident throughout (a sharp contrast to the company's aggressiveness in product and marketing strategies). There is precise attention to detail at Wang and a certain disdain for frills. An Wang runs a lean operation—something that is immediately evident to any visitor to corporate headquarters. All this was brought home to me when at a meeting of security analysts I discovered An Wang temporarily tending bar prior to the luncheon. With Wang in firm control—he continues to own 48% of the stock and actively runs the company as chairman—there is clearly heavy dependence on his continuing leadership.

Wang's preeminent position in the computer industry of the 1980s stems from the company's uncanny ability to be in the right market at the right time with the right product. Some examples are: scientific electronic programmable calculators in the late 1960s; small business computers in the late 1960s and early 1970s; word processing in the early 1970s; superminicomputers in the late 1970s; and integrated office automation systems in the early 1980s. The company is not only into the markets early, staking out a big share, but also out early, before there is any debacle and decline.

Wang's start in office automation began a decade ago with the introduction of a memory typewriter that used the IBM Selectric as its typing element. The world laughed. How could a tiny company with a product dependent on IBM's typewriter for its innards compete against the IBM magnetic tape and card Selectric typewriters, both 10 years old but the only such devices around? Little Wang roared and was soon the leader in word processing. The world stopped laughing and started buying. Over the years Wang has successfully carved out an identity as a supplier of office systems. It avoided being cast as a minicomputer or for that matter even a word processing company. Individual product types are always a passing phase. While the market remains, the products change. Wang never wanted to be compared to or identified with Digital Equipment. For ultimate credibility it preferred to be contrasted to IBM. Wang created a local area network, Wangnet, just to be compared against IBM and Xerox; its purpose was that of an image-builder, until the company had time to really get into telecommunications and local area networks in a meaningful way.

The strategy is to sell innovative, leading-edge products directly to end users. Wang will provide the entire system—voice, image, text, data—all the technology disciplines for the office.

Wang's customer base is 85 to 90% end users—customers that buy computers directly for use themselves, as opposed to original equipment manufacturers or systems houses. As the OEM business is a more economically sensitive area, Wang is protected from these fluctuations. Its sales force is large, 1500 salespeople selling directly to customers both in the United States and abroad.

These strategies and strengths have made Wang the fastest growing billion dollar company in the industry and have catapulted it into the Top 10 lineup. It has come a long way fast. The transition year was 1975, the last time profits fell, amid the shift from a dependence on scientific calculators and small business computers to an emphasis on word processing, larger computers, and office systems. Since 1975, sales have skyrocketed 46% annually, from $75 million that year to $1.5 billion in 1983. In 1984 revenues will reach $2 billion. Profits over the 8-year stretch have surged 61% annually. R&D spending, the life blood of the company, has gone from $3 million to $118 million a year. Sales of office systems (including word processing) are half the company, expanding 25 to 30% annually. Superminicomputers and personal computers comprise about 40% of sales, climbing 50% per year. Small business computers are around 10% of the total and are in decline.

Despite Wang's record and position, there are more hurdles and challenges confronting the company than ever before. It will be more difficult to triple in size over the next 5 years than it was to triple over the past 3 years. As the office market develops, Wang is confronting IBM directly in what has become IBM's bread-and-butter market. IBM's introduction in 1983 of several personal computer-related products (such as the PC 370 and the PC 3270) indicates intensified efforts to move more aggressively in the office market. IBM's personal computers are sweeping the office market and may be a basic building block for many office automation systems. Wang's expansion into integrated office systems for large national customers will require more attention to maintenance, support, and service. These are aspects of the business that Wang once neglected, although a major buildup has been evident in the past few years. Wang's management structure remains highly centralized despite the company's large size. The effectiveness of the company's financial and managerial control is uncertain.

That's not all. Though the company has made great strides in cracking the Fortune 500 (such customers accounted for 45% of its revenues in 1983), it is getting more difficult now that IBM is on the move. Wang is threatened by a few big customer defections and has failed to obtain even a small megacontract, such as the Data General win of E. F. Hutton's office system, worth $40 million. Wang's capacity for innovation is prone to exaggeration. Its products sometimes promise more than they deliver or are too far ahead of the market. The intelligent printer introduced a few years ago, the Mailway (voice-mail store and forward system), and Wangnet (local area network) are all cases in point. We will have to wait and see about the Professional Image Computer, the computer introduced in 1983 that can process photo images, not just text and numbers. Of course, when a company strives for creative products and very early entry into markets, it can't hit home runs 100% of the time.

Wang may also find it more difficult to hold off the new-wave hardware companies as they offer powerful, 32-bit desk-top work stations for the office market. Personal computers have already become a major piece of the office systems market, and Wang is playing a minor role there. It sold only 20,000 in 1983 and possibly will sell over 50,000 in 1984, well under 5% of that market sector. Wang once had the office automation market more to itself. Now IBM is calling the tune. IBM has established the compatibility standards in the office. Wang and others have had to settle for an open-access strategy so as to allow tie-in to IBM systems. Pricing competition has intensified in personal computers, word processors, and 32-bit superminis. Now that the office market has arrived, a lot of competitors want to be involved, and we have yet to hear much from AT&T. Wang's profit margins will suffer as it goes head-to-head for large Fortune 500 contracts against IBM.

By the end of the decade, Wang's goal is to reach $5 billion in sales, to derive 60% of its revenues from large national customer accounts, and to have integrated office automation systems (computers, word processors, etc.) as its largest product line. This could happen by 1988. Several factors will help Wang achieve these ambitious goals. The company is deeply involved in technology, spending 7.5% of its revenue on R&D. Products are creative and (in terms of performance) are in the forefront of the industry. Technology is particularly good in data processing, word processing, and networking. Wang has been emphasizing communications capability in its products for some time, and it has taken a 15% ownership position in VLSI Technology (a manufacturer of very large scale integrated custom semiconductor circuits) to insure access to such components. It will also be moving more into communications (as, for example, the Bolt, Beranck, and Newman wide-area network project) and probably more into data services and software.

The history of the computer and electronics industries is strewn with companies that grew at a pell-mell rate and thought it would never stop, so it may seem presumptuous to assume Wang will grow 25 to 30% annually for the next 10 years, to reach $10 billion by the early 1990s. But if any company in the industry has a chance to make it really big, to challenge for No. 2 status eventually, it is Wang. It appears An Wang is interested in giving it a try. Though closing in on 65 years of age, he has given up smoking and has taken to squeezing a tennis ball instead. One obvious up-and-coming member of management is Fredrick A. Wang, the son of An Wang, currently vice-president, development. It would appear that the younger Wang is being groomed for higher office and, in fact, is his father's likely successor. The company retains its flexibility, acuity, entrepreneurial creativity, and spirit, and it is still a fun place. An Wang is humble, not counting his accomplishments yet. He is still concerned for the future. He does more than think. He's involved, hands on. Wang Laboratories will squeeze a lot more than tennis balls for several years to come. It will squeeze many competitors. This company will be a giant in the 1990s, and the office is its domain.

NBI: BUILDING A NAME IN OFFICE AUTOMATION

NBI is one of several word processing firms struggling today to become full-line office automation suppliers. It got its start back in the days when word processing per se was an underdeveloped, emerging market, when offices were amenable to buying office automation gear piece by piece. There were no personal computers, work stations, integrated networks, or even office automation in the systems sense. The only question asked by the customer was: "Should our secretaries have a word processing machine, and if so which one?" The purchase decision was similar to that for a typewriter or copier. Buy it. Let it stand alone. Make sure it's serviced. One good product and a sales strategy were all that was needed.

NBI was by no means the biggest of the independents, but it has come the farthest in terms of moving away from the world of boxes to the new era of office systems. NBI opened its doors in 1975. Thomas S. Kavanagh, a cofounder of Storage Technology and an engineer by background, wanted a shot at running his own show in Boulder, Colorado. By 1978 this "nameless" company (NBI stands for "nothing but initials") was in business in a big way, with $13 million in sales and some profits. Sales reached almost $150 million in 1983. NBI's strategy was to sell office automation products to a customer piece by piece. Actually, that was the only strategy possible. No organization was ready for sweeping office automation. IBM customers could view NBI as a unique secondary niche vendor and use the products selectively so as not to put all their office product eggs in one basket (IBM). NBI established a direct end-user sales force, branch offices, and service organization. It uses dealers and distributors only as secondary channels. As a result, it has an outstanding record for maintenance service, a key way for a small company to establish credibility. (NBI is rated No. 1 in word processing maintenance.) NBI also went after the small-business market, where IBM and Wang were weaker. Its products utilize an open architecture to coexist with IBM.

This approach worked beautifully before, but now NBI has reached a crossroads. The office automation era has arrived. Word processing is only one piece of a big pie. A full system is required. This is where the IBMs and Wangs take over and the early suppliers of stand-alone systems, such as NBI, start to fade. But NBI won't give up without a fight. Its hand was forced prematurely in 1983 to reveal its new strategy: to expand beyond traditional word processing into data processing and local area network communications. NBI took the wraps off its IBM-compatible personal computer, its System One work station, and its Ethernet local area network scheme. This new strategy has clout. NBI's work station is UNIX 68000-based with a powerful new architecture. It puts NBI in the ranks of the new wave with Apollo and Convergent. The personal computer has twice the power and screen resolution of IBM's PC.

While this new, broad-based office system approach is necessary, and the new NBI products in the data processing realm are first rate, the risks have magnified as a result. The new System One work station is a wholly different architecture than past products and therefore incompatible. NBI's customers must make a painful, costly upgrade from the old products to take advantage of the new. By going into the computer systems market, NBI spreads itself thin and may have overreached. Its sales force and maintenance group must learn a new skill; they must make a transition that will be costly, time consuming, and maybe impossible. The R&D budget is already overburdened. The company's narrowness of focus and concentration is now dissipated. NBI is attempting to go head to head, across the board, in the office market against IBM and Wang. Yet it is one-fifteenth Wang's size, and even smaller relative to IBM.

The initial new product foray in 1983 had a wrenching self-impact. Orders for the older products stopped prematurely while customers awaited future delivery of the new products. Profits were hit severely. NBI is also confronted with several other hurdles. Its overall presence in office automation is slight. Penetration of Fortune 1000 customers is low. NBI must establish an identity beyond word processing just when more office automation purchase decisions may be gravitating back toward the data processing, computer center manager.

It would be wrong to dismiss NBI's chances in office automation too quickly. This is a feisty company, with a cooperative, hardworking management team, high morale, small-company spirit, a humble attitude, with its head screwed on right. Its very style—an open-door atmosphere; open-air and glass-partitioned offices; natural, modern decor; lack of ornateness or presumptuous manifestations—reveals that this company still has its mind on its business. NBI is attuned to its market. Top management spends 1 week a month in the field with customers. NBI's goal is to become the largest independent office automation company, to top Wang. Well, you have to think big, don't you? NBI is making the moves to hang in there for several years yet, and it may end up in a second source role to Wang, as Wang itself may be to IBM. It has the best chance of the small independents to make it in office automation, but the odds are stacked against it. The battle to make it will be lonely and bloody. That's the way it was for the pioneers that settled Colorado. So it will be for NBI of Boulder.

CPT: A SCHEFF KEEPS THE POT BOILING

Dean Scheff, founder and president of CPT, has a management style best termed *negative*. He does a lot of yelling. Not surprisingly, his management has gone through revolving doors for years. As Scheff puts it, bluntly, "If you have no talent, I'm the hardest guy in the world to work for." CPT is usually in turmoil or controversy of one type or another—management changes, dealer complications, product strategy upheaval, or the modern decor chosen for the new headquarters near Minneapolis. As a company, CPT seems to have more faults and weaknesses than strengths. Until recently, it has had only one product—word processing. It is small and relies on dealers for marketing, and then there is Scheff's management style. Still, the company is doing something right. It is hard to put your finger on it, but the record speaks for itself: from $2 million in sales in 1973 to $178 million in 1983. Profits expanded 10 straight years through 1982. Since 1978, sales have been ahead 55% per year and profits 45%. The secret, one must conclude, is Scheff himself. CPT has done better for longer than anyone expected. Dean Scheff's imprint is on every aspect of the company.

CPT started more than a decade ago with a unique twist: a word processor with a white background display and black letters so that the screen would more closely resemble a typed page. Beyond that, the product strategy was nothing unusual. The marketing concept was to have office equipment dealers in every town around the country sell the product. Once you have the small cities (sales, maintenance, customers), the large ones would be sure to follow. And they did, at least to a modest degree. Larger customers were easier to sell once CPT's presence was established at local, remote sites, where branch offices were located. Dealer marketing, over 75% of sales, is a mixed situation. It got CPT up and running fast. Business, even large contracts, such as a $16 million deal with the Tennessee Valley Authority, is easier to pull off if pursued by local, established dealer organizations, rather than by a new salesperson in a new office. The dealers develop innovative software and provide maintenance. And dealers are more loyal (or rather, locked in) because of inventory investments. The disadvantages, however, are also notable. Dealers restrain CPT from introducing aggressive new products that would make their existing inventory obsolete. Once dealers get comfortable marketing a familiar product, they are hesitant to switch and learn a new one. The manufacturer becomes dependent on those uncontrollable outside sources for the vital marketing function. When it comes time to establish a direct sales organization, inevitable conflict and competition emerge with the dealers. It's a two-edged sword.

CPT's office automation product strategy has broadened beyond word processing, but as this continues to occur, the company will no longer play to its previous word processing strength. Products are now being designed from a software standpoint: stand-alone and shared systems with software for engineers, publishers, software programmers, draftsmen, and technical personnel, providing capabilities to show designs, pictures, and schematics. Scheff wants CPT to be the "Nieman Marcus of office automation [a collection of boutiques], rather than a K Mart." The product strategy sounds fine, but in fact it's a little confused. It's a piece-by-piece strategy, with no one all-encompassing system. There have been false starts. Some of the technology has come from as far away as Germany. Word processing remains the keystone, what the company does best, but it seems CPT almost wishes for a return to the salad days when stand-alone word processing units were king and CPT's white screen was unique. Today CPT is being forced to go head to head against Wang, IBM, Apollo, and Convergent. It's a different ball game in a new stadium.

CPT has some resources. Its dealer network remains loyal. Its products have communications capability to attach to IBM, Honeywell, Digital Equipment, and other computer companies' systems. CPT will not be cornered and frozen out of the market. The company is small enough to retain its creativity, flexibility, and adeptness, and the founder is still in control. Increasingly, though, the office market is expanding outward from traditional word processing, toward Apollo-type microprocessor-based work stations at one end and larger computer systems capability, such as offered by IBM, Wang, and probably in the future AT&T, at the other end. CPT is caught in the middle. The company will undoubtedly find its niches and avenues of growth, but it will not be a leader, a major competitor, nor will it be in the billion dollar class.

ROLM: THE WAY TO WIN OFFICE AUTOMATION'S HEART IS THROUGH ITS COMMUNICATIONS

ROLM believes that the best way to approach the office automation market is with communications, the PBX and most recently the digital PBX. A PBX can route voice and low-speed data more effectively and cheaply than can a local area network. It is a more elegant way of tying together telephones, personal computers, terminals, and other computer devices and is better suited to handling both voice and data—as long as the speed requirements are not too onerous. In the Office of the Future, communications, not the computer devices, is the vital glue, the critical factor. That's the way ROLM, and of course AT&T, sees things.

ROLM's communications strategy began to unfold in 1975. Prior to that it had been a builder of ruggedized, military-specification

Data General minicomputers. That's how it acquired its digital computer expertise. ROLM saw the communications revolution on the horizon, a deregulated market that would gradually foster open competition, rather than an AT&T monopoly. It seized the opportunity. The PBX—or as ROLM calls its product, the CBX (computer-controlled branch exchange)—was the opening wedge. Ten years ago, AT&T owned 100% of the U.S. PBX market. Then the upgrade replacement business commenced, after the Carterphone decision was handed down allowing non-AT&T equipment to be attached to the AT&T system. Independents like ROLM, Northern Telecom, and Mitel beat AT&T to the market with new products, at cheaper prices. By 1983 AT&T had only 35% of U.S. shipments; ROLM and Northern, 15% each; and Mitel a little under 15%. There are 250,000 PBXs installed in the United States with an average of 65 telephone lines on each one. The market is basically a replacement business, though, with the old AT&T analog PBXs being replaced with new analog and now digital PBXs. In digital PBXs, ROLM and Northern own the show. AT&T's System 85 was still in the start-up phase as 1984 began. But the PBX business itself is a finite market. It's what comes later that counts. The strategy goes that, if a company (ROLM) controls the PBX, then it will have a major influence over office automation terminals, work stations, personal computers, and even telephones that will tie into the PBX at a later time. The PBX is smack-dab in the middle of it all. Every internal communication will go through the PBX if ROLM has its say (through a local area network if the computer manufacturers win out). To this end, ROLM has introduced a vast product line of peripheral office automation devices, such as electronic telephones and the Cypress personal communications terminal (an electronic telephone and intelligent computer terminal with CRT screen and keyboard, all combined into one unit).

ROLM's most ambitious product undertaking is its CBX II, which transmits voice and data communications between telephones and computers at speeds of up to 192,000 bits per second compared to the 9600 bits per second of older PBXs. (Local area networks have speeds of up to 10 million bits per second.) The CBX II can handle up to 22,000 telephone lines (a huge number) and is a complete end-to-end digital business communications system, linking work stations, computers, telephones, and other office automation devices. It is said to be the architecture for the 1990s.

ROLM has considerable strengths: digital PBX experience, the broadest array of office automation products to attach to the PBX, exceptional customer service and support, and a half billion in cash. Its most glaring advantage, though, is its IBM connection. IBM owns 22% of ROLM, purchasing $229 million of ROLM stock from the company in mid-1983 and more since. Kenneth Oshman, president and founder of ROLM, sought out IBM to avoid being locked out of the market by AT&T. With IBM's endorsement, PBX communications protocols are being kept open. There are industry-wide standards, instead of an exclusive standard set by AT&T (as IBM set for the personal computer market—and look what that did to most personal computer vendors). Other benefits from IBM could be substantial but are secondary—investment capital for R&D, the entry into international markets, incremental volume as IBM sells ROLM products, and joint R&D efforts. ROLM products are compatible with IBM's SNA communications protocol and the IBM PC, and they tie into IBM 3270 terminals.

In just 8 years since ROLM pioneered the independent thrust into PBXs, it has reached over $433 million in business communications sales, over three-fourths of the company's total revenues. (Military-specification computers were $70 million in sales in 1983.) Total revenues will exceed $650 million in 1984. Sales have climbed by over 40% annually since 1975, and profits by over 30%. All growth has been internal—no acquisitions. ROLM has each of the top 20 Fortune 500 as customers and 80 of the top 100. An almost $20 million contract to install PBX in 700 Bank of America branches over the next two years is a fine example of the company's penetration in the large corporate market. The objective is to continue expanding at a 25 to 50% rate. ROLM is likely to reach the exalted Top 10 industry status sometime in the 1990s. It will be a major office automation leader.

Even with IBM on its side, all is not roses. Competition is heating up in PBXs as a new wave of companies (Ztel, Intecom, CXC, among others) are using all new architectures and computer designs. The PBX market itself suffers from vicious price cutting (led by Northern Telecom), while newer office automation devices for attachment to the PBX are only beginning to develop into a profitable business.

Some foreign competition, Northern Telecom, Ericsson, and Nippon Electric Company, are subsidized by their governments and can afford to be less profit conscious. ROLM, straining to introduce an assortment of new products, put pressure on its profits in 1983 that continues in 1984.

Ken Oshman will lead this company through its continuing transition. He has an informal style, typical of Silicon Valley, greeting me personally in the lobby the day I went to interview him. ROLM's facilities are not elaborate or overly plush, but the atmosphere is extremely pleasant and stimulating. Japanese botanical gardens surround the sprawling two-story buildings, complete with fauna, flora, ponds, moats, and allegedly even alligators. It's a pleasant place to work. How can AT&T and Northern Telecom compete for the best personnel against this?

Any way you slice it, ROLM is in a strong position. This company should be a leader in the communications side of office automation, although AT&T will have a say in that. ROLM could be the next Wang, staking out a specialty market that will play an essential role in the automated office. The PBX market is the stepping-stone that could make ROLM one of the information titans in the 1990s.

HARRIS: READY TO TAKE THE PLUNGE

Harris is a $1.8 billion diversified operation, almost a high-technology conglomerate, that has been on the periphery of the computer industry for years. Its traditional strengths have been in defense and communications systems, to say nothing of its niche in semiconductors or, for 88 years, until 1983, its role as the leading manufacturer of printing presses. Yet, in casting around for a high-growth market for the future, Harris shied away from the markets it knows best and chose instead to cast itself in the role of an office automation company. It intends to forge a presence in that sector with the 1983 acquisition of Lanier Business Products, and its ongoing data terminals and superminicomputer business. Steeped in technology, Harris is hoping that Lanier will give it the broad marketing presence that it needs in order to crack this new market. Unfortunately, when it comes to marketing office automation systems, Lanier has a few problems of its own.

The Lanier acquisition was actually the latest in a series that has transformed Harris from a manufacturer of printing presses into a leading high-technology firm. As late as 1969, printing presses accounted for half of the company's total profits, but by 1983 electronic-based technologies were the whole show. The pivotal move was the 1967 combination with Radiation, Inc., headed by Joseph A. Boyd, now the chairman of Harris.

Radiation's business was NASA and defense-oriented communications and data processing equipment. Harris brought to the deal a commercial orientation, diversification, and solid financial backing. The result was the development of several new commercial product lines in semiconductors, satellite communications, and fiber optic systems. Other key electronics acquisitions included RF Communications (two-way radio communications) in 1969 and the 1980 purchase of Farinon (microwave and communications switching equipment).

These acquisitions have kept Harris on the periphery of the computer industry. Harris had scientific superminicomputers, IBM-compatible data terminals, and (via Farinon) PBXs, but only now, with the Lanier merger—a $450 million acquisition that now accounts for one-fifth of the merged company—will computer and office systems products account for the leading portion of the company, 40% of total sales.

Lanier sells low-end, conventional equipment: copiers (25% of revenues), dictating equipment (less than 33%), and word processors and business computers (more than 33%). Although it recently started up its first plant, Lanier does little manufacturing, acquiring most of its products from Japanese sources. Its forte is marketing to small customers. The Fortune 1000, for example, represents only 12% of its revenues. Lanier's 2200-person sales force is highly motivated by an all-commission income structure, and its service and maintenance are broad based. Lanier was an early player in the word processing market. It profited greatly from the boom in the stand-alone word processing market and was the top company in that market a few years ago. The company continues to be a leader in the dictating equipment business and is expanding fast in the sales of 3M-Toshiba copiers to small businesses. The new 3M copier territories added in 1982 will lead to healthy growth in that sector for a while.

Unfortunately, like all vendors of conventional office equipment (Xerox, Pitney-Bowes; see Chapter 6), Lanier is at a crossroads. Dictating machines are not the high-growth, high-profit items they once were. But with a sales force accustomed to marketing such items, it is questionable how successful Lanier can be in the new systems-oriented office automation market. Harris can help by providing Lanier with access to good technology and product development resources, but in marketing and manufacturing, Lanier is on its own. For its part, Lanier has recently come out with a shared word processing system that it developed in house and initially trained a select group of 100 sales representatives to market it. Harris will also try to do its share and is preparing to introduce a 10,000 line PBX. Despite these thrusts, penetrating the corporate market from such a small base will be a mammoth undertaking.

Harris wants to grow at a 20% rate and achieve a return on equity that is as good as the top one-third of the companies in the industry. It wants to join the ranks of Digital Equipment, Hewlett-Packard, and Wang. To do this, it is following a different approach than most other companies, spreading itself across a number of different technology markets. However, it may be spreading itself a bit thin.

Harris must undergo a fundamental transition in order to successfully address broader markets that require a larger direct sales force. To grow from its existing $1.8 billion revenue base, the company can no longer focus on niche markets and large custom systems, but rather it must become more broadly based and marketing oriented. Harris has chosen to place heavy emphasis on the computer and office automation systems market and is directing heavy capital resources to this area. Harris has always been steeped in technology and is developing products, such as its local area network, for this market. However, the company is starting from a minor industry position, a relatively small customer base, a modest ability to market to the Fortune 1000 market, and little expertise in volume manufacturing. The opportunities are substantial, but the challenge to obtain a fair-sized piece of the office automation market is immense.

Meanwhile, Harris has become a more cyclical company, and there has been some top-management turnover. The company clearly has the communications, semiconductor, and computer technology. And it will flourish in those markets. The office automation market, though, takes more than just technology. I expect Harris to expand at a rate of 20% long term, despite a potentially modest penetration in the office automation market. To top this pace, it will have to achieve major success in the broad-based computer and office systems market.

According to Dr. Joseph A. Boyd, Harris's chairman, "To be successful, you have to be different." Boyd himself has a broad intellect and a keen interest in books, especially history (I have swapped many a book recommendation with him). An engineer by background (and a university dean early in his career), he is certain Harris can deliver the technology. But can Lanier kick in the marketing? That's the weak point that may very well keep Harris's presence in office automation a modest one.

DIEBOLD: PUTTING BANKS EVERYWHERE

Corporate offices are not the only ones that face an electronic future. Banks are doing the same thing with automated teller machines (ATMs). As of the end of 1983, there were some 41,000 ATMs accepting deposits and dispensing cash. Everyone used to say that computers would introduce the cashless society, but ATMs seem to be doing exactly the opposite.

ATMs are popping up all over, in supermarkets, shopping centers, office buildings, airports, gas stations, college campuses, and aboard ships (the Navy has two on the aircraft carrier U.S.S. Ranger). And then there are the banks themselves. There are some 35,000 bank branches across the country, in addition to savings and loans, and credit unions.

Since 1978, sales of ATMs have expanded each year by 45% (although they slowed to 35% recently). In the United States in 1983 alone, 13,000 ATMs were shipped at an average price of about $25,500. The total U.S. market came to $400 million (including service). Worldwide, the market is double the size of the U.S. market, with the heaviest concentration in Japan.

At first, banks had to install ATMs just to stay competitive with other banks that were offering them as a customer convenience. Now, however, cost savings are outweighing customer convenience to stimulate more ATM sales. In 1983 there were some 300,000 bank tellers in the United States with an average annual salary (plus fringe benefits) of $12,500, a figure that keeps rising with inflation. The ATM has a one-time cost of $17,000 to $30,000. The cost of a transaction using a teller is expected to be $1.61 by 1986, compared to 22 cents for the ATM. It's not hard to see why more and more banks are turning to ATMs. Today, most banks have one or two through-the-wall ATMs outside the lobby and an average of eight tellers handling customers in the lobby. In the future the ATMs may very well outnumber the tellers.

The placement of ATMs in nonbank locations will keep this market active long after all bank branches have their own ATMs. Moreover, there are many nonbank uses for them. Tickets, vouchers, and even stamps can be sold through ATMs. The Grand Ole Opry uses ATMs to sell tickets. Avis uses them for quick, convenient car return. By 1990, according to the *Nilson Report*, a banking industry newsletter, there will be 120,000 ATMs in the United States and more than that in international markets.

The one influence that could rob the ATM boom of some of its luster is a rise in ATM theft or fraud. The potential for robbery after users withdraw funds at remote locations is always there (and may well cause ATMs to be kept out of some areas). The ATMs themselves are also targets for attack. In the summer of 1983, there were three assaults on ATMs over a 4-day period in Dallas. A demolition-style hit team blew up the ATMs with explosive charges and escaped with the cash that wasn't burned in the process. In New York City, the state attorney general forced Citibank to refund money to customers who were victimized by a fraud scheme in which a con artist, posing as another bank customer, would interrupt the victim during a transaction, causing the person to leave the transaction uncompleted. After the customer left, the con artist was able to go into the customer's account and withdraw money. Overall, however, considering the speed at which they have become an established fixture in banking, ATMs have been remarkably free of such problems.

One company that has a lot banking on the ATM market is Diebold. Diebold was founded in 1859 and has come a long way since the Civil War days—although it has not been an easy road for the company. Diebold's safes survived the Great Chicago Fire in 1871; the 1907 depression nearly drove Diebold out of business; and during World War II, Elliot Ness (of Untouchables fame), as chairman, put Diebold into the military and defense business only to see the company left high and dry after the war. The Murchison family of Dallas took over Diebold in 1950, reestablishing the company's preeminent position in safes, security systems, and, thereafter, bank branch equipment, such as drive-in tellers. The Murchison family has subsequently liquidated its interest in the company.

In 1973, Docutel introduced the first ATM; Diebold followed with an off-line, stand-alone model that came on the market during the height of the 1974–1975 recession, resulting in little market penetration. Diebold's ATM business was in the red until the company's total automatic banking system (TABS) product line was introduced in 1978. The first significant shipment volume, 778 units, was achieved in that year. Since 1978, Diebold's share of the ATM market has soared from 18% to over 45%. Sales have expanded 14% a year, and profits 39% without a decline since 1978. IBM is No. 2 in ATMs, with a 25% share, while Docutel-Olivetti is at 17% and NCR is at 13% of the market.

It won't be easy for anyone, including IBM, to knock off Diebold. Of all the companies in the business, Diebold has the widest array of ATM products, including through-the-wall, in-lobby, drive-in, and parking lot ATM kiosks, with both on- and off-line capability. The company is innovative and a technological leader, as it demonstrated by being first in cassette-cash loading, drive-up ATMs, software compatibility with IBM computer/controllers, and teller dispensing/depository equipment.

Diebold offers a fully integrated, turnkey system. It provides installation (IBM and NCR contract out for through-the-wall installation), maintenance (Docutel uses TRW), software programming, supplies, and spare parts. No competitor can offer such a complete turnkey system—a great convenience to the operator.

Diebold is also a leader in service. It has service contracts with 10,000 of the 14,000 U.S. banks, and has a sales and service organization that has called on virtually all U.S. banks for more than 100 years. Diebold's more than 3500 service personnel, 1000 of whom are trained to maintain ATMs, have helped to give the company the best service record for timeliness and performance in the ATM industry. Service contracts have always been a critical factor in the security business. A typical ATM service contract generates $3000 annually per machine, so, as the installed base grows, this represents a major profit center and an ongoing base of repeat business.

Diebold has the broadest array of software and the best software R&D capability dedicated to ATMs. Diebold's ATMs are software driven. To change a machine's functions, only a simple program change is required. Software can be tailored to the individual needs of a bank, such as Spanish language or differently configured credit cards.

As a result of its economies of scale, experience, and vertical integration in both protection equipment and ATMs, Diebold is the low-cost producer in the ATM market. Diebold's cash reserves total over $138 million, making the company almost embarrassingly cash rich. Cash flow has been positive virtually every year. Diebold is more of a money machine than its ATMs.

While the ATM side of Diebold's business couldn't be better, its business in conventional security equipment (which accounts for one-third of the company's sales) is in the doldrums. It is a mature, cyclical, no-growth business. In addition, Diebold had a series of labor strikes (1970, 1977, and 1983) at its Canton, Ohio, safe and alarm systems plant. The company is now phasing out the plant.

Although Diebold has grabbed on to one of the hot growth areas of the 1980s, this is not your typical high-tech high flier. Management at Diebold is cut from the same cloth as the company's banking customers: conservative, low-key, courteous bankers through and through. Diebold is a pillar of the banking community. Just look at its balance sheet. Although Diebold has been innovative and aggressive in tackling the ATM market, you won't find any schemes or daring new thrusts from this company.

For my own tastes, Diebold should be doing a bit more. It has the financial resources, the customers, the service, the sales force, and the manufacturing. It could offer different products, enter other financial markets, or even make a complete break from its conventional security business. What this company needs is a push. If it is not careful, a hungry acquirer with some more innovative ideas about the financial services business may come along, take a look at all of Diebold's fine attributes, and make a grab. In fact, that might be just what the company needs. There is some movement afoot though. Robert W. Mahoney came over from NCR in mid-1982, was promoted to president at the beginning of 1984, and will likely be chairman soon. He brings a more aggressive, technology bent to Diebold. In the meantime, Diebold's friends in the banking community will continue to take care of the company. Diebold is not out for a fast buck. It wants to stick around for its third century.

Conclusion

16

Rules for Survival in the Shakeout

When things seem more confused and unfamiliar than ever, its time to fall back on some basic rules of thumb. Herewith are some of the distinguishing features that will help you tell the winners from the losers in computers, as well as McClellan's Laws: 15 tried-and-true axioms based on years of experience to help protect both the neophyte as well as the experienced investor or industry observer from the snares and pitfalls that lurk behind every corner.

CORPORATE CHARACTER

1. Look for something unique or different about the company's business: the product or service, the selling approach, manufacturing (low cost or unusual quality), timing, . . . something.
2. Check management background. What companies were they involved with the last time around? What did they accomplish? Why did they leave?

3. Is founder management still in place, or has professional management taken over? The founders are usually necessary for success.

4. Assess the company's approach to the business. Is it out for a quick buck—selling through dealers, using outside maintenance service, buying the product from another company, recording up-front sales on several-year installment payment terms, going public early while only barely profitable so the founders can cash in? Or is the company sewing the seeds for sustained long-range growth (building a direct sales and maintenance force, R&D, manufacturing, and doing it right)?

5. How many press releases has the company issued? A large number is usually a sign of overhype. The same goes for overly active, aggressive investor relations.

6. How open and accessible is management in bad times, when there has been a disappointment, as compared to when everything is going well? Hiding behind stockholder suits as reason not to communicate to the outside world is an excuse, a cover-up.

7. Look for humbleness, a low-key understated style in dress, corporate headquarters, facilities, and publications. This indicates whether the company is all show or whether there is substance, whether management is in business for themselves or for customers, investors, and employees.

8. Call the company at 8:30 A.M. or 5:30 P.M. and see if anyone is there.

9. It's the little things that count in assessing a company—the small customers, the low-level employees, the small investor, attention to details. Talk to a small customer or a low-level employee.

FINANCIAL CHARACTER

Analyze the income statement:

1. A varying rate of growth in sales and profit is preferable to a steady one. This tells you the company is not managing earnings. The profits that are reported are more credible

because business patterns and trends are not perfectly smooth. Don't trust smooth profit patterns. Perfection is usually faked and always comes undone when least expected.

2. Computer company profit margins before taxes (the profit before tax, divided by revenues) should be at least in the low teens, preferably better.

3. Sales growth should be at least 20% annually.

4. The tax rate should be relatively full, over 30%.

5. Check to see what accounting firm, lead commercial banker, and investment banker is used.

Analyze the balance sheet:

6. Cash levels should be high.

7. Debt should be low, under 25% of capitalization (that is, debt divided by the total of debt and deferred taxes and stockholders equity). The technology business is risky enough; a company should not be taking a financial risk by leveraging itself.

8. Look for reasonably tight inventory and accounts receivable control.

9. Complicated or unusual items, such as deferred costs, goodwill, or leases (products it leases to its customers, instead of outright sales) must be carefully scrutinized.

10. Operating cash flow (i.e., net income and depreciation minus capital expenditures and dividends) should be positive.

McCLELLAN'S LAWS

1. **It Never Rains Bad News, It Pours.** When you first hear bad news about a company, always expect more of the same to follow. What you first heard is usually only the tip of the iceberg.

2. **When Management Says Things Are Bad, Assume They Are Terrible.** Anytime a company announces a negative setback, assume that it is worse than they are telling you.

Remember, it had to be pretty bad for them to admit anything in public in the first place. Never be misled by management calm or confidence in the eye of a storm. Managers get paid to act that way. And after all, they own the stock too.

3. **When Insiders Sell, You Should Too.** When management begins to sell off its stock, it means that the stock is overpriced. In short, management knows that the stock is about to take a tumble and why, but no one outside the company does yet. Don't buy the excuse that the company needs the money. No one ever raised cash by selling a stock that they thought would rise further.

4. **Beware of Stock Price Fixation.** When management is intensely concerned with the stock price, that means trouble. It means management is short term oriented, willing to shortchange such areas as R&D. What goes up must come down. Management should be paying attention to its business and let the stock price take care of itself.

5. **The First Drop in Profits Is Never the Last.** Profit declines, like bad news, always come in bunches. A modest drop is usually followed by an even sharper falloff. A 1-year decline is followed by an even worse one the next year.

6. **Don't Hold Your Breath When a New Product Is Delayed.** There is never just a brief, one-time postponement in new product shipments. Once a delay is announced, in either R&D or production, expect the stretch-out to worsen before the product gets shipped.

7. **Managers, Like Lemmings, Never Go Alone.** Rarely is there an isolated management resignation. Managers usually resign because the company has problems or is no longer exciting, so more than one member of top management is likely to leave.

8. **The Bigger Their Egos, the Harder They Fall.** Beware of smugness or cockiness in management. Lack of humility is dangerous. Those who have overly high opinions of themselves usually have other blind spots as well.

9. **Companies That Stand Pat, Go Broke.** Any company that is not constantly changing and adjusting to this rapidly changing industry is on a fast track to obsolescence. Don't believe the axiom: "If it isn't broken, don't fix it."

10. **If You Can't Understand a Company's Business, Management and Employees May Not Either.** Beware of complicated business or accounting techniques. If you cannot understand the business, obviously you cannot make a judgment. Moreover, the more complicated it is, the more likely there will be a screw-up down the road.

11. **Turnarounds Are Usually too Little, too Late.** Turnarounds almost never work in this business. Once a company falls behind, it never catches up. Turnarounds only work if a company enters a new and different market, becoming, in effect, a different company.

12. **When a Company Talks Bad, That Ain't Good.** Beware of a management that seems to take pleasure in casting negative aspersions on the competition. It usually means they are hiding something, running scared, trying to divert attention.

13. **Don't Be Fooled by New Digs.** Invariably, when a company ensconces itself in a plushy new headquarters, it is getting fat and happy and is ripe for a downfall.
    ...or Filet Lunches. Sumptuous lunches are intended to cover up a lack of substance with superficial impressions. Any company that spends big bucks on entertaining investors, the media, or customers is overreaching for a reason.

14. **If You Read It in This Morning's Paper, You're too Late.** The media is always a lagging indicator of what is really happening at a company. It's usually the last to get the real story. Acting on what appears in the press is like preparing for the last war.

15. **It's Never too Late to Sell a Stock.** Stock prices decline in stages, and, like bad news, there is usually more to come. Get out while you can.

CONCLUSION: THE PERMANENT SHAKEOUT

My inclination as a computer industry observer at this point is to don the guise of a fortune teller, whip out my trusty crystal ball, and offer up some wild prognostications on what the computer industry will be like in the year 2000. That might be fun, and it would probably satisfy some readers' idle curiosity, but my instincts as a stockbroker tell me to do otherwise. It really won't do anyone much good. You would go broke waiting for any such predictions to come true or prove false, as the case may be. In the technology business, 10 or 15 years is eons away, too far to consider. Between now and then, there will be several generations (at least) of new products, new computer architectures, new companies, successes and failures, turmoil and upheaval, fragmentation and specialization—in short, torrid capitalism at its best.

The pace of the industry will continue to accelerate. Markets and companies will mature faster than before. The rapid appearance (or disappearance) of phenomena like Apple will become more commonplace. There will always be another whirlwind about to take off. For every market segment that matures and consolidates, other new ones will emerge. There will be constant regeneration and new life.

Somewhere along the way maturity will begin to creep up on the industry as a whole. That will bring consolidation (already being forced by IBM's grip on the field). There will be concentration, like Big Steel or the Big Three in automobiles. By then, however, essential control of the market will hardly be envied. Computers will be a no-growth, cyclical business, like home construction or televisions. What good did it do to be a powerful titan in the steel or farm equipment industry during the recession? It didn't prevent a downturn.

It would be foolish to try to predict any more closely than that where the industry is headed. The computer industry isn't like other industries. It operates by its own rules, or should we say lack of rules. The microprocessor and the shift to software have created an industry in which the shakeout is for all practical purposes a permanent condition, not just a temporary aberration. The galloping pace of fragmentation and specialization are part of the new industry landscape. The ground rules are being rewritten in computers, and perhaps in the rest of the economy as well.

The computer industry, the crowning achievement of the industrial era, is now a reluctant midwife in the birth of the information era. It is no mean trick being in the vanguard of a sweeping societal change. Somehow, somewhere, sometime, things will begin to even out, regain a semblance of normalcy. But not in the forseeable future. In some basic and very profound ways, things will never be the same again.

GLOSSARY OF TERMS

Accounts Receivable Money owed to a company by its customers for previously delivered products or services.

Applications Programs or Software Programs designed to do specific jobs, like general ledger or inventory record keeping.

Architecture The way a computer or a computer system is designed. It refers to the arrangement of components inside the cabinet.

Automated Teller Machine (ATM) A bank machine for customers' self service, performing such functions as cash dispensing, deposits, balance inquiries, or transferring money between accounts. Installed through the wall of bank branches, in the lobby, or at remote locations.

Bit The smallest unit of information, 0 or 1, in a computer's binary arithmetic system—a positive or negative electric charge. A string of bits or characters, usually 8, 16, or 32, comprises a computer's word length.

BUNCH The five non-IBM mainframe computer manufacturers that make mainframe computers incompatible to IBM. They are Burroughs, Sperry (Univac), NCR, Control Data, and Honeywell.

Byte Eight bits of data. The computer space required to store one character (letter, number, or symbol).

CAD/CAM Computer aided design/computer aided manufacturing. The use of high resolution graphics terminals, intelligent work stations, and computers to aid in designing products or structures. Replaces manual blue prints and drawings.

CAE Computer aided engineering.

Capitalization The financial structure of a company—its permanent financial underpinnings, usually including long-term debt, deferred taxes, and stockholders' equity.

Central Processing Unit (CPU) Technically, the logic and arithmetic circuitry inside a computer. The place where data actually get processed. In jargon, sometimes used to describe a big computer. The term originated when manufacturers started incorporating processing capabilities in peripherals to avoid slowing down the central computer. CPU differentiates between the computer and these peripheral devices.

Commercial OEM A company, also known as a systems house, that purchases a computer, adds specialized application software, and resells it to the ultimate end user of the equipment.

Communications Protocol The set of rules governing the operation of different units of a communications network to be uniformly adhered to in order to achieve communications. The format and timing of information to be exchanged.

Compatibility The ability of one manufacturer's computer to operate with different models from the same manufacturer or with computers from other manufacturers. Also, a computer's ability to work with other devices like printers, data storage units, etc.

Computer An electronic machine that manipulates text and numbers at high speed using a prewritten set of instructions (software programs).

Controller A peripheral device that controls the input-output operations between a computer and its storage or other peripherals, that is, a disk drive controller or a tape drive controller.

CP/M Control Program Microcomputer. A widely used personal computer operating system developed by Digital Research for the early 8-bit microcomputers, prior to IBM's entry into PC's.

CRT Cathode Ray Tube. The output display of a computer terminal; looks like a small television screen.

Database An organized set of data accessible by computer for the purpose of updating, deletion, and reporting.

Data Processing A general term for all facets of computing. The use of computers to manipulate, classify, sort, calculate, summarize, and record large quantities of data.

Data Services The variety of computing services, which includes performing or supplying all types of computing, time sharing, systems integration, and maintenance.

Debt Borrowed money to finance a company, usually in the form of bonds, necessitating interest expenses and the commitment to eventually pay back the principal.

Digital Pertaining to digits or to the representation of data or physical quantities by digits.

Digital Computer A computer in which there is discrete representation of data. A computer that operates on discrete data by performing arithmetic and logic processes on these data.

Disk Drive A data storage device, used in conjunction with computers, having read/write heads that store data on the disk and retrieve data from it. Data are retrieved by searching any section of the disk directly without scanning over intermediate information.

Equity   Financing a company by the sale of stock. This capital never has to be paid back to the investors, but it does represent ownership in the company by the shareholders.

Facsimile (FAX)   A system for the transmission of images (printed copy, pictures, maps, diagrams, etc.). The image is scanned at the transmitter, reconstructed at the receiving station, and duplicated on some form of paper.

Floppy Disk   A flexible plastic (magnetic) disk resembling a 45 RPM record, used in a floppy disk drive. An inexpensive yet high capacity storage device, used mostly with small computers and word processors.

General Purpose Computer   A computer which has the ability to store programs in a volatile manner so that they may be changed easily and very rapidly. Consequently the computers can be quickly set up to perform any of a relatively unlimited number of mathematical, logical, or data processing operations.

Hardware   In data processing, the mechanical, magnetic, electrical, and electronic components of a computer and its peripheral equipment.

Information Float   When key information is inaccessible or takes too long to obtain.

Intelligent Terminal   Input and output device with built-in programmable intelligence. Can process data and information without the assistance of another computer.

Interactive   A computer or program that is able to carry on a textual conversation with its operator. The computer prompts the operator, helping him through a routine, checks the information it receives for accuracy, and notifies the operator when a mistake is made.

Interactive Computing   A computer system designed to receive, process, and transmit at rates commensurate with the input/output rate, such as for airline reservations, bank transaction posting, and manufacturing processes. Input/output and other peripheral equipment under direct control of the computer.

K The letter "K" means kilobyte or approximately 1,000 bytes of computer memory.

Keyboard A device similar to a typewriter keyboard. An operator uses a keyboard to enter information into a computer and to retrieve data from it.

Kilobyte Eight bits make a byte. One thousand bytes make a Kilobyte of data or information.

Local Area Network A communications system within a building enabling any number of computers and peripheral devices to talk with each other and share data.

Mainframe The central processor of a large computer system. Contains the main storage, arithmetic unit, and special memory registers. Same as central processing unit. Usually over $100,000 in price with over 16 megabytes of main memory.

Megabyte Eight bits make a byte. One million bytes make a megabyte of data or information.

Microcoding Building software program instructions directly into the semiconductor circuitry of a computer.

Microprocessor An extremely small computer with its processing circuitry on a single chip.

Microcomputer A very small computer with a microprocessor that serves as its central processing unit (CPU). Usually under $15,000 in price. Up to 2 megabytes of main memory.

Minicomputer Small computers designed to be used as tools, not solutions. Usually dedicated to special classes of applications, such as scientific and engineering computing, process control, or communications. Often used by original equipment manufacturers as components integrated into other systems. Discounted in volume buys, but usually under $100,000 in price with at least 2 megabytes of main memory. Designed for interactive, on-line processing.

MIPS Millions of instructions per second. A measure of a computer's speed.

MS-DOS   The software operating system for the IBM 16-bit Personal Computer, developed by Microsoft, essentially setting an industry standard in PC's in the early 1980s. The acronym stands for Microsoft Disk Operating System.

Memory   The part of a computer where programs and information are stored.

Network   A group of computers interconnected by telephone or telegraph lines for communications.

OEM   Original Equipment Manufacturer. Any company that purchases computer hardware for enhancement, alteration, or software programming, prior to its sale to the ultimate user.

Office Automation   The use of computer devices in the office, such as personal computers, word processing machines, and desktop work station terminals, to make clerical, administrative, secretarial, as well as analytical and professional tasks easier.

On Line   Any data processing work under the direct control of the computer.

Operating Cash Flow   The result of adding net income (profits) and depreciation, then subtracting out capital expenditures and dividends paid to stockholders.

Operating System   Software that controls the execution of computer programs and that may provide scheduling, debugging, input/output control, accounting, compilation, storage assignment, or data management.

PABX or PBX   Telephone switching equipment used for interconnecting the telephones located on a customer's premises and also connecting the phone system with the outside public telephone network. The connection is made automatically. PABX stands for Private Automatic Branch Exchange.

Packaged Software   Computer application programs that can be purchased off the shelf to perform common jobs such as financial spread sheet analysis or accounts receivable processing.

Parallel Processing   Concurrent or simultaneous operation of two or more computers in a tight network, in close proximity, to enable multiple computers to all work on the same task.

PCM   Plug-compatible manufacturer. A company that makes computers or peripherals that can be easily plugged into and operate with another computer made by another company (usually IBM). PCM's are, in almost every case, IBM-compatible.

Plug-Compatible   Two devices that can be made to work together simply by plugging one into the other. No special interface devices are needed.

Peripheral   External device, such as a printer or tape drive, that is not required for the basic operation of a computer.

Personal Computer (PC)   An inexpensive, (usually under $5000) more or less portable computer, with relatively easy to use software for an individual user.

Printer   A peripheral device that prints data output from a computer.

Product Cycle   The life span during which a computer product is commercially viable or salable prior to its being made obsolete by another, newer product.

Profit Margin   Profits, either before taxes are paid, or after taxes, as a percentage of sales.

Program   A set of instructions given to a computer to perform a specific task. Programs are written in computer languages such as BASIC or COBOL.

RAM   Random Access Memory. Items stored can be retrieved as needed regardless of their location in storage. In other words, the 100th item can be retrieved without the computer having to read the first 99.

Relational Database   A new method of organizing and accessing a database where the software determines the relationship among the data during processing, rather than having the structure of the database determine the relationships.

Return on Equity   Annual percentage profit return on the net worth of the company. Net profits as a percent of stockholders' equity.

Rigid (Hard) Disk   A flat, hard, rotating plate-like object used in a disk drive to record information magnetically. High capacity yet fast access form of computer data storage.

Semiconductor   Material whose electrical conductivity is somewhere between that of an insulator and that of a conductor and whose conductivity varies with temperature. The hotter the material, the better the conductivity. Silicon is a semiconductor. Semiconductors make up many of the electronic components in computers and are much more reliable than the vacuum tubes they replaced. Also referred to as "solid state" circuitry.

Software   A term for all programs, routines, instructions, and other support necessary for a computer to perform its assigned tasks.

Stockholders' Equity   The stock investment portion of a company's finances and its accumulated retained earnings (profits).

Storage Device   A functional unit into which data can be entered, retained, and retrieved.

Supercomputer   The fastest and most powerful computers available, operating at more than 20 MIPS.

Superminicomputer   A computer that has the power of a mainframe at the price of a minicomputer. 32-bit word length like a mainframe, able to support 16 to 128 or more terminals, and has 6 to 16 megabytes of main memory.

Systems House   Usually describes an independent, third party firm (a commercial OEM) that sells computer systems made up of hardware acquired from one or more manufacturers, after adding specialized applications software.

Systems Integration   The job of attaching a far flung proliferation of computer equipment into one large network.

Systems Network Architecture (SNA)   IBM's communication protocol, which allows its computers to communicate.

System Software The package of programs that organizes the memory of a computer system. The most fundamental component is known as the operating system. Usually furnished by the manufacturer.

Technical OEM A company that purchases a computer for resale after embedding in it another device such as a machine tool or simulator. Usually a capital equipment manufacturer that uses computers as components of a larger piece of equipment.

Terminal A device similar to a typewriter that is used to communicate with a computer. It is usually connected to a printer or CRT for data output.

Time Sharing A method of operation in which a computer is shared by several users for different purposes (apparently) at the same time.

Turnkey System When a systems house purchases a computer, adds application software programs, and sells the resultant system to an end user who needs only to "turn the key" to operate the system.

UNIX Operating System The computer operating system developed by AT&T (Bell Labs), rapidly becoming an industry standard for multiuser microcomputers and work stations. Especially well suited to computers in interactive, shared networks.

Word Processor A computer designed for text entry, processing, formatting, and presentation of written communications. Word processing equipment allows storing, editing, and displaying or printing of paragraphs and pages of text.

Work Station A desk top computer capable of doing its own computing, as well as hooking into a larger network of terminals and computers to send and receive data to perform a job.

Index